Learn PowerShell Toolmaking
in a Month of Lunches

Learn PowerShell Toolmaking in a Month of Lunches

DON JONES
JEFFERY HICKS

MANNING

Shelter Island

Manning Publications Co.   Development editor: Cynthia Kane
20 Baldwin Road   Technical proofreader: James Berkenbile
PO Box 261   Copyeditor: Linda Recktenwald
Shelter Island, NY 11964   Proofreader: Maureen Spencer
                                  Typesetter: Gordan Salinovic
                              Cover designer: Leslie Haimes

ISBN 9781617291166
Printed in the United States of America
1 2 3 4 5 6 7 8 9 10 – MAL – 17 16 15 14 13 12

brief contents

v

contents

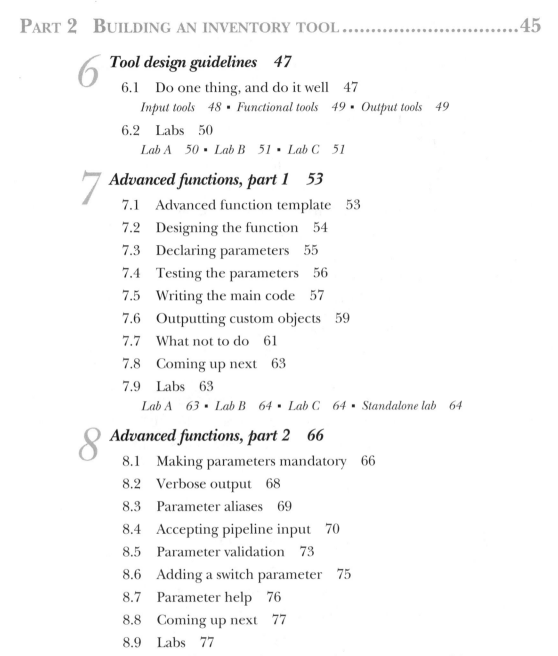

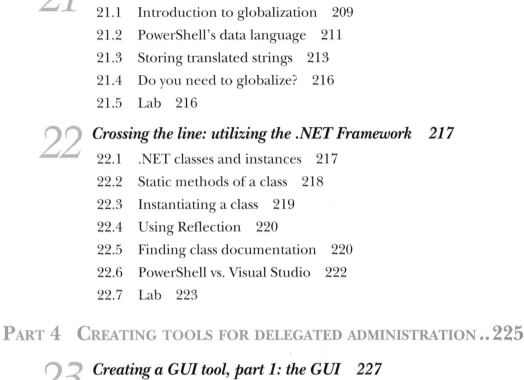

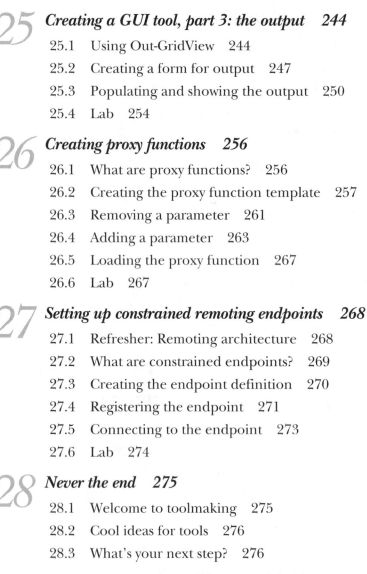

preface

I have a unique outlook on scripting. In my first career as an aircraft mechanic, I worked with machinists—folks who used tools and dies to carve metal into aircraft parts. A step above machinist, career-wise, was the tool and die maker. Those were the highly-trained folks who actually created the tools and dies used by machinists. Folks aspired to be toolmakers, as they were nicknamed, because it was considered a bit cushier job. You didn't work on the hot shop floor around screaming machines and flying shards; you worked in a cool office, on a computer-aided design (CAD) station. You wore nicer clothes.

It turns out that PowerShell can be treated in much the same way. Imagine working in a nice, cool office, with no users demanding your attention. You cruise through your organization's help desk ticketing system, looking for recurring problems that eat up a lot of time, or that end up having to be solved by higher-tier technical staffers. You write tools, in PowerShell, to solve those problems. You deploy those tools to the help desk and your lower-tier colleagues. They can now solve those problems more quickly and more consistently—and with less involvement from you. Your job is cushier. Maybe you get paid more, too. Sounds awesome, right?

It'll happen. That same pattern has repeated itself, over and over, throughout the history of IT, in almost every corner of IT except the Microsoft space, mainly because we haven't had the right tool-making tools. Well, we do now: Windows PowerShell. If you're ready to stop thinking like a button-clicker and command-runner, and to start thinking like a toolmaker, you've picked up the right book.

DON JONES

about this book

Most of what you'll need to know about this book is covered in chapter 1, but there are a few things that we should mention up front.

First of all, if you plan to follow along with our examples and complete the hands-on exercises, you'll need a virtual machine or computer running Windows 8 or Windows Server 2012. We cover that in more detail in chapter 1. You can get by with Windows 7, but you'll miss out on a few of the hands-on labs.

Second, be prepared to read this book from start to finish, covering each chapter in order. Again, this is something we'll explain in more detail in chapter 1, but the idea is that each chapter introduces a few new things that you will need in subsequent chapters. You shouldn't try to push through the whole book—stick with the one chapter per day approach. The human brain can only absorb so much information at once, and by taking on PowerShell in small chunks, you'll learn it a lot faster and more thoroughly.

Third, this book contains a lot of code snippets. Most of them are quite short, so you should be able to type them easily. In fact, we recommend that you do type them, since doing so will help reinforce an essential PowerShell skill: accurate typing! Longer code snippets are given in listings and are available for download at http://Morelunches.com (just click on this book's cover image and look for the "Downloads" section).

That said, there are a few conventions that you should be aware of. Code will always appear in a special font, just like this example:

```
Get-WmiObject -class Win32_OperatingSystem
➥ -computerName SERVER-R2
```

That example also illustrates the line-continuation character used in this book. It indicates that those two lines should actually be typed as a single line in PowerShell. In other words, don't hit Enter or Return after `Win32_OperatingSystem`—keep right on typing. PowerShell allows for very long lines, but the pages of this book can only hold so much.

Sometimes, you'll also see code font within the text itself, such as when we write `Get-Command`. That lets you know that you're looking at a command, parameter, or other element that you would type within the shell.

Fourth is a tricky topic that we'll bring up again in several chapters: the backtick character (`` ` ``). Here's an example:

```
Invoke-Command –scriptblock { Dir } `
-computerName SERVER-R2,localhost
```

The character at the end of the first line isn't a stray bit of ink—it's a real character that you would type. On a U.S. keyboard, the backtick (or grave accent) is usually near the upper left, under the Escape key, on the same key as the tilde character (~). When you see the backtick in a code listing, type it exactly as is. Furthermore, when it appears at the end of a line—as in the preceding example—make sure that it's the very last character on that line. If you allow any spaces or tabs to appear after it, the backtick won't work correctly, and neither will the code example.

> **NOTE** Frankly, it'd be easier to just download the code samples and not worry about typing them in. They're posted at http://MoreLunches.com—just click on this book's cover image and head for the Downloads section.

You can also download the code from the publisher's website at www.manning.com/LearnPowerShellToolmakinginaMonthofLunches.

Finally, we'll occasionally direct you to Internet resources. Where those URLs are particularly long and difficult to type, we've replaced them with Manning-based shortened URLs that look like http://mng.bz/S085 (you'll see that one in chapter 1).

Author Online

The purchase of *Learn PowerShell Toolmaking in a Month of Lunches* includes access to a private forum run by Manning Publications where you can make comments about the book, ask technical questions, and receive help from the authors and other users. To access and subscribe to the forum, point your browser to www.manning.com/LearnPowerShellToolmakinginaMonthofLunches and click the Author Online link. This page provides information on how to get on the forum once you are registered, what kind of help is available, and the rules of conduct in the forum.

Manning's commitment to our readers is to provide a venue where a meaningful dialogue between individual readers and between readers and the authors can take place. It's not a commitment to any specific amount of participation on the part of the authors, whose contribution to the book's forum remains voluntary (and unpaid). We suggest you try asking the authors some challenging questions, lest their interest stray!

The Author Online forum and the archives of previous discussions will be accessible from the publisher's website as long as the book is in print.

about the authors

DON JONES is a multiple-year recipient of Microsoft's prestigious Most Valuable Professional (MVP) Award for his work with Windows PowerShell. He writes the Windows PowerShell column for *Microsoft TechNet Magazine,* blogs at PowerShell.org, and authors the "Decision Maker" column and blog for *Redmond Magazine.* Don is a prolific technology author and has published more than a dozen print books since 2001. Don is a Senior Partner and Principal Technologist for Concentrated Technology (ConcentratedTech.com), an IT education and strategic consulting firm. Don's first Windows scripting language was KiXtart, going back all the way to the mid-1990s. He quickly graduated to VBScript in 1995 and was one of the first IT pros to start using early releases of a new Microsoft product code-named "Monad"—which later became Windows PowerShell. Don lives in Las Vegas and travels all over the world delivering IT training (especially in PowerShell) and speaking at IT conferences.

JEFFERY HICKS is a multi-year Microsoft MVP in Windows PowerShell, a Microsoft Certified Trainer, and an IT veteran with 20 years of experience, much of it spent as an IT consultant specializing in Microsoft server technologies. He works today as an independent author, trainer, and consultant with clients all over the world. Jeff writes the popular Prof. PowerShell column for MPCMag.com and is a regular contributor to the Petri IT Knowledgebase. If he isn't writing books then he's most likely recording training videos for companies like TrainSignal or helping out in discussion forums. You can keep up with Jeff at his blog, http://jdhitsolutions.com/blog.

acknowledgments

Books simply don't write, edit, and publish themselves. Don would like to thank everyone at Manning Publications who decided to take a chance on a very different kind of book for Windows PowerShell, and who worked so hard to make this book happen. And Jeff would like to thank Don for inviting him along for the ride, as well as the PowerShell community for their enthusiasm and support.

We are both grateful to Manning for allowing us to continue the "Month of Lunches" series with this next book in the line-up.

Thanks also to the following peer reviewers who read the manuscript during its development and provided feedback: Bryan Clark, Chad McAuley, Christoph Tohermes, David Smith, Karl Mitschke, Manuel Ruf, Marc Johnson, Mark Schill, Mike Stevenson, Nathan Shelby, and Thomas Lee. Special thanks to James Berkenbile for his technical proofread of the final manuscript shortly before we went to press.

Part 1

Introduction to toolmaking

Before you can dive into PowerShell scripting and toolmaking, you need to know exactly what those entail—and you need just a crash course in PowerShell's scripting language. That's what we'll accomplish in this part of the book.

If the material in this part seems high level and brief, it's okay. That's our intent: At this point, all of these foundation topics are a bit conceptual and abstract, so we're going to try to get them out of the way quickly. Stick with it, because we'll be revisiting all of them later, when we can do so in a more real-world and meaningful context. If you're looking for more complete coverage, grab a copy of *Learn PowerShell in a Month of Lunches*, 2nd edition. Or if you feel like going all in, pick up *PowerShell in Depth*, also from Manning Press.

Before you begin 1

Windows PowerShell is an interesting product. It's one of the few Microsoft products that were explicitly designed for several different audiences. Within those audiences will be beginners, intermediate users, and experts, but in many cases there's little crossover between the audience categories. Folks who use the shell as a command-line interface—*tool users*, in our terminology—aren't always interested in approaching the shell in any other way. Folks who use the shell to create tools—*toolmakers*, as we would call them—might use the shell as a development tool most of the time and only rarely use PowerShell as an interactive command-line interface. This book is for people—primarily administrators—who are getting started in that second, toolmaking audience.

1.1   What is toolmaking?

We borrowed the term *toolmaking* from the tool and die industry, because we think it's a particularly apt fit for PowerShell. In that industry, there are machinists who produce a variety of different parts and products. To do so, they use tools—drill bits, dies, and so forth—which are manufactured by tool and die makers. Both audiences—machinists and the tool and die makers—utilize many of the same skills and equipment, but they do so for different reasons. Toolmakers know that the tools they make aren't an end product but are rather a means to an end. They know their work product will be consumed by another expert, albeit an expert with a slightly different set of goals and a different inventory of skills.

In the PowerShell world, the broadest audience of shell users is just using the tools provided to them. They're running commands and at most combining a bunch of those commands in a script to automate some complex, multistep process. Toolmakers, on the other hand, are focused less on getting a production task accomplished and more on making a reusable, packaged tool that can complete that task—and doing so in a way that enables the tool to be handed down to the tool users, who can consume the tool in their own, simpler scripts.

Sure, there's crossover. Today, Bob might be focused on getting a bunch of new users provisioned in Active Directory. After doing that manually for a while, Bob might think, "You know, I bet I could put this all into a script that someone from Human Resources could run, and get this off of my plate entirely." Bob has just set himself up to become a toolmaker: using PowerShell not to accomplish a task directly but instead enabling someone else—often someone less technically proficient—to accomplish the task themselves.

We use the term *toolmaking* instead of *scripting* in order to highlight what we believe is a key difference between the two. For us, a script is something you make for yourself. It might be a bit ugly, but you're the only one who'll know. You can make a lot of assumptions about how it will be run, because you'll be the one running it. *Scripts* are often quick and dirty, and although they might be long and complicated, they're just a way for you to automate something that only you will ever do. For a tool, on the other hand, you can make fewer assumptions. You're going to be handing it over to someone else, and you won't be around to babysit it. Your tool needs to be more structured and more resilient to errors. You need to check the input your tool is given to make sure it's correct and usable. Your tool needs to be a bit more professional, and a bit more robust, than something that you'd only ever run yourself.

Toolmaking is a step below full-on software development. Toolmakers still operate entirely within PowerShell, rather than moving into, say, Visual Studio and a .NET Framework language like C#. Toolmakers still need to exhibit some of the discipline and maturity of a developer—anticipating and handling errors, validating user input, and so forth—but toolmakers work in a simpler environment than developers and often produce less-complex tools. Developers often tap into broad portions of the .NET Framework; PowerShell toolmakers rely more heavily on PowerShell commands and may not directly access the Framework at all or may do so only minimally. We admit that it's a fine line; in the end, it becomes more about the person. If Visual Studio just ain't your cup of tea, and you'd rather stick with a simpler, scripting-like environment, then you're a toolmaker. Welcome aboard.

1.2   *Is this book for you?*

At a minimum, you should be a confident and skilled Microsoft administrator. Whether you work with Windows, Exchange Server, SharePoint Server, or even third-party products like VMware vSphere, you should know how to quickly accomplish whatever tasks you need within your chosen technology. We're going to keep the examples in this book pretty generic, so that you can focus on the skills and techniques rather than on the technology being managed; we'll also keep the examples very template-ized, so that you can more easily rip them apart and repurpose them for your own uses, in your own environment. Remember, the goal here is to teach you how to make tools in PowerShell, not to teach you how to accomplish tasks in

Exchange or SharePoint or whatever. The skills we're teaching are universal and can be applied to any technology that's administered through PowerShell.

You should also have a strong background as a tool user in Windows PowerShell. You should be confident typing and running commands, dealing with command-line errors, and even stringing commands together into a simple script. If you're not, we suggest starting with *Learn Windows PowerShell v3 in a Month of Lunches* (http://MoreLunches.com), which is a better way to learn those foundational skills.

Ideally, you should even have a little bit of programming or scripting in your background. Any language is fine—C++, C#, Perl, PHP, VBScript, Python, whatever. Just enough to let you recognize an if statement, to understand what a loop does, and so forth. You won't need major programming skills in this book, and if you have zero programming background you'll still get along just fine; having that background will just make things a teeny bit smoother for you.

1.3   Prerequisites

Before you get started, there are a few things you need. First, make sure you've read "Is this book for you?" because that section describes the skills and background we're expecting you to bring to the table.

1.3.1   PowerShell v3

In addition, we expect that you have access to a Windows computer that has PowerShell v3 installed. If you have PowerShell but aren't sure if it's v3, open it up, type $PSVersionTable, and hit Enter. The PowerShell version should be 3.0. If it isn't, visit http://download.microsoft.com, punch "PowerShell" into the search field, and download v3 of the Windows Management Framework, the package that includes PowerShell appropriate for your operating system. We strongly recommend that your Windows computer be running either Windows 8 or Windows Server 2012, and we even more strongly recommend that you be running it in a virtual machine of some kind. That way, if you mess anything up, you've only messed up a virtual machine and not your real computer.

You must make sure script execution is enabled for PowerShell by running Set-ExecutionPolicy and specifying either Unrestricted or RemoteSigned, based on your organization's preferred setting. If you do so and receive a warning that the execution policy is being set via Group Policy, make sure that the execution policy is either Unrestricted or RemoteSigned. If it isn't one of those, contact your Active Directory administrator to discuss the situation. For this book, we're assuming you can run scripts without needing to digitally sign them. Again, working in an off-the-domain virtual machine is a good way to resolve that problem.

1.3.2   Admin privileges

For much of this book, we assume that you will have local Administrator privileges on your machine or within your test virtual machine. When you run PowerShell, the window title bar should say "Administrator"; if it doesn't, close the shell, right-click the icon, and select Run As Administrator. If that isn't available or doesn't work, then you'll need to resolve that before continuing.

1.3.3 *Multiple computers*

Many of the tools you'll build in this book are designed to query multiple computers. If you only have one computer to work with, you can always specify "localhost" multiple times, to simulate connecting to multiple machines. But if it's possible to have two or three machines to work with, it makes for a more exciting experience. We used a web-based virtual lab service called CloudShare.com to set up our environment for this book. We created a domain controller in a domain named AD2008R2 and then added a client computer and a member server to that domain. That gave us three computers to play with. Figure 1.1 shows our test environment, which we'll use throughout this book.

> **NOTE**   CloudShare.com is a commercial service and has a monthly or annual fee. It isn't the only service of its kind (you may know of others that are free or cost less), and you may well have the resources at your job to bring up a couple of virtual machines to use as a lab. Whatever you choose to do, we think it's worth it—even the monthly fee for a service like CloudShare.com—so that you can use PowerShell in a more realistic environment. Toolmaking is a big-league set of tasks, and that means you'll need to be willing to invest a bit in order to have the best learning experience. You *can* do this entire book on a single machine—but we don't think that'll fully prepare you for the real world. We like CloudShare.com mainly because it lets us spin up virtual machines, completely configured (even as domain controllers) in a few seconds, so it's super convenient for us.

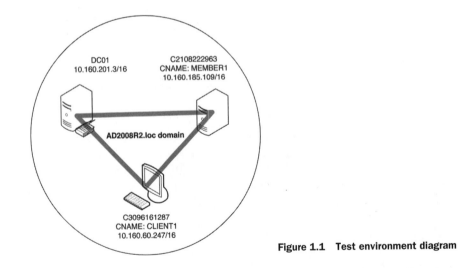

Figure 1.1   Test environment diagram

> **NOTE**   It's not our goal in this book to teach you how to set up a domain controller or a test environment; we expect that you already have those skills. We consider these to be baseline skills that every Microsoft network administrator should have. If you don't have them, then it's very likely this isn't the right book for you.

For some of our multi-computer examples, we're assuming that Windows Management Instrumentation (WMI) can communicate between these machines, which typically requires that they not have a local firewall blocking any ports. You may even wish to disable the Windows Firewall, or other local firewall software, on your test machine. You wouldn't do that in a production environment, of course, but doing so in a lab environment (or a test virtual machine) will let you follow along without having to worry about complex configurations.

For other examples, we utilize PowerShell Remoting. You can enable Remoting by running `Enable-PSRemoting` on each of your test machines (make sure you're running this as Administrator). We're assuming that any multi-machine environment that you set up will have all machines in a single domain, so that Remoting will work in its simplest, default configuration. If you only have a single machine, running the command on it and always using localhost as the remote computer name (even if you use localhost multiple times) will also work, even if your single machine isn't in a domain at all. Make sure `Enable-PSRemoting` completes without error.

If you need to learn more about Remoting, consider the free *Secrets of PowerShell Remoting* guide available at http://PowerShellBooks.com.

1.3.4 SQL Server

For portions of this book, you're also going to need SQL Server. We recommend downloading SQL Server Express (whatever the latest version is) and that you specifically download the package that includes the Express Management Tools (sometimes, you'll need to download SQL Server Express and independently download the matching Express Management Tools for that version—Microsoft frequently changes their mind on how they package those). That way, you'll get both the SQL Server backend and the GUI-based management tools. Install these packages into your test computer or virtual machine using the default installation options. SQL Server Express is free, and you'll find it at http://download.microsoft.com—just enter "sql express" into the search field.

Note that PowerShell v3 requires Microsoft .NET Framework v4; SQL Server, depending on the version you download, will also require one or more specific Framework versions. Read the prerequisites on the download page and make sure you have everything required.

1.3.5 PowerShell ISE

If you choose to work on a Windows Server operating system, install the Windows PowerShell ISE. To do so, from the PowerShell console, run `Add-WindowsFeature powershell-ise` and wait a few minutes. No restart should be needed for that.

1.3.6 Optional prerequisites

There are a few other things you can choose to have on hand if you want to. They're not absolutely necessary, but if you choose to further pursue certain topics in this book, you'll want some tools to make life easier. These include the following:

- *PowerShell Studio, formerly known as PrimalForms*—This will be useful in chapters 21 though 23. This is a commercial product, available through http://primaltools.com. A free trial is available.
- *An XML editor*—This will come in handy a few times throughout this book. We tend to hand-code XML in a text editor like Notepad, but if you get really serious with it, a dedicated editor can be useful.
- *Microsoft InfoPath*—If you start authoring multilanguage help files for the tools you make, then InfoPath can be an easy way to produce the necessary source files. We tend to stick with single-language comment-based help that doesn't require XML or InfoPath, but you may feel differently when you get to chapter 9.

1.4   *How to use this book*

This book is designed to be read one chapter at a time, in order. Each chapter builds on the ones before it, so we don't recommend skipping around, especially on your first read-through. Each chapter is sized to be readable in about an hour, and that should in most cases include enough time to complete the hands-on lab at the end of each chapter.

We can't emphasize the benefit of the hands-on labs enough. Make sure you're doing those. They truly help to reinforce the concepts. If you get stuck on one, hop on http://bit.ly/AskDon and ask for help. You can also visit http://MoreLunches.com, click this book's cover image, and download sample lab answers. But don't peek until you've at least given the lab a shot on your own! The website will also direct you to additional supplementary resources, including bonus chapters, tools, narrated demo videos, and more.

Finally, stick with the one-chapter-a-day program. It can be tempting to zoom through the book, but trust us: By reading one chapter a day, you're giving your brain time to process the day's learning in the background. If you feel ready to move forward the next day, do one more chapter. If not, reread the previous day's chapter and let your brain process it a bit. Hop online (http://bit.ly/AskDon) and ask questions to clarify any problems or sticking points. Above all, don't move on to the next chapter until you're sure you've gotten the previous one *completely*. The goal here is for you to be successful and learn something, not to just race to the end of the book!

Your Month of Lunches starts with the very next chapter. Good luck!

PowerShell scripting overview

2

When you start using PowerShell's scripting language, it's easy to run into a number of gotchas and hurdles that you wouldn't ordinarily see when you're running commands. In this chapter, we'll try to get those hurdles out of the way up front, so that you can start creating tools with fewer hassles.

2.1 What is PowerShell scripting?

From our perspective, PowerShell is first and foremost a command-line interface (CLI). That means you run commands and get immediate results. Like many good CLIs, PowerShell contains a scripting language, but using that language is optional. To make tools, we'll definitely be using that language! The good news is that compared to languages like VBScript, Perl, PHP, and others, PowerShell's language is incredibly simplified, consisting of only about three dozen keywords.

At its simplest, scripting might just involve running several specific commands in a specific sequence. More complex scripts might start applying logic—only execute *this* command if *that* condition exists. Scripts might have to execute some task across a number of different targets—checking a number of different files, reconfiguring a number of different services, and so on. The point is *automation*, in most cases, typically completing some series of steps that you could do manually but that you'd rather codify into a tool that can be reused and repeated more easily, perhaps by folks other than yourself.

2.2   *PowerShell's execution policy*

PowerShell goes to some lengths, by default, to prevent scripts from executing. That's mainly because in the past (think VBScript era, here) scripts were used maliciously. A detailed discussion of PowerShell security is out of scope for this book; you should already be familiar with the execution policy, what it does, and what setting is appropriate for your organization. If you're not, review the help for PowerShell's `Set-ExecutionPolicy` command, including the "See Also" help files that it references. You can also refer to the "Security Alert!" chapter in *Learn Windows PowerShell v3 in a Month of Lunches*, which includes a more detailed discussion of PowerShell's security concepts and mechanisms.

For now, you need to decide which execution policy is right for you in terms of this book's hands-on labs. Ideally, you'll be working in a standalone, isolated virtual machine, giving you the ability to set your execution policy to RemoteSigned or Unrestricted without any potentially negative consequences. You should also know what your production environment's execution policy is and take the time to think about how that will affect the script-based tools that you'll create and use in that environment.

2.3   *Running scripts*

If you're writing scripts, then it goes without saying that you'll want to run them. This is where another PowerShell security feature can create a gotcha. As shown in figure 2.1, you can't simply type the name of a script file in order to run it. Even with the execution policy configured to permit scripts, you must precede the script filename with a path. In figure 2.1, you'll see the .\path in use, which refers to the current directory. You could also provide any other absolute or relative path in order to run a script—but you *must* provide a path of some kind.

If you're working in the PowerShell ISE—and we expect that you'll spend most of this book doing so—then you can click the green Play icon to run whatever script is

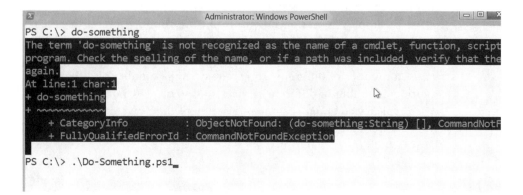

Figure 2.1   Running a script requires you to provide a path to it.

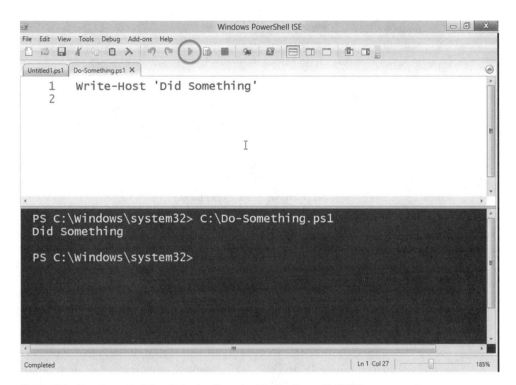

Figure 2.2   Running a script and viewing its output in the PowerShell ISE

open in the current tab. Figure 2.2 shows what this looks like and how you can configure the ISE to display both your script and its output in different panes.

Note that the one way you can't run scripts, at least by default, is to double-click them in Windows Explorer. The .PS1 file type, which is used for PowerShell scripts, isn't configured as an executable file type. Again, that's a security precaution, so that double-clicking a script opens it in Notepad rather than running it. We don't recommend changing that setting.

Scripts, you'll notice, continue to use a .PS1 filename extension even though they're running under PowerShell v3. The 1 designates the version of PowerShell's scripting language, which hasn't really changed since PowerShell v1.

2.4   *Editing scripts*

Whatever you do, please don't use Notepad to edit PowerShell scripts. Notepad might be free, but it does nothing to make the process easier. What's far better, and equally as free, is the PowerShell ISE, which was shown in figure 2.2. Version 3 of the ISE (which comes with PowerShell v3) is robust, offers numerous handy features like IntelliSense code completion, and color codes your commands to help you make sure you're typing them correctly. For example, as shown in figure 2.3, the ISE uses IntelliSense pop-up menus to help you complete command names more quickly—and to help prevent typos.

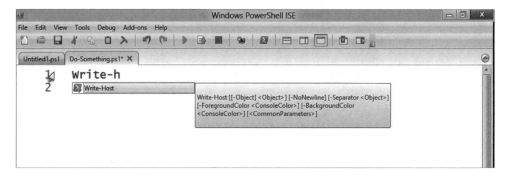

Figure 2.3   Using IntelliSense to complete command names

We strongly encourage you to get used to this feature, pressing Enter or Tab to select an item from the menu rather than typing entire command names manually. What you don't type, you can't mistype!

> **TRY IT NOW**   Now's a good time to dive into the ISE and start trying this feature. It's new in version 3, so if you don't see the IntelliSense menus, you need to install PowerShell v3.

Figure 2.4 shows another ISE feature: parameter completion. Just type a command name, a space, and a dash, and the ISE prompts you with all of that command's available parameters. Again, you can't mistype what you don't type, so choosing a parameter from the list will ensure that it's typed correctly and completely and that it's a legitimate parameter for that command.

Figure 2.5 shows how the ISE can help you prevent errors, too. Notice the squiggly red underline (we've added an arrow to point it out)? That's telling you that there's a syntax problem. In this case, it's because we typed a comma but didn't type anything after it. This is a great feature that helps you avoid error messages later: Just make sure you clear up all the red squiggles, and you're one step closer to an error-free script!

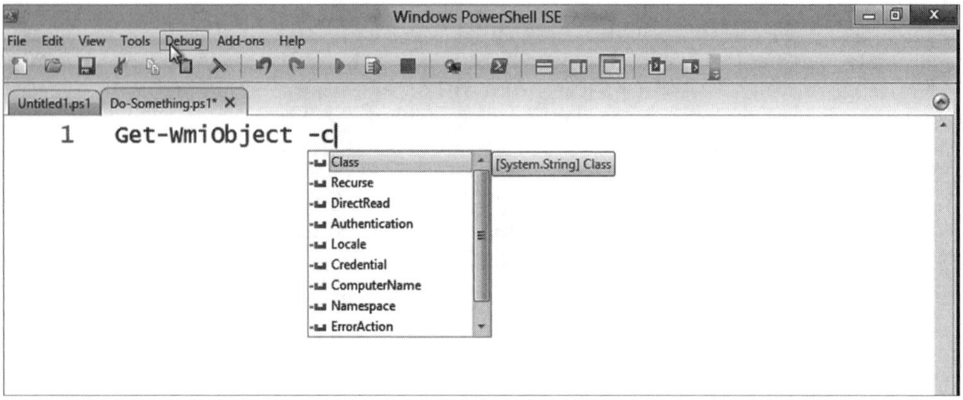

Figure 2.4   Using parameter name IntelliSense in the ISE

Figure 2.5   Red squiggly underlines call your attention to syntax errors.

You should pay close attention to the ISE's color coding, because it's another way the ISE can cue you to potential errors. For example, figure 2.6 shows a command we've typed incorrectly, forcing the ISE's color coding to be incorrect and displaying a red squiggle. By getting used to what the colors *should* be, you'll become more alert to errors when the colors look wrong.

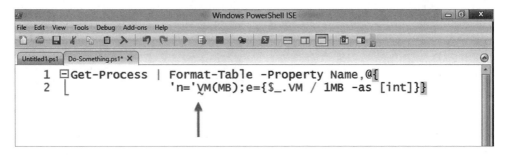

Figure 2.6   Color coding is another way the ISE alerts you to possible syntax errors.

Color coding errors can also come from improperly paired elements, like curly brackets, quotes, and so on. Just look for the spot where the color goes wrong—it'll often be accompanied by a red squiggle—and that's close to where you'll need to put your fix. As shown in figure 2.7, the ISE goes a step further by highlighting matching paired elements. For this example, we put our cursor right next to a closing curly bracket, and the ISE subtly highlighted it and its pairing opening bracket. That helped us make sure that everything was properly nested, closed, and error free.

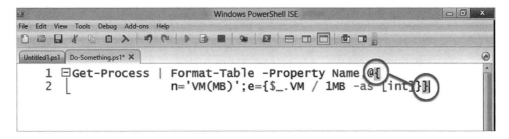

Figure 2.7   Highlighting matching brackets is another way the ISE helps you avoid syntax errors.

NOTE   It can be tough to see some of the ISE's more subtle visual features in a black-and-white book—so we encourage you to retype these examples in the ISE yourself, so that you can more clearly see what's happening. Also, keep in mind that you can select the Options item from the ISE's Tools menu to customize the color coding, in case you find some elements too low contrast to read comfortably.

2.5   *Further exploration: script editors*

Of course, the ISE isn't the only game in town. Numerous free editors—Notepad++ is one that folks often turn to—provide color coding for PowerShell scripts, although color coding is really the least of the features the ISE provides. There are also many commercial and free editors that provide more specific PowerShell support along the lines of the ISE. Some of the major choices include these:

- PowerShellPlus by Idera (http://idera.com)
- PrimalScript by SAPIEN Technologies (http://primalscript.com)
- PowerShell Studio (formerly PrimalForms) by SAPIEN Technologies (http://primaltools.com)
- PowerGUI (free and commercial Pro edition) by Quest Software (http://powergui.org and http://quest.com/powershell)
- Admin Script Editor (http://adminscripteditor.com)
- PowerSE (free and integrated with the commercial PowerWF product) by DevFarm Software (http://powerwf.com).

We don't intend this as a comprehensive list, merely the major titles we're aware of at the time of this writing. Concentrated Technology made a pretty detailed comparison of many of these, which you'll find at http://Library.ConcentratedTech.com. Note that, as of this writing, PowerGUI doesn't seem to be under active development, although it's still in wide use by administrators everywhere. We weren't able to evaluate its compatibility with PowerShell v3, though. Most of the commercial tools are available in a free trial, which often extends to 30 or 45 days, giving you ample time to try them all and decide which, if any, you like.

2.6   *Lab*

You'll start this book with a simple lab: Make sure you can get the ISE open. Enter, save, and run a simple script (like `Write-Host "It's working!"`) to make sure your execution policy is set properly. There's no sample answer for this lab, because all you're doing is verifying base PowerShell functionality.

Also ensure that you're running PowerShell v3: If your ISE doesn't look a lot like our screen shots and doesn't provide the pop-up IntelliSense menus, download version 3 (it's in the Management Framework package) from http://download.microsoft.com.

PowerShell's
scripting language

Before we dive into scripting and toolmaking, we need to cover a few background concepts—some of which are unique to PowerShell. We're also going to do a lightning overview of PowerShell's scripting constructs. If this seems a bit brief, don't worry—we'll be re-explaining a lot of these when you see them in a more practical context. The idea now is to familiarize you with what's ahead.

3.1 One script, one pipeline

A PowerShell script isn't exactly like a command-line batch file, and running a script isn't precisely the same as running the same commands yourself in the same sequence. For example, open a console window and run the following, pressing Enter after each line:

```
Get-Service
Get-Process
```

Now type those exact same lines into a script file, or into the ISE's script editing pane, and run the script. You'll get different results.

In PowerShell, each time you hit Enter you start a new pipeline. Whatever commands you typed are run in that single pipeline, and at the end of the pipeline PowerShell converts the contents of the pipeline into a text display. When you ran the two commands in the normal console, you did so in two distinct pipelines. Therefore, PowerShell was able to construct a unique display for each set of output. When entered into a script, however, both commands ran in the same pipeline, and PowerShell's formatting system isn't sophisticated enough to construct the same unique output for two different sets of results. Try running this in the console:

```
Get-Service;Get-Process
```

Those results should look the same as they did when you ran the script containing those two commands. That's because in this case both commands ran in a single pipeline—which is what happened when you ran the script.

The practical upshot of all this is that a script should produce one kind of output only. It's a bad idea—due in large part to the limitations of the formatting system, but also due to other considerations—to have a script that's dumping several different kinds of things into the pipeline at the same time.

Focus on that as a rule for everything that we'll cover: A script should output one, and only one, kind of thing.

3.2   *Variables*

Variables provide a named, temporary place in memory that you can store objects—whether those are simple values like the number 5 or a collection of complex objects like the output of Get-Service.

Think of variables as a box, into which you can put one or more things—even dissimilar things. The box has a name, and in PowerShell that name can include almost anything. Var can be a variable name, as can {my variable}. In that second example, the curly brackets enclose a variable name that contains spaces—which is pretty ugly. As a good practice, stick with variable names that include letters, numbers, and underscores.

Using a variable's name references the entire box, but if you want to reference the contents of the box you need to add a dollar sign: $var. Most commonly, you'll see PowerShell variables preceded with the dollar sign because the whole point of using one is to get at the contents. It's important to remember, however, that the dollar sign isn't part of the variable name: It's just a cue to tell PowerShell that you want the contents rather than the box itself.

```
$var = 'hello'
$number = 1
$numbers = 1,2,3,4,5,6,7,8,9
```

These examples show how to place items into a variable, by using the assignment operator (=). The first example assigns a string object to the variable var, with the characters in the string contained within quotation marks. The second example creates a variable with an integer. Note the last example: It creates an array, because PowerShell interprets all comma-separated lists as an array, or collection, of items.

One thing that can sometimes confuse newcomers is that PowerShell doesn't understand any meaning you may associate with a variable name. A variable like $computername doesn't tell the shell that the variable will contain a computer name. Similarly, $numbers doesn't tell the shell that a variable will contain more than one number—the shell doesn't care if you use a variable name that happens to be plural. $numbers = 1 is equally valid to the shell, as is $numbers = 'fred'.

Variable names normally consist of just letters, numbers, and the underscore character. But ${this is also a legal variable name} is also a valid variable name. In this example, the curly brackets enclose the entire name. We don't recommend using that approach—it's confusing to read, and there's really no need to have such a long variable name. But you may run across that in others' scripts, so we wanted you to know what to look for.

When a variable does contain multiple values, you can use a special syntax to access just a single one of them. $numbers[0] gets the first item, $numbers[1] is the second, $numbers[-1] is the last, $numbers[-2] is the second to last, and so on.

PowerShell includes a number of commands for working with variables (run Get-Command -noun variable to see them), but by and large they're unnecessary. PowerShell doesn't force you to declare variables in advance and technically provides no way to do so. So we'll just work with variables by referring to them, and for the most part we won't use the cmdlets. Keep in mind that if you choose to use those cmdlets, they ask for a variable name, which does not include a dollar sign. If you run New-Variable -Name $x, you won't be creating a new variable named x; you'll be creating a new variable named whatever is inside of $x, because the dollar sign draws out the contents of $x.

> **NOTE** Variables are something you should already be pretty familiar with from using the shell as a command-line interface. *Learn Windows PowerShell 3 in a Month of Lunches* has a whole chapter on this introductory topic.

3.3 Quotation marks

As a best practice, you should use single quotes to delimit a variable unless you have a specific reason not to. There are three specific instances where you'd want to use double quotes.

The first is where you need to insert a variable's contents into a string. Within double quotes only, PowerShell will look for the $ and will assume that everything after the $, up to the first character that's illegal in a variable name, is a variable name. The variable name and $ will be replaced with the contents of that variable.

```
$name = 'Don'
$prompt = "My name is $name"
```

$prompt will now contain My name is Don because $name will be replaced with the contents of the variable. This is a great trick for joining strings together without having to concatenate them. If you need to insert something more complex than a single variable's contents, you can use a *subexpression*, for example:

```
$processes = Get-Process
$prompt = "The first process is using $($processes[0].vm) bytes of VM."
```

The $() is the subexpression; anything inside it is evaluated as code, and the entire subexpression is replaced with the results of that code. Using this technique, you should almost never have to concatenate strings together—simply insert items into double quotation marks using either variables or subexpressions.

Within double quotes, PowerShell will also look for its escape character, the back-tick or grave accent, and act accordingly. Here are a couple of examples:

```
$debug = "`$computer contains $computer"  #the first $ is escaped
$head = "Column`tColumn`tColumn"           #`t is the tab character
```

In the first example, the first $ is being escaped. That removes its special meaning as a variable prefix, so if `$computer` contained `'SERVER'`, then `$debug` will contain `computer contains SERVER`. In the second example, `` `t `` represents a horizontal tab character, so PowerShell will place a tab between each `Column`. You can read about other special escape characters in the shell's `about_escape_characters` help topic.

Finally, use double quotes when a string needs to contain single quotes:

```
$filter1 = "name='BITS'"
$computer = 'BITS'
$filter2 = "name='$computer'"
```

In this example, the literal string is `name='BITS'` and the double quotes contain the whole thing. Both `$filter1` and `$filter2` end up containing exactly the same thing; `$filter2` gets there by using the variable-replacement trick of double quotes. Note that only the outermost set of quotes matters when it comes to that trick—the fact that single quotes are used within the string doesn't matter to PowerShell. Those single quotes are just literal characters; PowerShell doesn't interpret them.

3.4   *Object members and variables*

Everything in PowerShell is an object. Even a simple string like `'name'` is an object, of the type `System.String`. You can pipe any object to `Get-Member` to see its type name (that is, the kind of object it is) as well as its members, which include its properties and methods.

```
$var = 'Hello'
$var | Get-Member
```

Use a period after a variable name to tell the shell, "I don't want to access the entire object within this variable; I want to access just one of its properties or methods." After the period, provide the property or method name. Method names are always followed by parentheses `()`. Some methods accept input arguments, and those go within the parentheses in a comma-separated list. Other methods require no arguments, and so the parentheses are empty. But don't forget the parentheses!

```
$svc = Get-Service
$svc[0].name          #get the first object's name property
$name = $svc[1].name
$name.length          #get the length property
$name.ToUpper()       #invoke the ToUpper method
```

Notice line 2. It starts by accessing the first item in the `$svc` variable. The period means "I don't want that entire object—I just want a property or method." We've then accessed just the name property. Line 5 illustrates how to access a method, by providing its name after a period, and then following that with the parentheses.

A period is normally an illegal character within a variable name, because the period means we want to access a property or method. That means line 2 below won't work the way you might expect:

```
$service = 'bits'
$name = "Service is $service.ToUpper()"
$upper = $name.ToUpper()
$name = "Service is $upper"
```

On line 2, $name will contain Service is BITS.ToUpper() whereas on line 4 $name will contain Service is BITS.

3.5   *Parentheses*

Aside from their use with object methods, parentheses also act as an order-of-execution marker for PowerShell. Just like in algebra, parentheses tell the shell to "execute this first." The entire parenthetical expression is replaced by whatever that expression produced. Here's a mind-bending couple of examples:

```
$name = (Get-Service)[0].name
Get-Service -computerName (Get-Content names.txt)
```

On the first line, $name will contain the name of the first service on the system. Reading this takes a bit of effort: Start with the parenthetical expression, because that's what PowerShell will start with as well. Get-Service resolves to a collection, or array, of services. [0] accesses the first item in an array, so that'll be the first service. Because it's followed by a period, we know that we're accessing a property or method of that service rather than the entire service object. Finally, we pull out just the name of the service.

On the second line, the parenthetical expression is reading the contents of a text file. Assuming that file contains one computer name per line, Get-Content will return an array of computer names. Those are being fed to the -computerName parameter of Get-Service. Any parenthetical expression that returns an array of strings can be fed to the -computerName parameter in this case, because the parameter is designed to accept arrays of strings.

3.6   *Refresher: comparisons*

We're about to dive into PowerShell's scripting constructs, and they require that you recall PowerShell's comparison operators. Specifically, you'll need to know the ones in table 3.1.

Table 3.1   Basic comparison operators

Operator	Purpose	Example
-eq	Equality (case-insensitive for strings)	"hello" -eq "HELLO" (True) 5 -eq 100 (False)
-ne	Inequality (case-insensitive for strings)	"hello" -ne "HELLO" (False) 5 -ne 100 (True)

Table 3.1   Basic comparison operators *(continued)*

Operator	Purpose	Example
-like, -notlike	Wildcard string comparison (case-insensitive)	"Power" -like "*ow*" (True) "Shell" -notlike "*he*" (False)
-gt	Greater than (numbers, dates, and times)	5 -gt 100 (False)
-ge	Greater than or equal to	50 -ge 10 (True)
-lt	Less than (numbers, dates, and times)	100 -lt 1000 (True)
-le	Less than or equal to	100 -le 100 (True)

You can learn more about these and other PowerShell comparison operators by reading the about_comparison_operators help file in the shell.

3.7   *Logical constructs*

Logical constructs are used to make decisions and to execute different commands based on the outcome of that decision.

3.7.1   *If construct*

This is PowerShell's main decision-making construct. In its full form, it looks like this:

```
If ($this -eq $that) {
  # commands
} elseif ($those -ne $them) {
  # commands
} elseif ($we -gt $they) {
  # commands
} else {
  # commands
}
```

The If keyword is the only mandatory part of this construct. Following it is a parenthetical expression that must evaluate to either True or False—although PowerShell will always interpret 0 (zero) as False and any nonzero value as True. PowerShell also recognizes the built-in variables $True and $False as representing those Boolean values. If the expression in parentheses works out to True, then the commands in the following set of curly brackets will execute. If the expression is False, then the commands won't execute. That's really all you need for a valid If construct.

Note that you don't necessarily have to put a comparison in those parentheses—so long as whatever you do put in there contains True or False. For example, if you have a variable $go_ahead that you know will contain either True or False, then this is a legal construct:

```
If ($go_ahead) {
  # do something
}
```

It isn't necessary to put If ($go_ahead -eq $True), though doing so won't hurt and will work properly also.

Optionally, you can go a bit further by providing one or more ElseIf sections. These work the same way: They get their own parenthetical expression, and if that's True the commands within the following curly brackets will execute. If not, they won't.

Finally, you can wrap up with an Else block, which will execute if none of the preceding blocks executed. Only the block associated with the first True expression will execute. For example, if $this did not equal $that, and $those did not equal $them, then the commands on line 4 would execute—and nothing else. PowerShell won't even evaluate the second ElseIf expression on line 5.

Note that the # character is a comment character, making PowerShell essentially ignore anything from there until a carriage return.

Also notice the care with which those constructs were formatted. You might also see formatting like this from some folks:

```
if ($those -eq $these)
{
  #commands
}
```

It doesn't matter where you place the curly brackets. But what does matter is that you be consistent about how you place them, so that your scripts are easier to read. It's also important to indent, to the exact same level, every line within the curly brackets. The PowerShell ISE lets you use the Tab key for that purpose, and it defaults to a four-character indent. Indenting your code is a core best practice—fail to do so and you'll have a tough time properly matching opening and closing curly brackets in complex scripts. Also, all of the other PowerShell kids out there will make fun of you, deservedly. Imagine looking at a script that's poorly formatted:

```
function mine {
if ($this -eq $that){
get-service
}}
```

That's a lot harder to read, to debug, to troubleshoot, and to maintain. Although the space after the closing parenthesis isn't necessary, it does make your script easier to read. The indented code isn't necessary, but it makes your script easier to follow. Placing a single closing curly bracket on a line by itself isn't required by the shell, but it's appreciated by human eyes. Be a neat formatter, and you'll have fewer problems in your scripts and in your life.

3.7.2   *Switch construct*

The Switch construct examines a single object, often contained in a variable, and compares it to a number of possible values. This is essentially like having an If statement with a whole bunch of ElseIf statements. Many people prefer to just use If and ElseIf and to ignore Switch completely. You're welcome to do so. But you should be aware of what `Switch` does, so that you can recognize it in someone else's script. Here's the basic construct:

```
Switch ($status) {
  0 { $status_text = 'ok' }
  1 { $status_text = 'error' }
  2 { $status_text = 'jammed' }
  3 { $status_text = 'overheated' }
  4 { $status_text = 'empty' }
  default { $status_text = 'unknown' }
}
```

With this construct, `$status_text` will be assigned a value based on the value of `$status`. The `Default` section will run only if no other section matched the contents of `$status`. One reason to keep `Switch` in the back of your mind is that it has some unique capabilities not shared by the `If` construct, for example:

```
$result = ""
Switch -wildcard ($servername) {
  "*DC*" { $result += ' Domain Controller ' }
  "*FILE*" { $result += ' File Server ' }
  "*SQL*" { $result += ' SQL Server ' }
  "*EXCH*" { $result += ' Exchange Server ' }
}
```

In this example, the `Switch` construct's `-wildcard` option allowed us to use wildcard characters in the possible values. We set `$result` to be an empty string by default and then concatenated a value based on the contents of `$servername`. If `$servername` was `DCFILE01`, then `$result` would contain `Domain Controller File Server`. You see, `Switch` will execute each matching comparison, rather than stopping after the first match. That's different from the `If` construct, which will only execute the first match.

If you don't want `Switch` executing multiple matches, you can add a `break` keyword. We'll cover that more toward the end of this chapter, but here's a sneak preview:

```
$result = ""
Switch -wildcard ($servername) {
  "*DC*" { $result += ' Domain Controller '; break }
  "*FILE*" { $result += ' File Server '; break }
  "*SQL*" { $result += ' SQL Server '; break }
  "*EXCH*" { $result += ' Exchange Server '; break }
}
```

We're using an old C programming trick that works well in PowerShell: A semicolon separates the two commands within each condition section. It's the same as if we'd formatted each on a separate line:

```
$result = ""
Switch -wildcard ($servername) {
  "*DC*" {
          $result += ' Domain Controller '
          break
          }
  "*FILE*" {
```

```
                    $result += ' File Server '
                    break
                }
    "*SQL*" {
                    $result += ' SQL Server '
                    break
                }
    "*EXCH*" {
                    $result += ' Exchange Server '
                    break
                }
}
```

When our conditional code contains only a couple of commands, we often find that using a semicolon to separate them provides for a more concise and readable code listing, but you're welcome to format your code however you like. Switch has other capabilities, too; read the about_switch help file in PowerShell to learn about them.

3.8   *Looping constructs*

Looping constructs are designed to execute some action over and over, either a specified number of times or until some condition is met.

3.8.1   *Do...While construct*

This is a primary looping construct in PowerShell. It's designed to repeat a block of commands so long as some condition is True or until a condition becomes True. Here's the basic usage:

```
Do {
  # commands
} While ($this -eq $that)
```

In this variation of the construct, the commands within the curly brackets will always execute at least one time, because the While condition isn't evaluated until after the first execution. You can move the While, in which case the commands will only execute if the condition is True in the first place:

```
While (Test-Path $path) {
  # commands
}
```

Notice that this second example doesn't use a comparison operator like -eq. That's because the Test-Path cmdlet happens to return True or False to begin with; just as with the If construct, there's no need to compare that to True or False in order for the expression to work. Remember, the parenthetical expression used with these scripting constructs merely needs to simplify down to True or False—if you're using a command like Test-Path, which always returns True or False, then that's all you need.

As always, there's an "about" topic in the shell that demonstrates other ways to use this construct, along with information on one additional variation that uses the Until keyword.

3.8.2   *ForEach construct*

This construct is similar in operation to the `ForEach-Object` cmdlet and differs only in its syntax. The purpose of `ForEach` is to take an array (or collection, which in Power-Shell is the same as an array) and enumerate the objects in the array so that you can work with one at a time.

```
$services = Get-Service
ForEach ($service in $services) {
  $service.Stop()
}
```

It's easy for newcomers to overthink this construct. Here are a few things to remember:

- The fact that `$services` happens to be a plural English word doesn't mean anything at all to PowerShell. That variable name is used to remind us, as human beings, that the variable contains one or more services. Just because it's plural doesn't make the shell behave in a special fashion.
- The `in` keyword on line 2 is part of the `ForEach` syntax.
- The `$service` variable is one we made up. It could as easily have been `$fred` or `$coffee` and it would have worked in just the same way. We chose `$services` because the variable name describes what's in the variable; we chose `$service` because the name describes what the variable will hold—one service at a time. That's entirely for our benefit—PowerShell doesn't care what we call the variables.
- PowerShell will repeat the construct's commands—the ones contained within curly brackets—one time for each object that's in the second variable (`$services`). Each time, a single object will be taken from the second variable (`$services`) and placed into the first variable (`$service`).
- Within the construct, use the first variable (`$service`) to work with an individual object. On line 3, we've used the period to indicate that we don't want to work with the entire object but rather want to work with one of its members—the `Stop()` method.

There are times when using `ForEach` is inevitable and even desirable. But if you have a bit of programming or scripting in your past, you can sometimes leap to using `ForEach` when it isn't the best approach. The previous example isn't a good reason to use `ForEach`. Wouldn't this be easier?

```
Get-Service | Stop-Service
```

The point here is to really evaluate your use of `ForEach` and to make sure it's the only way to accomplish what you're trying to do. Here are some instances where `ForEach` is probably the only way to go:

- When you need to execute a method against a bunch of objects, and there's no cmdlet that performs the equivalent action.

- When you have a bunch of objects and need to perform several consecutive actions against each one.
- When you have an action that can only be performed against one object at a time, but your script may be working with one or more objects, and you have no way of knowing in advance.

3.8.3 *For construct*

This construct—similar to VBScript's `For...Next` construct—is designed to execute the construct's contents a specific number of times. Here's the basic syntax:

```
For ($i=0;$i -lt 5;$i++) {
  #do something
}
```

For some starting condition, (`$i=0`), while some condition is True, (`$i less than 5`), do the code in the curly braces. Then increment $i by 1 (`$i++`).

PowerShell seems to always provide a lot of alternative ways to do things. For example, if you need to execute something 10 times, some folks will use a `For` construct, whereas others will do something like this:

```
1..10 | ForEach-Object -process {
  # code here will repeat 10 times
  # use $_ to access the current iteration
  # number
}
```

That doesn't technically use any constructs at all. It uses PowerShell's range operator (`..`, or two periods right next to each other) to produce 10 objects (the integers 1 through 10) and then uses `ForEach-Object` to enumerate them. The Process script block of `ForEach-Object` will therefore execute 10 times. It's up to you how to do this type of thing; if you're browsing the internet for scripts, be prepared to run across any and all variations!

3.9 *Break and Continue in constructs*

`Break` and `Continue` are two special keywords. You've already seen `Break` in the section on `Switch`, but here's a bit more about it:

- `Break` will immediately exit any construct except the `If` construct. If you use `Break` within an `If` construct, and the `If` construct is nested within another construct, then it'll break out of that parent construct. In other words, in the following example, once $i reaches 5, the loop will exit completely:

```
$i = 0
do {
    if ($x -eq 5) { break }
    $i++
} while ($i -lt 100)
```

- If you use `Break` and there are no constructs to exit from, then it will exit the current script, ceasing execution.

The Continue keyword, when used within any looping construct, will immediately jump to the end of the construct and loop again (if the loop would normally continue). For example, the following would attempt to stop only the BITS service:

```
$services = Get-Service
foreach ($service in $services) {
    if ($service.name -ne 'BITS') { continue }
    $service.Stop()
}
```

That's just meant as an easy-to-read example; it's certainly not as easy as running Stop-Service -Name BITS, but hopefully it illustrates how the Continue keyword works.

3.10   *Lab*

There's no lab for you in this chapter; our goal was to expose you to some of these basics for the first time. You'll be using them plenty in upcoming chapters and labs, and you should remember to refer to this chapter if you need a quick refresher in how each of these items works.

Simple scripts and functions 4

Depending on how much you've worked with PowerShell already, this chapter may be a bit of a refresher. That's okay, because we're going to quickly build on what this chapter covers. In fact, you can think of this chapter as your true starting point in tool-making, now that we've reviewed some of the foundation topics. This chapter represents the point where tool *users* usually stop and where true tool *maker* begins.

4.1 Start with a command

Whenever we set out to build a tool, we usually start at the shell's command line. Internally, tools run PowerShell commands in a specific sequence, so we'll start by getting our command working properly. After all, at the command line we have less complication to worry about and fewer moving parts. It's a lot easier to get the command working there and to then move it into a script than to start in a script where many other things are going on. Start simple and then build complexity!

For this chapter, we'll start with a simple tool that retrieves some basic operating system information from a remote computer. Here's the command, along with a sample of its output:

```
PS C:\> Get-CimInstance -ClassName Win32_OperatingSystem -ComputerName DONJ
ONES1D96

SystemDirect Organization BuildNumber  RegisteredU SerialNumbe Version
ory                                     ser         r
------------ ------------ -----------   ----------- ----------- -------
C:\Window...               8250         Don Jones   00127-82... 6.2.8250
```

> **TRY IT NOW** It's a good idea to try this command on your own. We'll be building on this throughout this and subsequent chapters, so making sure the command runs in this simpler form will help ensure you don't run into problems later.

27

We've chosen to use Get-CimInstance, which is new in PowerShell v3. It requires that Windows Remote Management, or WinRM, be enabled on the remote computer (run Enable-PSRemoting on the remote machine to enable WinRM and configure a default remoting configuration), and it requires that you be running PowerShell as a user who is also a local Administrator on the remote machine. If you only have a single machine to test with, just provide your computer's name instead of the name of a remote computer.

4.2   Turn the command into a script

For the next step, we're going to turn to the PowerShell ISE. We'll copy our command to the clipboard (if you started in the PowerShell console, highlight the command and press Enter to copy it) and then paste the command into the ISE. As you can see in figure 4.1, our copy-and-paste operation included some of the PowerShell prompt, as well as an unnecessary carriage return. We'll need to edit those out before running the command again.

Figure 4.2 shows the edited script, which includes the complete command on a single line. We'll run this by clicking the green Play icon in the toolbar (you could also press F5). This is an important step, because it ensures that our command—which ran fine in the console—has been properly copied over to the ISE. As shown in figure 4.2,

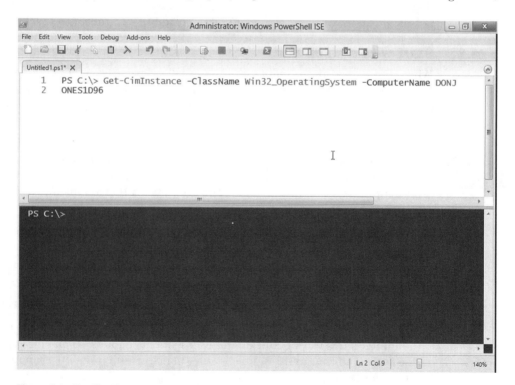

Figure 4.1   Pasting the command into the ISE

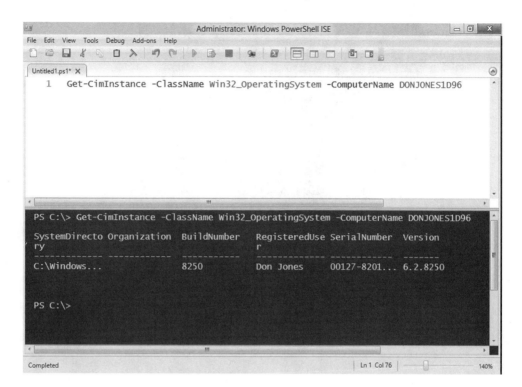

Figure 4.2   Ensuring the command runs correctly after editing it

we can confirm that the ISE is displaying the same output, thus confirming that we pasted and then edited the command correctly.

TRY IT NOW   Once again, make sure you can follow along and get this command running within the ISE. The computer name we used will need to be replaced, with either your computer's name, the name of a remote computer on your network, or even localhost.

At this point, you can save the file. Figure 4.3 shows that we're saving this as C:\Get-OSInfo.ps1. We chose the root of the C:\ drive for two reasons: First, it makes our script easy to get to, and we plan to run it a lot throughout this chapter, so it makes for a shorter path to type. Second, saving to that location ensures we've run the shell as Administrator (you can also see that the window title bar for the ISE says "Administrator," which also confirms our permissions). You might opt to save this into an alternate path with a short name, like C:\Scripts or something similar.

We chose a script filename that looks like a PowerShell cmdlet name: It uses a verb, followed by a singular noun. If at all possible, try to stick with standard and approved verbs. If you don't know what they are, run `Get-Verb`. The .ps1 filename extension lets Windows know that this is a PowerShell script file. Having saved the script, we want to again test it by running it from the console (you can use the console in the ISE or

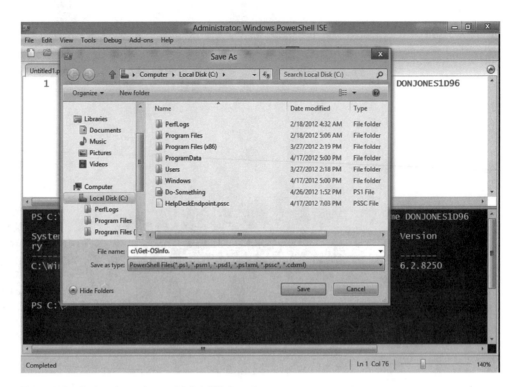

Figure 4.3   Saving the script as C:\Get-OSInfo.ps1

switch back to the normal console window), as shown in figure 4.4. Running a quick
test after each change we make helps us make sure we've done everything right. The

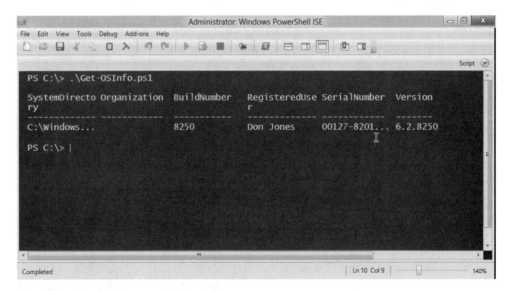

Figure 4.4   Running the new script file

worst thing you can do is make a bunch of changes and then test them all at once, because if something's broken it's more difficult to figure out which of your many changes caused the problem.

> **TRY IT NOW** Once again, make sure you're able to follow along to this point. Notice that we had to type a path (.\, which means "the current folder") in front of our script name to get it to run, and that we've already used `Set-ExecutionPolicy` to enable script execution on our computer.

4.3 *Parameterize the command*

Let's consider what we've done so far, with the perspective of a toolmaker. We've created this script, which can query information from a remote computer. We want to give this to someone else to use. But they're likely to want to query other computers as well as the one we've been testing with. We could just tell them, "Look, whenever you want to use this, open it up in Notepad or the ISE. You have to change the computer name, but be sure not to change anything else, or you could break it." What could possibly go wrong?

It would make a lot more sense to not have other folks editing our script on a routine basis—the less they edit, the less they'll break. Besides, when someone runs a regular PowerShell command, they don't have to edit anything—they just provide information to a parameter. That's what we should do, too: provide a parameter to accept any changeable information. Looking at our script, there's probably only one piece of information we'd change: the computer name. So we'll parameterize that.

Before we do so, we need to choose a parameter name. The goal here should be to remain consistent with the rest of what PowerShell does. So when you see a PowerShell command that accepts a computer name, what parameter does it use to do so?

> **NOTE** You'll find that "remaining consistent with the rest of PowerShell" is a major theme in this book. As we build tools, we want them to look and work as much like "real" PowerShell commands as possible. We'll be continually asking you to look at the rest of the shell for inspiration and to stick as close as possible to what PowerShell already does.

Looking at commands like `Get-Service`, `Get-Process`, `Invoke-Command`, and even `Get-CimInstance`, we see that PowerShell always uses a `–computerName` parameter for commands that can accept a computer name. So we'll use that same parameter name in our script. Listing 4.1 shows our revised script, with the changes in boldface.

> **ONLINE** As a quick reminder, you can download all numbered listings from this book by visiting http://MoreLunches.com. Click this book's cover on the main page and then look under the Downloads section.

Listing 4.1 Parameterizing Get-OSInfo.ps1

```
Param(
    [string]$computerName = 'localhost'
```

```
)
Get-CimInstance -ClassName Win32_OperatingSystem `
                -ComputerName $computerName
```

There are several things we need to point out—and please read these carefully:

- We defined the parameter in a `Param()` block that uses parentheses to enclose our parameters. Within the parentheses, we indented everything by using the Tab key. PowerShell doesn't require the indentation, but it's very important to keeping the script readable and easier to troubleshoot.

  CAUTION We always welcome your questions at http://bit.ly/AskDon. But if you can't take the time to format your scripts nicely, then our reply is going to be "Fix your formatting first." We can't help you troubleshoot a hard-to-read script—so please, please, please, pay attention to formatting. It'll make troubleshooting easier for you, too.

- We defined a data type, `[string]`, for our parameter.
- The parameter is basically a variable, so it gets a dollar sign (`$`) in front of its name.
- We've assigned a default value, `localhost`, which will be used if someone runs the script and doesn't provide a value for the parameter.
- We replaced our hardcoded computer name with the new `$computerName` variable. This is what puts the parameter to use.
- Just because we passed the parameter to a `-ComputerName` parameter didn't force us to use `$computerName` as our parameter name. We could have easily used `$fred` or `$x` or `$anything`. We used `$computerName` for consistency: Power-Shell commands use `-computerName` as the parameter name whenever a computer name is being accepted, and we wanted to remain consistent with that practice.
- After `Win32_OperatingSystem`, you'll notice a backtick (`` ` ``) character. That isn't a stray piece of toner on the page—it's important! You see, we didn't have enough room in this book to put that entire command on a single line. The backtick escapes the following carriage return, allowing us to continue the command on the next line. What's crucial, if you're typing this in yourself, is that the backtick be immediately followed by a carriage return, not by spaces or tabs or anything else. If the carriage return isn't right after the backtick, the trick won't work and the script won't run. Of course, in your version you aren't limited by space, so feel free to make this a one-line command.

With all of that out of the way, try running the script. Take a look at figure 4.5, where you can see that PowerShell is opening the script file and reading that `Param()` block, so that it can offer IntelliSense hinting for the `-computerName` parameter. Cool! This is starting to work just like a real PowerShell cmdlet!

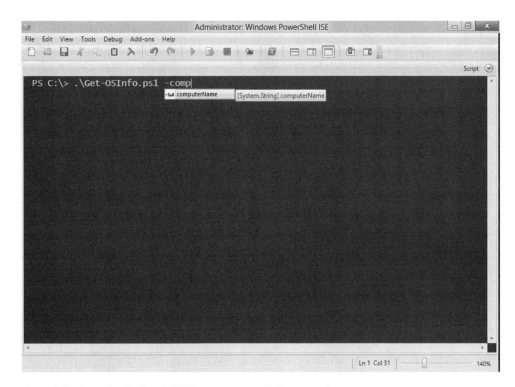

Figure 4.5   PowerShell offers IntelliSense for our script's parameter.

We should now be able to run the script with any of the following commands:

```
.\Get-OSInfo -computerName SERVER2
.\Get-OSInfo -comp SERVER2
.\Get-OSInfo SERVER2
.\Get-OSInfo
```

The first three of those query a computer named SERVER2; if you're following along, you'll need to provide a valid computer name. These demonstrate that we can type the full parameter name, a truncated parameter name, or even no parameter name at all—we can provide the value in the first position after the script name. The last example shows that our default value of localhost will also work.

> **TRY IT NOW**   Make sure you can get this script working in your own copy of Power-Shell—it's important that it be functional and bug free before you continue.

4.4   *Turn the script into a function*

Throughout much of this book, you'll find our general approach will be to do something, discuss how cool it is, and then point out something we don't like about it—thus creating a clever segue into the next topic. Right now, we have a parameterized script that anyone can run, which is cool. What we don't like is that every tool we create in this fashion has to be in its own file. As we create more and more and more and more tools, that's going to be a lot of files to manage, which we don't like. We'd rather bundle a bunch of tools into a single file, which is what a function lets us do. Listing 4.2 shows our modified script, with our code contained inside a function. We've resaved this as C:\Tools.ps1—because this file can now contain multiple tools, it makes sense to give it a generic name rather than a cmdlet-style, verb-noun name.

> **Listing 4.2   Tools.ps1**

```
function Get-OSInfo {
    param(
        [string]$computerName = 'localhost'
    )
    Get-CimInstance -ClassName Win32_OperatingSystem `
                    -ComputerName $computerName
}
```

As always, there are a few specifics we want to point out:

- We've given the function itself a cmdlet-style, verb-noun name.
- The contents of our old script are now the contents of the function, contained within curly brackets {}.
- In the ISE, we highlighted the contents of the function and pressed Tab to indent everything one level. This is really, really important, because a well-formatted script is an easier-to-debug script. The function's opening { should appear either after the function name or at the beginning of a line by itself after the function name. The closing } should be on a line by itself.
- Nothing else changed—we haven't added more features to our script. We've just added some structure to it.

Let's talk a bit more about the formatting. Here's the deal: You've spent decent money, we expect, buying this book. You did so because you thought we'd teach you something important, and that's our plan. Trust us when we tell you that the formatting is one of those important things. We know people like to just fudge the formatting and move on to cooler stuff, like writing scripts that solve real tasks, but you have to pay attention to the formatting. Here's an alternate formatting approach that's also acceptable:

```
function Get-OSInfo
{
    param(
        [string]$computerName = 'localhost'
    )
    Get-CimInstance -ClassName Win32_OperatingSystem `
                    -ComputerName $computerName
}
```

You see, with either this or the original (in listing 2.2), it's easy for us to tell where the contents of the function begin and end. The curly brackets line up—the closing bracket is indented to the same level as the opening bracket. We've also taken some care to line up our parameter names in the `Get-CimInstance` command, making it more visually apparent which command those parameters are attached to. Skip these niceties at your own risk—but, at the risk of sounding harsh, if you can't be bothered to do the right thing with your formatting, then please don't come asking us to help debug your script. Help yourself by paying attention to the formatting, and we'll be more than glad to help you debug any further issues.

4.5 Testing the function

So how do we test this function? We could just run the script, as shown in figure 4.6.

But, er, nothing happened. As you'll learn in the next chapter, each script file acts as a kind of container. When we ran the script, it *defined* the `Get-OSInfo` function, but it didn't run that function. Further, once the script finished, PowerShell removed everything defined by the script as part of a sort of automatic cleanup process. So now our function is gone, and we didn't even get to see it run!

You see, once you put your commands into a function, they do become a tad bit more difficult to test. You have two possible approaches for right now and a third approach that we'll get into much later. Let's briefly look at all three.

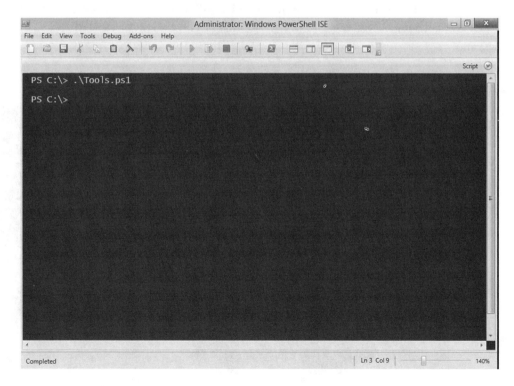

Figure 4.6 Running C:\Tools.ps1

4.5.1   Dot sourcing

This approach is shown in figure 4.7. What we've done is typed a dot, a space, and then the path and filename to our script. When you're using the .\ path (which again means "the current directory"), this can look a little confusing, so pay close attention.

Here's the command again:

```
PS C:\>. .\tools.ps1
```

That ran the script, which defined the function, but told PowerShell to skip the post-script cleanup process (that's a simplification, and in the next chapter we'll explain what actually happened in more detail). The result is that the script finished running, but the Get-OSInfo function remained defined. We were therefore able to execute it—and want to point out that we did so without providing a path. Get-OSInfo isn't a script now, so you don't provide a path to it. It's a command (specifically, a function) that's sitting in PowerShell's memory. You can run Dir function: to see the function sitting in PowerShell's function "drive."

> **TRY IT NOW**   Make sure you're able to follow along and that you can run Dir function: to see the function in memory.

Dot sourcing is a useful technique. There are downsides, though: One is that you'll often be making changes to your script and then wanting to test them. With dot sourcing, you

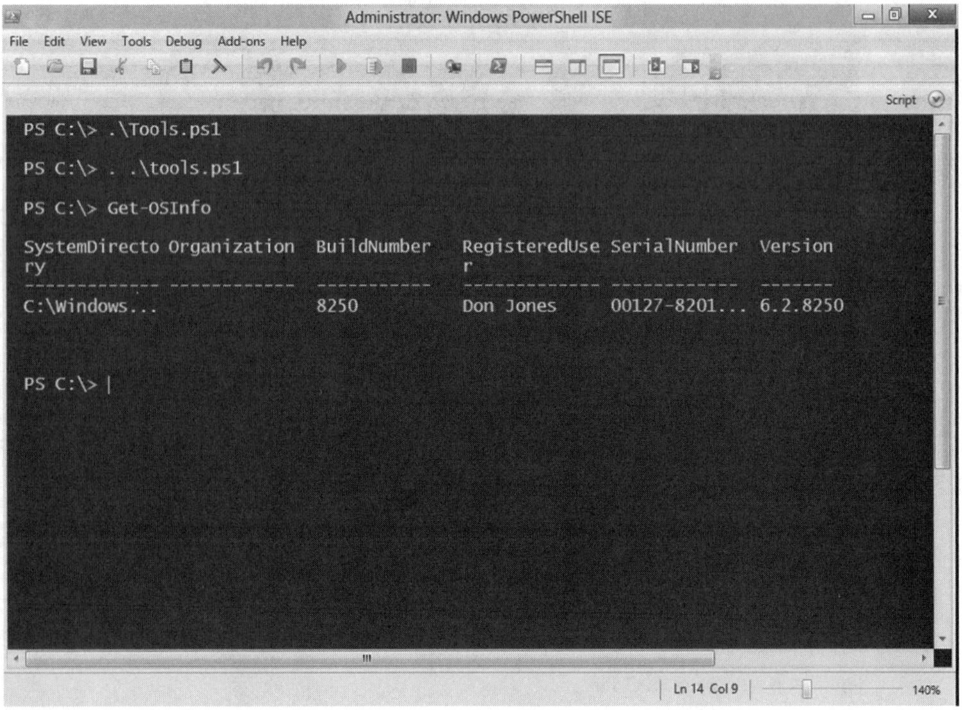

Figure 4.7   Dot sourcing C:\Tools.ps1 and then running the Get-OSInfo function

have to re–dot source your script file each time you want to test your most recent changes. That can be kind of annoying, and it's the biggest downside to dot sourcing. Also, should you decide you want to remove your script's functions from PowerShell's memory, there's no super-easy way to do so; you have to manually delete each one from the drive, which again is kind of annoying.

4.5.2 *Calling the function in the script*

We think it's easier—just for testing purposes, you understand—to have the script *define* the function and also *run* the function. That way, PowerShell can still clean up after the script finishes, removing the function from memory—but we get to see the function work. The following listing shows the revised Tools.ps1 script, which adds a line to the end.

Listing 4.3   Revised Tools.ps1

```
function Get-OSInfo {
    param(
        [string]$computerName = 'localhost'
    )
    Get-CimInstance -ClassName Win32_OperatingSystem `
                    -ComputerName $computerName
}
Get-OSInfo -computername SERVER2
```

TRY IT NOW   You should modify your Tools.ps1 to look like this, although you'll want to provide a valid computername (or localhost) so that your script actually works. Run it to make sure!

Figure 4.8 shows that this is a bit easier to test—just run the script normally.

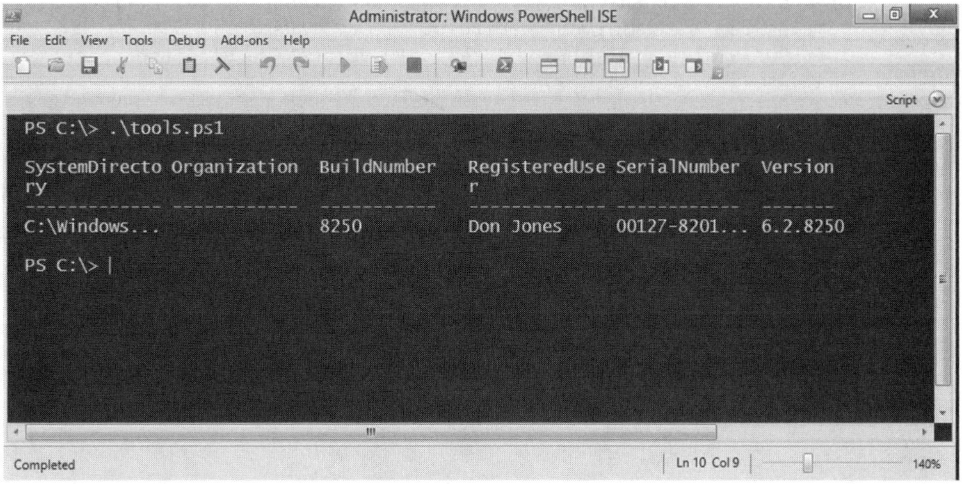

Figure 4.8   Running Tools.ps1 to define and test our function

Now it's easier to modify, test, modify, test, and repeat. Now we could just click the Play button on the ISE's toolbar, or press F5 while looking at the script, to quickly test it.

> **NOTE** If you want to have your script run your function, you must have it do so after your function's definition. PowerShell has to see the function before it can run it, so you'll often stack up all of your functions at the top of the file and then run one or more at the very end of the file.

4.5.3 *A better way ahead: modules*

Neither dot sourcing nor having the script run the function is appropriate outside of testing. What would be better is to provide a defined way to load the script (and its functions) into memory, allow those functions to be run on demand, and also provide a way to quickly and easily remove them all from memory if needed. That way is called a *module*, and we'll eventually show you how to turn your script into one. It isn't difficult, but we have a few other things we want to cover first. Until that happens, we suggest you use the technique we just showed you—have the script run the function.

4.6 *Lab*

WMI is a great management tool and one we think toolmakers often take advantage of. Using the new CIM cmdlets, write a function to query a computer and find all services by a combination of startup mode such as Auto or Manual and the current state, for example, Running. The whole point of toolmaking is to remain flexible and reusable without having to constantly edit the script. You should already have a start based on the examples in this chapter.

For your second lab, look at this script:

```
Function Get-DiskInfo {
Param ([string]$computername='localhost',[int]$MinimumFreePercent=10)
$disks=Get-WmiObject -Class Win32_Logicaldisk -Filter "Drivetype=3"
foreach ($disk in $disks) {$perFree=($disk.FreeSpace/$disk.Size)*100;
if ($perFree -ge $MinimumFreePercent) {$OK=$True}
else {$OK=$False};$disk|Select DeviceID,VolumeName,Size,FreeSpace,`
@{Name="OK";Expression={$OK}}
}}

Get-DiskInfo
```

Pretty hard to read and follow, isn't it? Grab the file from the MoreLunches site, open it in the ISE, and reformat it to make it easier to read. Don't forget to verify that it works.

5 *Scope*

Like the previous chapter, this chapter may be a bit of a refresher. But because the concept of scope continues to trip people up, we feel it's worth our time and yours to get on the same page. More than likely your toolmaking projects will be on the complex side, and if you don't understand scope, you may end up with a bad tool.

5.1   *What is scope?*

Scope is a system of containerization. In some senses, it's designed to help keep things in PowerShell from conflicting with one another. For example, if you ran a script that defined a variable named $x, you'd be pretty upset if some other script also used $x and somehow messed up your script. Scope is a way of building walls between and around different scripts and functions, so that each one has its own little sandbox to play in without fear of messing up something else.

There are several elements within PowerShell that are affected by scope:

- Variables
- Functions
- Aliases
- PSDrives
- PSSnapins (but oddly not modules—so as things migrate mainly to modules and away from PSSnapins, this won't matter much)

The shell itself is the top-level, or *global*, scope. That means that every new Power-Shell window you open is an entirely new, standalone, global scope—with no connection to any other global scope. The ISE lets you have multiple global scopes within the same window, which can be a bit confusing. In the ISE, when you select

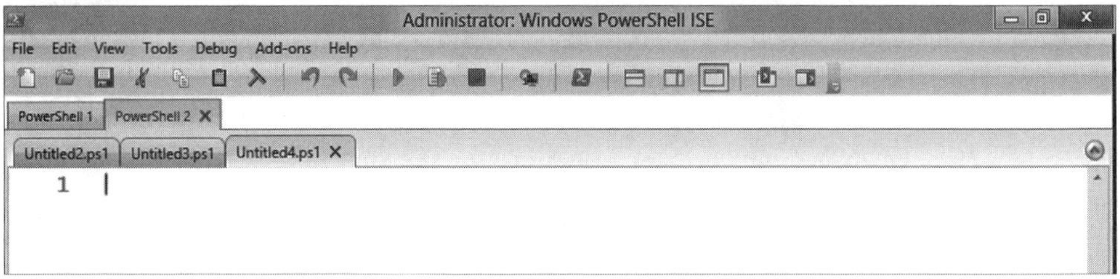

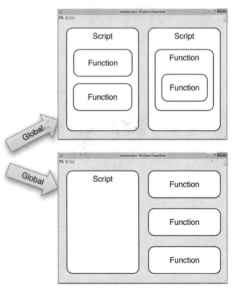

Figure 5.1   This ISE window has two runspaces (global scopes); the second one, which is selected, has three script file tabs.

New PowerShell Tab from the File menu, you're creating a new PowerShell runspace—which is equivalent to opening a new console window. Each of those tabs within the ISE is its own global scope. Figure 5.1 shows what that looks like in the ISE— note that it's the top, rectangular tabs that represent separate global scopes; the more rounded tabs that hold script files all live within that runspace, or global scope.

Each script that you run creates its own *script scope*. If a script calls a script, then that second script gets its own script scope as well. Functions all have their own scope, and a function that contains a function gets its own scope. As you can imagine, this can result in a pretty deep hierarchy, which figure 5.2 illustrates with a few global scope examples. There's even terminology for the scopes' relationships: a scope's containing scope is called its *parent*; any scopes contained within a scope are its *children*. So the global scope is only ever a parent (because it's the top-level scope), and it contains children.

So here's the deal: If you create a variable within a script, that variable belongs to that script's scope. Everything inside that same scope can "see" that variable and its contents. The scope's parent can't see the variable.

Any child scopes, however, have an interesting behavior. Imagine a script named C:\Tools.ps1, in which we create a variable named $computer. Within that script, we have a function named Get-OSInfo (sound familiar?) If Get-OSInfo attempts to access the contents of $computer, the operation will work. But if Get-OSInfo attempts to change the contents of $computer, it will create a brand-new variable, also named $computer, within its own scope. From then on, the function will be accessing its own private version of $computer, which will be

Figure 5.2   Scopes within scopes within scopes within scopes

independent of the $computer in the script scope. This, as you imagine, can be crazy confusing, so let's see it in action to clarify.

5.2 Seeing scope in action

The following listing is a script that will help demonstrate scope.

Listing 5.1 Script.ps1 will be used to demonstrate scope

```
$var = 'hello!'

function My-Function {
    Write-Host "In the function; var contains '$var'"
    $var = 'goodbye!'
    Write-Host "In the function; var is now '$var'"
}

Write-Host "In the script; var is '$var'"
Write-Host "Running the function"
My-Function
Write-Host "Function is done"
Write-Host "In the script; var is now '$var'"
```

Let's run that and check out the results:

```
PS C:\> .\script.ps1
In the script; var is 'hello!'
Running the function
In the function; var contains 'hello!'
In the function; var is now 'goodbye!'
Function is done
In the script; var is now 'hello!'
```

TRY IT NOW Please, definitely run this script on your own—we want you to see the results for real, right in front of your eyes. It'll make it all clearer.

Read through the script's output. Notice that at the start of the script, $var contains hello! because that's what the first line in the script set it to. Then the function runs, and it sees that $var contains hello! That's because $var doesn't exist in the function's scope, so when it tries to access $var, PowerShell goes up to the scope's parent. Lo and behold, there's a $var there! So that's what the function sees.

But then the function assigns goodbye! to $var. PowerShell sees that $var still doesn't exist in the function's scope, and so it creates the variable and puts goodbye! into it. There are now two copies of $var running around: one in the function's scope and one—which still contains hello!—in the script's scope. The global scope is still clueless about either of these; there's no $var in its scope, and it can't see the variables of its child scopes.

5.3 Working out of scope

The basic rule is this: If you try to create or change something in your own scope, it's created in your scope. Run New-Alias inside a function, for example, and the alias will only be created within that scope. If you try to access (that is, read) something, and it doesn't already exist in the current scope, PowerShell will go to the parent scope and its parent and its parent and so forth, until it finds that something. If it doesn't find it, then the item truly doesn't exist, and you'll get an error message, or a null value, or whatever's appropriate for the kind of thing you're accessing.

But PowerShell has some techniques for working with out-of-scope items. There are two techniques, which we call the long-form way and the short-form way. We'll look at the long-form way first.

All of the cmdlets that deal with scoped items have a –scope parameter, which lets you explicitly work with items in a different scope. The parameter takes one of two value types:

- A number, where zero (0) represents the current scope, 1 is your parent, 2 is your parent's parent, and so on.
- A word: Local, meaning the current scope; Script, meaning the script scope that's nearest to you in the hierarchy; or Global, which refers to the shell's top-level scope.

The default value is 0, or Local. So, if you were to write a function that did this

```
New-Variable -Name Color -Value Purple -Scope 1
```

you'd be creating a variable named $Color, setting it to Purple, and doing so in your parent script's scope—not within the function itself. You'll find the –Scope parameter on all of the cmdlets using the variable noun, on New-Alias, and so forth.

The short-form way is designed only for variables and involves adding Global, Script, or Local. Using it looks like this:

```
$global:color = 'purple'
```

This would create or set a global variable named $color, setting it to contain purple, no matter where this command was executed. Even if executed within a deeply nested scope, it would modify the top-level scope.

> **NOTE** Commands like New-Variable and New-Alias also have an –Option parameter. Setting this to AllScopes causes the variable or alias to be created in all child scopes created from that point on within that shell session. The item isn't retroactively added to any existing child scopes, but it will be added, automatically, to any new scopes. Those scopes can then modify the item in any way they want, without affecting any other scope's copy of the item.

5.4 *Getting strict with scope*

PowerShell offers a cmdlet named Set-StrictMode, which configures some options that affect how scope works. There are two strict modes, v1.0 and v2.0. Here are the differences:

- In v1.0 mode, if you try to access a variable that doesn't exist in your scope or in any parent scope, you'll get an error. The exception is a variable contained within double quotes, which will be treated as an empty string.
- In v2.0 mode, if you try to access a variable that doesn't exist in your scope or in any parent scope, you'll get an error—even if the variable is inside double quotes. Also, if you attempt to access nonexistent properties of an object, you'll get an error.

You can also use the `-Off` parameter to shut off strict mode entirely. It's worth reading the help for `Set-StrictMode` to learn a bit more about what it can do.

5.5   *Best practices for scope*

The basic rule is "Don't mess with other people's scopes." It's a bad idea. You can't ever know what lingering, cascading effects those changes will have. By the same token, don't rely on other people's scopes. Other people are *so* unreliable! Don't access any variable that you haven't assigned a value to right within your own scope— that way, you'll always know what it contains.

These rules don't apply to the built-in aliases that ship with PowerShell: Although aliases like `Dir` exist in the global scope, it's fine to use them in a script or function, because it's always there, and it's always defined the same. It's reliable, because it's "in the box."

We get particularly irritated when we see people writing scripts that dump things into some `$global:variable` in order to pass information from one function to another. That's a bad, bad idea. You can't always guarantee that your global scope will be preserved between calls (sure, the basic PowerShell host application will, but you might not always be running in that). There are proper ways to pass data between functions, and we'll be showing you how to do those. Typing `$global` means you're doing it wrong, wrong, wrong.

5.6   *Lab*

This script is supposed to create some new PSDrives based on environmental variables like %APPDATA% and %USERPROFILE%\DOCUMENTS. But after the script runs, the drives don't exist. Why? What changes would you make?

```
Function New-Drives {

Param()

New-PSDrive -Name AppData -PSProvider FileSystem -Root $env:Appdata
New-PSDrive -Name Temp -PSProvider FileSystem -Root $env:TEMP

$mydocs=Join-Path -Path $env:userprofile -ChildPath Documents
New-PSDrive -Name Docs -PSProvider FileSystem -Root $mydocs

}
New-Drives
DIR temp: | measure-object -property length -sum
```

Part 2

Building an inventory tool

Now you're ready to start constructing a practical, real-world tool. We're going to create an inventory tool called Get-SystemInfo, and over the next few chapters we'll continue to build on it. Each chapter will address a new aspect of the tool, from its basic functionality through error handling, debugging, and packaging the tool for distribution.

Each chapter will also provide you with a series of hands-on labs. Completing all of them may take more than the hour that you've allotted for your lunchtime reading, but we encourage you to take the extra time, if you can, to complete each of the labs. Repetition is an important part of cementing this new knowledge, and each lab will throw a slightly different twist on the subject matter to help build your experience and prepare you for real-world toolmaking.

Tool design guidelines

We have a confession to make. When we first started outlining this book, we were just going to jump right into the get-it-done stuff. That's actually in the next chapter. You see, our original plan was to dig in, and then after it was all over, to explain our design philosophy. One of our early reviewers suggested, very politely, that we were being dumb. We just wanted to get to the fun stuff, but that reviewer was right: We need to explain why we're going to do what we're going to do.

We know it's easy to skip past this philosophy stuff. But we plan to keep it brief and to the point—and honestly, this stuff is important. People really struggle to make PowerShell do the right thing, and they honestly end up working a lot harder than they need to, because nobody wants to cover these basic design guidelines. So here we go.

6.1 Do one thing, and do it well

Here's a basic tenant of good PowerShell tool design: Do one thing, and do it well. Broadly speaking, a function should do one—and only one—of these things:

- Retrieve data from someplace
- Process data
- Output data to some place
- Put data into some visual format meant for human consumption

This fits well with PowerShell's command-naming convention: If your function uses the verb Get, that's what it should do: get. If it's outputting data, you name it with a verb like Export, or Out, or something else. If each command (okay, function) worries about just one of those things, then they'll have the maximum possible flexibility.

For example, let's say we want to write a tool that will retrieve some key operating system information from multiple computers and then display that information in a nicely formatted onscreen table. It'd be easy to write that tool so that it opened up Active Directory, got a bunch of computer names, queried the information from them, and then formatted a nice table as output. The problem?

Well, what if tomorrow we didn't want the data on the screen but rather wanted it in a CSV file? What if one time we needed to query a small list of computers rather than a bunch of computers from the directory? Either change would involve coding changes, probably resulting in many different versions of our tool lying around. Had we made it more modular and followed the basic philosophy we just outlined, we wouldn't have to do that. Instead, we might have designed the following:

- One function that gets computer names from the directory
- One function that accepts computer names, queries those computers, and produces the desired data
- One function that formats data into a nice onscreen table

Suddenly, everything becomes more flexible. That middle function could now work with any source of computer names: the directory, a text file, or whatever. Its data could be sent to any other command to produce output. Maybe we'd pipe it to Export-CSV to make that CSV file or to ConvertTo-HTML to make an HTML page. What about the onscreen table we want right now? We're betting Format-Table could do the job, meaning we don't even have to write that third function at all—less work for us!

So let's talk about function design. We're going to suggest that there are really three different categories of functions, or tools: input, functional, and output.

6.1.1   *Input tools*

Input tools are the functions you write that don't produce anything inherently useful themselves but are rather meant to feed information to a second tool. So a function that retrieves computer names from a configuration management database is an input tool. You don't necessarily want the computer names, but there might be an endless variety of other tools that you want to send computer names to—including any number of built-in PowerShell commands!

That's a good example of how to draw a line between your functions. Let's say you're writing a hunk of commands intended to retrieve computer names from your configuration management database. Your intent *today* is to query some WMI information from those computers—but aren't there other tools that need computer names as input? Sure! Restart-Computer accepts computer names. So does Get-EventLog, and Get-Process, and Invoke-Command, and a dozen more commands. That's what suggests—to us, at least—that the getting-names-from-the-database functionality should be a standalone tool: It could potentially feed a lot more than just today's current need.

PowerShell already comes with a number of input tools. Sticking with the theme of getting computer names, you might use Import-CSV, Get-Content, or Get-ADComputer to retrieve computer names from various sources. To us, this further emphasizes the fact that the task of getting computer names is its own, standalone capability rather than being part of another tool.

6.1.2 Functional tools

This is the kind of tool you'll be writing most often. The idea is that this kind of tool doesn't spend any time retrieving any information that it needs to do its main job. Instead, it accepts that information via a parameter of some kind—that parameter being fed by manually entered data, by another command, and so on. So if your functional tool is going to query information from remote computers, then it doesn't internally do anything to get those computers' names but instead accepts them on a parameter. It doesn't care where the computer names come from—that's someone else's job.

Once it's been given the information it needs to operate, a functional tool does its job and then outputs objects to the pipeline. Specifically, it outputs a single kind of object, so that all of its output is consistent. This functional tool also doesn't worry about what you plan to do with that output: It just puts objects into the pipeline. This kind of tool doesn't spend a nanosecond worrying about formatting, about output files, or about anything else. It does its job, perhaps produces some objects as output, and that's it.

Note that not all functional tools will produce output of any kind. A command that just does something—perhaps reconfiguring a computer—might not produce any output, apart from error messages if something goes wrong. That's fine.

6.1.3 Output tools

Output tools are specifically designed to take data—in the form of objects—that's been produced by some functional tool and then put that data into some final form. Let's stress that: *final form.* We looked up *final* in our dictionary, and it says something like, "pertaining to or coming at the end; last in place, order, or time." In other words, once you've sent your data to an output tool, *you're finished with it.* You don't want anything else happening to the data. You want to save it in a file or a database, or display it onscreen, or fax it to someone, or tap it out in Morse code, whatever. PowerShell verbs for this include Export, Out, and ConvertTo, to name a few.

Consider the inverse of this philosophy: If you have a tool that's putting data into some final form, like a text file or an onscreen display, then that tool should be doing nothing else. Why? Well, consider a function that we've created, named Get-ComputerDetails. This function goes and gets a bunch of information from a bunch of computers. It then produces a pretty, formatted table on the screen. That's a text-based display. Doing so means we could never do this:

```
Get-ComputerDetails | Where OSBuildNumber -le 7600 |
Sort ComputerName | ConvertTo-HTML | Out-File computers.html
```

Why couldn't we do that? Because—in this example—Get-ComputerDetails is producing text. Where-Object, Sort-Object, and ConvertTo-HTML can't deal with text—they deal with objects. Our Get-ComputerDetails has put our data into its final form, meaning—according to the dictionary—that `Get-ComputerDetails` is "coming at the end" and should be "last in place." Nothing can come after it—meaning we have less flexibility.

A better design would have had `Get-ComputerDetails` just produce objects and to create a second command, perhaps called `Format-MyPrettyDisplay`, that handles the formatting. That way we could get our originally desired output:

```
Get-ComputerDetails | Format-MyPrettyDisplay
```

But we could also do this

```
Get-ComputerDetails | Where OSBuildNumber -le 7600 |
Sort ComputerName | ConvertTo-HTML | Out-File computers.html
```

meaning we could change our minds about using `Format-MyPrettyDisplay` from time to time, instead sending our data objects on to other commands to produce different displays, filter the data, source the data, create files, and so on.

6.2 *Labs*

In these labs, we aren't going to have you write any actual scripts or functions. Instead, we want you to think about the design aspect, something many people overlook. Let's say you've been asked to develop the following PowerShell tools. Even though the tools will be running from PowerShell 3.0, you don't have to assume that any remote computer is running PowerShell 3.0. Assume at least PowerShell v2.

6.2.1 *Lab A*

Design a command that will retrieve the following information from one or more remote computers, using the indicated WMI classes and properties:

- `Win32_ComputerSystem`:
- `Workgroup`
- `AdminPasswordStatus`; display the numeric values of this property as text strings
- For 1, display Disabled
- For 2, display Enabled
- For 3, display NA
- For 4, display Unknown
- `Model`
- `Manufacturer`
- From `Win32_BIOS`
- `SerialNumber`
- From `Win32_OperatingSystem`
- `Version`
- `ServicePackMajorVersion`

Your function's output should also include each computer's name.

Ensure that your function's design includes a way to log errors to a text file, allowing the user to specify an error filename but defaulting to C:\Errors.txt. Also plan ahead to create a custom view so that your function always outputs a table, using the following column headers:

- `ComputerName`
- `Workgroup`
- `AdminPassword` (for `AdminPasswordStatus` in `Win32_ComputerSystem`)
- `Model`
- `Manufacturer`
- `BIOSSerial` (for `SerialNumber` in `Win32_BIOS`)
- `OSVersion` (for `Version` in `Win32_OperatingSystem`)
- `SPVersion` (for `ServicePackMajorVersion` in `Win32_OperatingSystem`)

Again, you aren't writing the script but only outlining what you might do.

6.2.2 Lab B

Design a tool that will retrieve the WMI `Win32_Volume` class from one or more remote computers. For each computer and volume, the function should output the computer's name, the volume name (such as C:\), and the volume's free space and size in GB (using no more than two decimal places). Only include volumes that represent fixed hard drives—don't include optical or network drives in the output. Keep in mind that any given computer may have multiple hard disks; your function's output should include one object for each disk.

Ensure that your function's design includes a way to log errors to a text file, allowing the user to specify an error filename but defaulting to C:\Errors.txt. Also plan to create a custom view in the future so that your function always outputs a table, using the following column headers:

- `ComputerName`
- `Drive`
- `FreeSpace`
- `Size`

6.2.3 Lab C

Design a command that will retrieve all running services on one or more remote computers. This command will offer the option to log the names of failed computers to a text file. It will produce a list that includes each running service's name and display name, along with information about the process that represents each running service. That information will include the process name, virtual memory size, peak page file usage, and thread count. But peak page file usage and thread count will not display by default.

For each tool, think about the following design questions:

- What would be a good name for your tool?
- What sort of information do you need for each tool? (These might be potential parameters.)
- How do you think the tool would be run from a command prompt, or what type of data will it write to the pipeline?

Advanced functions, part 1

PowerShell has a number of types of functions: basic functions that just return a value, filtering functions that work in the pipeline, and so on. We're going to jump straight to the top of the food chain and build an *advanced function*—what some people call a script cmdlet. Frankly, we think this is where you should be aiming for any tool you build—even if it's just a tool for your own personal use. Advanced functions do a lot of heavy lifting for you, giving you a great deal of functionality essentially for free. You can end up with the equivalent of a cmdlet without having to program in Visual Studio.

If you have any programming background, this will require you to reach into your mind, locate whatever you already know about functions, and delete that information—or at least willfully forget it for a while. PowerShell functions are a different beast, especially if you're building them to truly leverage PowerShell's functionality. Stick with us through the chapters in this part of the book, because one step at a time we're going to show you how to build something truly awesome.

7.1 Advanced function template

At the end of the day, advanced functions all end up looking remarkably similar, so we tend to start with a template of one. It's in the following listing, and it's a good starting point any time you need to build a tool to do anything at all.

Listing 7.1 Advanced function template

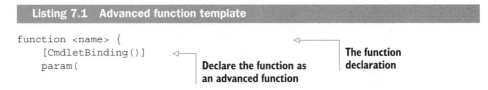

```
function <name> {
    [CmdletBinding()]
    param(
```

Declare the function as an advanced function

The function declaration

53

```
    )
    BEGIN {}
    PROCESS {}
    END {}
}
```

Defined script blocks

Input parameters go here

This starts with the keyword `Function` and is followed by the function's name—which should be in the familiar PowerShell verb-noun format. Try to use one of PowerShell's standardized, approved verbs—run `Get-Verb` in the shell to see a list of them all.

The first thing inside the function is the `[CmdletBinding()]` declaration, which identifies this as an advanced function rather than one of the lesser types. After that is the parameter block, where we'll stick our function's input parameters.

Following that are three named *script blocks*: `BEGIN`, `PROCESS`, and `END`. When the function is executed, PowerShell runs the `BEGIN` block first and the `END` block last. In between, it runs the `PROCESS` block, although how it does so depends a bit on exactly how the function got run. There are two possibilities:

- If the function is called with nothing more than its parameters, meaning no information is piped into it from the pipeline, then the `PROCESS` block runs once.
- If the function is called with pipeline input, then the `PROCESS` block runs one time for each object that was piped in from the pipeline.

We'll be covering both of those scenarios in more detail as we build out the function in the upcoming chapters, so if this doesn't make perfect sense right now, don't sweat it.

7.2   *Designing the function*

We need to start by remembering the previous chapter and deciding what kind of function we want to build. For this example, we're going to be creating a functional tool, meaning we're going to focus on doing something rather than on getting data to feed to another tool or on formatting the output. We're going to accept one or more computer names and query some information from the specified computers. To run the query, we'll use Windows Management Instrumentation (WMI). In order to make our tool compatible with older versions of Windows, we'll stick with the old-style WMI cmdlet, which uses remote procedure calls (RPCs) rather than Windows Remote Management for communications. Right there, we know our function is going to need a `-ComputerName` parameter, which will accept one or more strings.

We know it's possible for one or more of those computers to be offline when we try to query them, so we'll also keep a text log file of any computers we can't contact. That way, we can try them again later. Now, we're not going to *implement* that error-logging functionality in this chapter, but we want to be sure to include the capability in our *design*. We'll implement it eventually, but it means we need to plan for an `-ErrorLog` parameter that will accept a string.

Although we'll be querying information from several different places, we know that our function needs to output one and only one kind of object. There will be one output object for each computer that we query, and we want the properties of those objects to be as follows:

- ComputerName—The name of the computer
- OSVersion—The Windows version
- SPVersion—The service pack version
- BIOSSerial—The BIOS serial number
- Manufacturer—The computer's manufacturer
- Model—The computer's model description

The first piece of information will obviously be given to us. The second two will come from WMI's Win32_OperatingSystem class; the BIOS serial number will be from Win32_BIOS. The last two pieces of information can be found in the Win32 _ComputerSystem class.

We also need to decide how we want the function to be used. We like to do this by writing out some example commands using our function and then make sure we write the function to work that way. You can think of this as our end goal, which we're going to try to implement. First, we want to be able to specify one or more computer names via parameter:

```
Get-SystemInfo -computer one,two,three -errorlog retries.txt
```

We'd also like to be able to pipe in computer names. For example, suppose we have a text file that lists one computer name per line:

```
Get-Content computers.txt | Get-SystemInfo -errorlog retries.txt
```

7.3 *Declaring parameters*

We've identified the two parameters we intend to use, so let's go ahead and add them to our script. The next listing shows what we've done, with the changes in boldface.

Listing 7.2   Adding parameters to our script

```
function <name> {
    [CmdletBinding()]
    param(
        [string[]]$ComputerName,

        [string]$ErrorLog
    )
    BEGIN {}
    PROCESS {}
    END {}
}
```

We didn't do a lot, but we're establishing a pattern of good practices, so let's discuss some of the specifics of what we just did:

- PowerShell doesn't care about uppercase and lowercase much, but we like easy-to-read code, so we've been careful to type our parameter names nicely. -ComputerName looks better to us than -computername, and PowerShell will present the parameter exactly as we've typed it.

- We've declared a data type for each parameter. In the case of -ComputerName, it's a [string[]], and those extra square brackets after the g indicate that it can accept one or more values. -ErrorLog needs only one string, so it doesn't get the extra brackets.

- The parameters are a comma-separated list. We could have typed the entire parameter block on a single line, so the comma after the -ComputerName parameter separates it from the next parameter, -ErrorLog.

- We like putting each parameter on its own line, and we especially like putting a blank line between them. PowerShell doesn't care, but again, we love easy-to-read code. That extra blank line is going to make our lives a ton easier as we start adding things to this function later.

- Notice that we indented the contents of the Param() block. We're going to continue beating you up on formatting—it's important!

A lot of what we're focusing on at this point is just pretty formatting. That may come across as petty and annoying to you, but *please trust us*. The formatting is important. Don likes to tell people, "If you can't be bothered to format your script nicely, then you deserve all the bugs you get." It's true: Debugging—and even preventing bugs in the first place—is a ton easier when you keep your formatting neat and tidy. Plus, if your script is ugly, all the cool kids will point at you and laugh.

7.4   *Testing the parameters*

Let's not go one step further without testing what we've done. This is going to involve what we call throwaway code, meaning we're going to put in some commands that we'll then delete almost right away. The whole point is to make sure that our function is working properly. Listing 7.3 shows the revision—and note that we've added some commands to the bottom of the script that will actually run the function. That way, as we discussed in chapter 5, we can run the script in the ISE to test it. Also notice that we've finally given our function a real name.

Listing 7.3 Adding throwaway code to the function

```
function Get-SystemInfo {
    [CmdletBinding()]
    param(
        [string[]]$ComputerName,

        [string]$ErrorLog
    )
    BEGIN {}
    PROCESS {
        Write-Output $ComputerName
        Write-Output $ErrorLog
    }
    END {}
}

Get-SystemInfo -computername one,two,three -errorlog x.txt
Get-SystemInfo one x.txt
```

Here's the output of the script when we run it:

```
PS C:\> C:\test.ps1
one
two
three
x.txt
one
x.txt
```

TRY IT NOW   We expect that you're following along, so make sure that you can run the script and get identical output. If you can't, stop and fix it before you go on.

So we know that our parameter variables are accepting input, and we can display their contents from within the function's PROCESS block. Now it's time to clean out the test code—so we're going to proceed with the function shown in the following listing.

Listing 7.4   Removing the throwaway code

```
function Get-SystemInfo {
    [CmdletBinding()]
    param(
        [string[]]$ComputerName,

        [string]$ErrorLog
    )
    BEGIN {}
    PROCESS {
    }
    END {}
}
```

Now we're ready to make this thing work.

7.5   *Writing the main code*

Recall from the beginning of this chapter that we have two possible situations to deal with:

- If objects are piped into the function, the PROCESS block will execute multiple times. Since we plan to pipe in computer names, that means $ComputerName would only contain one computer name each time PROCESS executes.
- If data is provided solely via the function's parameters, PROCESS will execute just once. For us, that means $ComputerName would contain a collection of multiple computer names when PROCESS executes.

We haven't wired things up to even accept pipeline input yet, but we plan to, because we said so in our design. So we need to understand that $ComputerName might contain one name, or might contain multiple names. We can't know, so we have to write the function to deal with either situation. This is a common concern when writing advanced functions that accept pipeline input. Fortunately, there's an easy way to deal with it: We'll always assume that $ComputerName contains more than one name. PowerShell's ForEach construct can be used to enumerate them, so that we only have to deal with one at a time.

If `$ComputerName` turns out to only contain one name sometimes, that's fine—ForEach will still enumerate that one name, so our code will work fine. The next listing shows our modified function—notice that we've added a bit more throwaway code so that we can quickly test the function.

Listing 7.5   Beginning the functional code

```
function Get-SystemInfo {
    [CmdletBinding()]
    param(
        [string[]]$ComputerName,

        [string]$ErrorLog
    )
    BEGIN {
        Write-Output "Log name is $errorlog"
    }
    PROCESS {
        foreach ($computer in $computername) {
            Write-Output "computer name is $computer"
        }
    }
    END {}
}

Get-SystemInfo -ComputerName one,two,three -ErrorLog x.txt
```

Now let's run it:

```
PS C:\> C:\test.ps1
Log name is x.txt
computer name is one
computer name is two
computer name is three
```

Here are a few things to pay attention to:

- PowerShell will present our parameter names as they've been defined in the Param() block, so that's where we were careful about casing them nicely (ComputerName versus computername, for example). Elsewhere in the script we don't care, and neither does PowerShell, so we're a bit lazier, just using `$computername` and `$errorlog`.

- Notice the trick with variable names in double quotes, which lets us quickly check our work without having to concatenate strings or anything.

- We're explicitly testing the idea that the BEGIN block executes only once, and you can see in our output that we've confirmed it: `Log name is x.txt` appears only once, at the start of the output.

- Formatting, formatting, formatting! The contents of the ForEach construct—everything in its curly brackets {}—gets indented. Right now that's only one line, but we dutifully indented. The contents of the BEGIN and PROCESS blocks are indented too. Notice how easy it is to visually see what each block contains, because the contents are uniformly lined up.

Okay, now it's time to make a big leap and add the commands that will actually do what this function is supposed to do. Check out this listing.

Listing 7.6 Adding the WMI commands

```
function Get-SystemInfo {
    [CmdletBinding()]
    param(
        [string[]]$ComputerName,

        [string]$ErrorLog
    )
    BEGIN {
        Write-Output "Log name is $errorlog"
    }
    PROCESS {
        foreach ($computer in $computername) {
            $os = Get-WmiObject -class Win32_OperatingSystem `
                             -computerName $computer
            $comp = Get-WmiObject -class Win32_ComputerSystem `
                               -computerName $computer
            $bios = Get-WmiObject -class Win32_BIOS `
                               -computerName $computer

        }
    }
    END {}
}
```

There's the backtick again—three times in this function, mainly so that we could fit the code neatly within the printed pages of this book. We'll repeat our warning from earlier: Make sure the backtick is immediately followed by a carriage return and not by any spaces or tabs or anything else. Alternatively, just don't include the backtick, don't hit Enter, and string the entire Get-WmiObject command onto a single line.

Note that we haven't piped Get-WmiObject to anything else. Even though our intent is to only get certain properties from each of these WMI objects, we're putting the entire object—including the unwanted properties—into those three variables. There's no reason to do anything else at this point.

We've removed most of our throwaway code (we're leaving the BEGIN block alone for right now), and we can't test this again at this point. First, we need to construct our actual output.

7.6 *Outputting custom objects*

At this point, we have our WMI data stored in three variables. We can't just output those, because it would violate the "only output a single kind of object" rule. Instead, we need to combine the bits of information we want into a single object. The next listing shows how we do it.

Listing 7.7   Creating the custom output

```
function Get-SystemInfo {
    [CmdletBinding()]
    param(
        [string[]]$ComputerName,

        [string]$ErrorLog
    )
    BEGIN {
        Write-Output "Log name is $errorlog"
    }
    PROCESS {
        foreach ($computer in $computername) {
            $os = Get-WmiObject -class Win32_OperatingSystem `
                                -computerName $computer
            $comp = Get-WmiObject -class Win32_ComputerSystem `
                                -computerName $computer
            $bios = Get-WmiObject -class Win32_BIOS `
                                -computerName $computer
            $props = @{'ComputerName'=$computer;
                        'OSVersion'=$os.version;
                        'SPVersion'=$os.servicepackmajorversion;
                        'BIOSSerial'=$bios.serialnumber;
                        'Manufacturer'=$comp.manufacturer;
                        'Model'=$comp.model}
            $obj = New-Object -TypeName PSObject -Property $props
            Write-Output $obj
        }
    }
    END {}
}
```

`Get-SystemInfo -ErrorLog x.txt -ComputerName localhost,localhost`

We boldfaced the new stuff, including a new line of throwaway code at the end of the script file, so that we can test this. We've done three things within the function itself:

- We created a hash table, which is stored in $props. Given how we plan to use this, the syntax for this is the name of the property we want to create, then the value we want to put into that property, and then a semicolon. You'll notice that we've set up the exact properties we decided on in our original design, and we've filled them with data from our three variables that contain WMI objects.

- We then created a new object of the type PSObject, which is a special type of object that Microsoft gives us for this exact purpose. We tell it to populate the new object with the properties hash table, and we store the new object in $obj. Technically, we didn't need to store the object, but we plan to do more with this later, so it's easier to put it into a variable now.

- We then output the object to the pipeline by using Write-Object.

Let's run it. Notice that we've given our function the computer name localhost twice, just so we can test its ability to output multiple objects. Here's the result:

```
PS C:\> C:\test.ps1
Log name is x.txt

Manufacturer : Parallels Software International Inc.
OSVersion    : 6.2.8250
BIOSSerial   : Parallels-D5 A7 11 48 6C 63 42 80 AB E6 90 AF C4 D3 FC DC
ComputerName : localhost
SPVersion    : 0
Model        : Parallels Virtual Platform

Manufacturer : Parallels Software International Inc.
OSVersion    : 6.2.8250
BIOSSerial   : Parallels-D5 A7 11 48 6C 63 42 80 AB E6 90 AF C4 D3 FC DC
ComputerName : localhost
SPVersion    : 0
Model        : Parallels Virtual Platform
```

Perfect! Now we want to point out the advantage of the technique we're using. Because we're outputting a single kind of object to the pipeline, by means of Write-Output, we can send that output anywhere we want. All of these commands would work:

```
Get-SystemInfo -comp localhost -errorlog x.txt | Export-CSV
Get-SystemInfo -comp localhost -errorlog x.txt | ConvertTo-HTML
Get-SystemInfo -comp localhost -errorlog x.txt | Export-CliXML
Get-SystemInfo -comp localhost -errorlog x.txt | Sort OSVersion
Get-SystemInfo -comp localhost -errorlog x.txt | Format-Table
```

See? By not worrying about how the output will be used or what it should look like, we can send our output on to other commands. We can sort it. Filter it. Format it. Export it. Convert it. Doesn't matter—we get all of those options with no additional programming.

> **NOTE** You'll probably notice that our properties aren't displayed in the order in which we created them. That's normal: PowerShell displays the properties in more or less whatever order it wants to. There is a technique for retaining the order of the properties, but we're not going to use it. Why not? Eventually, we won't need to—in an upcoming chapter, we'll be exercising control over the visual display of our output.

7.7 *What not to do*

If you have some prior programming experience, you may start trying to use that to anticipate what PowerShell needs you to do. Use some caution, there, because it's easy to start running down a bad road to a bad place. Here are a few things we often see students do:

- Create an array variable, add the custom objects to that array, and then at the end of the script output the entire array. There's no need to do this. The whole point of the PowerShell pipeline is to accumulate output objects one at a time—it *is* your output array. Just write objects straight to the pipeline and let PowerShell worry about it.

- Use the Return keyword to output things. Again, there's no need. PowerShell's Return keyword is what some folks call syntax sugar, meaning it's only there so that people who expect it to be there will find it. Return does exactly the same thing as Write-Output, except that Return also immediately exits the function. Pointless! Just use Write-Output to write one object at a time to the pipeline. The function will exit when it reaches its end. Always be thinking about writing objects to the pipeline, not returning values.

We've also done something we shouldn't. Remember the rule, "only output one kind of object"? We've technically broken it. That line of throwaway code in the BEGIN block is using Write-Output, which is putting a String object into the pipeline. Our PROCESS block then puts out custom objects into the pipeline. Oops! The right thing to do at this point is to just remove the throwaway code from the BEGIN block. There's a better way to output that information, but we're not quite there yet. So we'll take the next listing as our final script for this chapter, which will become the starting point for the next chapter.

Listing 7.8   Removing the last line of throwaway code

```
function Get-SystemInfo {
    [CmdletBinding()]
    param(
        [string[]]$ComputerName,

        [string]$ErrorLog
    )
    BEGIN {
    }
    PROCESS {
        foreach ($computer in $computername) {
            $os = Get-WmiObject -class Win32_OperatingSystem `
                                -computerName $computer
            $comp = Get-WmiObject -class Win32_ComputerSystem `
                                -computerName $computer
            $bios = Get-WmiObject -class Win32_BIOS `
                                -computerName $computer
            $props = @{'ComputerName'=$computer;
                        'OSVersion'=$os.version;
                        'SPVersion'=$os.servicepackmajorversion;
                        'BIOSSerial'=$bios.serialnumber;
                        'Manufacturer'=$comp.manufacturer;
                        'Model'=$comp.model}
            $obj = New-Object -TypeName PSObject -Property $props
            Write-Output $obj
        }
    }
    END {}
}

Get-SystemInfo -ErrorLog x.txt -ComputerName localhost,localhost
```

We've left that last line in the script, which runs our function. We'll be testing this a lot more, so we might as well leave it in there.

> **TRY IT NOW**   Make sure you have this script and that it runs in the ISE without error. We're going to build on this in the next chapter, so it's important that we all be on the same page.

7.8   *Coming up next*

There are a few things about our function that we don't like, which provides the perfect segue into the next chapter. For one, we need to make sure that both of our parameters are mandatory, although we might just set a default value for -ErrorLog, so that we don't have to keep specifying that parameter.

We also need a better way of verifying the value of the -ErrorLog parameter, without using Write-Output (which was making our output pipeline contain multiple objects). There are also a few tweaks we'd like to make. For example, we're not sure that -ComputerName is the perfect parameter name. It's consistent with the rest of the shell, but we tend to think of words like -host first, so we'd like to see if we can make that work. It'd also be nice to put some limitations on our tool, so that it can (for example) only run against a small set of computers at a time. That'll keep performance from getting out of hand.

We'll address most of those issues in the next chapter.

7.9   *Labs*

Using your design notes from the previous chapter, start building your tools. You won't have to address every single design point right now. We'll revise and expand these functions a bit more in the next few chapters. For this chapter your functions should complete without error, even if they are only using temporary output.

7.9.1   *Lab A*

Using your notes from Lab A in chapter 6, write an advanced function that accepts one or more computer names. For each computer name, use CIM or WMI to query the specified information. For now, keep each property's name, using ServicePackMajorVersion, Version, SerialNumber, and so on. But go ahead and "translate" the value for AdminPasswordStatus to the appropriate text equivalent.

Test the function by adding <function-name> -computerName localhost to the bottom of your script and then running the script (replacing <function_name> with your actual function name, which would not include the angle brackets). The output for a single computer should look something like this:

```
Workgroup          :
Manufacturer       : innotek GmbH
Computername       : CLIENT2
Version            : 6.1.7601
Model              : VirtualBox
```

```
AdminPassword            : NA
ServicePackMajorVersion : 1
SerialNumber             : 0
```

It is possible that some values may be empty.

7.9.2   *Lab B*

Using your notes for Lab B from chapter 6, write an advanced function that accepts one or more computer names. For each computer name, use CIM or WMI to query the specified information. Format the `Size` and `FreeSpace` property values in GB to two decimal points. Test the function by adding `<function-name> -computerName localhost` to the bottom of your script and then running the script (replacing `<function_name>` with your actual function name, which would not include the angle brackets). The output for a single service should look something like this:

```
FreeSpace               Drive                 Computername       Size
---------               -----                 ------------       ----
0.07                    \\?\Volume{8130d5f3... CLIENT2           0.10
9.78                    C:\Temp\              CLIENT2            10.00
2.72                    C:\                   CLIENT2            19.90
2.72                    D:\                   CLIENT2            4.00
```

7.9.3   *Lab C*

Using your notes for Lab C from chapter 6, write an advanced function that accepts one or more computer names. For each computer name, use CIM or WMI to query all instances of `Win32_Service` where the `State` property is `Running`. For each service, get the `ProcessID` property. Then query the matching instance of the `Win32_Process` class—that is, the instance with the same `ProcessID`. Write a custom object to the pipeline that includes the service name and display name, the computer name, the process name, ID, virtual size, peak page file usage, and thread count. Test the function by adding `<function-name> -computerName localhost` to the end of the script (replacing `<function_name>` with your actual function name, which would not include the angle brackets).

The output for a single service should look something like this:

```
Computername : CLIENT2
ThreadCount  : 52
ProcessName  : svchost.exe
Name         : wuauserv
VMSize       : 499138560
PeakPageFile : 247680
Displayname  : Windows Update
```

7.9.4   *Standalone lab*

If time is limited, you can skip the three previous labs and work on this single, standalone lab. Write an advanced function named `Get-SystemInfo`. This function should accept one or more computer names via a `-ComputerName` parameter. It should then use WMI or CIM to query the `Win32_OperatingSystem` class and `Win32_ComputerSystem` class for each computer. For each computer queried, display the last boot time (in a standard date/time format), the computer name, and operating system version (all from `Win32_OperatingSystem`). Also, display the manufacturer and model (from `Win32_ComputerSystem`). You should end up with a single object with all of this information for each computer.

Note that the last boot time property does not contain a human-readable date/time value; you'll need to use the class's `ConvertToDateTime()` method to convert that value to a normal-looking date/time. Test the function by adding `Get-SystemInfo -computerName localhost` to the end of the script.

You should get a result like this:

```
Model         : VirtualBox
ComputerName  : localhost
Manufacturer  : innotek GmbH
LastBootTime  : 6/19/2012 8:55:34 AM
OSVersion     : 6.1.7601
```

NOTE Labs A, B, and C for chapters 7 through 14 build on what was accomplished in previous chapters. If you haven't finished a lab from a previous chapter, please do so. Then check your results with sample solutions on MoreLunches.com before proceeding to the next lab in the sequence.

Advanced functions, part 2

Once you've started creating advanced functions, it's easy to want them to do more and more and more. In this chapter, we'll take advanced functions a bit further, adding a number of useful features to them. We're going to try to get as much functionality as possible for as little work as possible, letting PowerShell do most of the work for us—meaning we won't have to do very much programming!

8.1 Making parameters mandatory

We want to ensure that our command has everything it needs when it runs, which means we might have to prompt someone for a computer name or an error log filename. We'd rather provide a simple default value for the error log filename, but we definitely want to prompt for that computer name if one isn't provided. Fortunately, there's no coding required to make that happen! Check out the following listing.

Listing 8.1 Adding parameter attributes

```
function Get-SystemInfo {
    [CmdletBinding()]
    param(
        [Parameter(Mandatory=$True)]
        [string[]]$ComputerName,

        [string]$ErrorLog = 'c:\retry.txt'
    )
    BEGIN {
    }
    PROCESS {
        foreach ($computer in $computername) {
```

```
            $os = Get-WmiObject -class Win32_OperatingSystem `
                            -computerName $computer
            $comp = Get-WmiObject -class Win32_ComputerSystem `
                            -computerName $computer
            $bios = Get-WmiObject -class Win32_BIOS `
                            -computerName $computer
            $props = @{'ComputerName'=$computer;
                    'OSVersion'=$os.version;
                    'SPVersion'=$os.servicepackmajorversion;
                    'BIOSSerial'=$bios.serialnumber;
                    'Manufacturer'=$comp.manufacturer;
                    'Model'=$comp.model}
            $obj = New-Object -TypeName PSObject -Property $props
            Write-Output $obj
        }
    }
    END {}
}

Get-SystemInfo
```

All we needed to do was add that default value to $ErrorLog, and we added a [Parameter()] attribute to the $ComputerName parameter. Inside that attribute, we indicated that the parameter is mandatory. One thing to be aware of is that if you set Mandatory to $True and provide a default parameter value, the default value will be ignored.

> **NOTE** This is where you can start to see the value of the blank line that we included between the two parameters. The [Parameter()] bit only goes with $ComputerName; we could include one with $ErrorLog, too, but right now there's no need.

Notice that the last line of the script is now just calling the function with no parameters, so that we can test our new configuration. Here's what happens when we run the script:

```
PS C:\> C:\test.ps1
cmdlet Get-SystemInfo at command pipeline position 1
Supply values for the following parameters:
ComputerName[0]: localhost
ComputerName[1]:

Manufacturer : Parallels Software International Inc.
OSVersion    : 6.2.8250
BIOSSerial   : Parallels-D5 A7 11 48 6C 63 42 80 AB E6 90 AF C4 D3 FC DC
ComputerName : localhost
SPVersion    : 0
Model        : Parallels Virtual Platform
```

Notice that we were prompted for ComputerName. Because the parameter is configured to accept multiple values (remember, that's the [string[]] part), PowerShell kept prompting us even though we'd entered a value. Just hit Enter on a blank prompt to tell the shell you're finished and have no more values to enter.

8.2 *Verbose output*

In the previous chapter, you'll recall that we wound up deleting some throwaway code from the function's BEGIN block because it was writing a String to the pipeline, which violated the "output only one kind of object" rule. Fortunately, PowerShell provides a specific way to write those kinds of messages without messing up the tool's intended output. Rather than writing to the pipeline, we can have text written to an alternate stream. Take a look at the next listing.

Listing 8.2 Adding verbose output

```
function Get-SystemInfo {
    [CmdletBinding()]
    param(
        [Parameter(Mandatory=$True)]
        [string[]]$ComputerName,

        [string]$ErrorLog = 'c:\retry.txt'
    )
    BEGIN {
        Write-Verbose "Error log will be $ErrorLog"
    }
    PROCESS {
        foreach ($computer in $computername) {
            Write-Verbose "Querying $computer"
            $os = Get-WmiObject -class Win32_OperatingSystem `
                            -computerName $computer
            $comp = Get-WmiObject -class Win32_ComputerSystem `
                            -computerName $computer
            $bios = Get-WmiObject -class Win32_BIOS `
                            -computerName $computer
            $props = @{'ComputerName'=$computer;
                    'OSVersion'=$os.version;
                    'SPVersion'=$os.servicepackmajorversion;
                    'BIOSSerial'=$bios.serialnumber;
                    'Manufacturer'=$comp.manufacturer;
                    'Model'=$comp.model}
            Write-Verbose "WMI queries complete"
            $obj = New-Object -TypeName PSObject -Property $props
            Write-Output $obj
        }
    }
    END {}
}

Get-SystemInfo -ComputerName localhost
```

We've added three uses of Write-Verbose. Let's see what that looks like when we run the script (we modified the last line of the script, which calls the function, so that we're providing a computer name, because we don't want to be prompted anymore):

```
PS C:\> C:\test.ps1

Manufacturer : Parallels Software International Inc.
OSVersion    : 6.2.8250
```

```
BIOSSerial    : Parallels-D5 A7 11 48 6C 63 42 80 AB E6 90 AF C4 D3 FC DC
ComputerName : localhost
SPVersion     : 0
Model         : Parallels Virtual Platform
```

Wait—where's the verbose output? Here's the cool part about Write-Verbose when it's used in an advanced function: It suppresses its own output by default. Want to turn it on? Run the script like this instead:

```
Get-SystemInfo -ComputerName localhost -verbose

PS C:\> C:\test.ps1
VERBOSE: Error log will be c:\retry.txt
VERBOSE: Querying localhost
VERBOSE: WMI queries complete

Manufacturer : Parallels Software International Inc.
OSVersion     : 6.2.8250
BIOSSerial    : Parallels-D5 A7 11 48 6C 63 42 80 AB E6 90 AF C4 D3 FC DC
ComputerName : localhost
SPVersion     : 0
Model         : Parallels Virtual Platform
```

Just by adding the -Verbose switch, we've enabled the output of Write-Verbose. Now, we can choose to have that output displayed or suppress it, depending on our needs at the moment.

> **TRY IT NOW**　　Make sure you're following along throughout this chapter—we want to make sure you have a working copy of this function that you can use as an example for your lab work.

8.3　*Parameter aliases*

At the end of the previous chapter, we mentioned that a word like *host* sprang more easily to our mind than *computername* when it came to our parameter. We need to use -ComputerName because it's consistent with the way the rest of PowerShell works, but that doesn't mean we can't have other options. Consider this listing.

> **Listing 8.3　Adding a parameter alias for -ComputerName**

```
function Get-SystemInfo {
    [CmdletBinding()]
    param(
        [Parameter(Mandatory=$True)]
        [Alias('hostname')]
        [string[]]$ComputerName,

        [string]$ErrorLog = 'c:\retry.txt'
    )
    BEGIN {
        Write-Verbose "Error log will be $ErrorLog"
    }
    PROCESS {
        foreach ($computer in $computername) {
            Write-Verbose "Querying $computer"
```

```
            $os = Get-WmiObject -class Win32_OperatingSystem `
                              -computerName $computer
            $comp = Get-WmiObject -class Win32_ComputerSystem `
                              -computerName $computer
            $bios = Get-WmiObject -class Win32_BIOS `
                              -computerName $computer
            $props = @{'ComputerName'=$computer;
                    'OSVersion'=$os.version;
                    'SPVersion'=$os.servicepackmajorversion;
                    'BIOSSerial'=$bios.serialnumber;
                    'Manufacturer'=$comp.manufacturer;
                    'Model'=$comp.model}
            Write-Verbose "WMI queries complete"
            $obj = New-Object -TypeName PSObject -Property $props
            Write-Output $obj
        }
    }
    END {}
}

Get-SystemInfo -Host localhost -verbose
```

The one new line is in bold. We've just added an [Alias()] attribute to the
-ComputerName parameter, so that the parameter can also be referred to as -HostName.
Because PowerShell still lets us truncate parameter names (as a kind of shortcut), we're
betting -Host will also work, and that's what we're now trying on the last line of the
script. Here's what we get when we run it:

```
PS C:\> C:\test.ps1
VERBOSE: Error log will be c:\retry.txt
VERBOSE: Querying localhost
VERBOSE: WMI queries complete

Manufacturer : Parallels Software International Inc.
OSVersion    : 6.2.8250
BIOSSerial   : Parallels-D5 A7 11 48 6C 63 42 80 AB E6 90 AF C4 D3 FC DC
ComputerName : localhost
SPVersion    : 0
Model        : Parallels Virtual Platform
```

Perfect! Again, this is where that blank line between the two parameters can be helpful. As our -ComputerName parameter becomes more and more complex, the visual
separation between the two parameters becomes more important.

8.4   Accepting pipeline input

In our original design of the function, we said that we wanted -ComputerName to
accept strings from the pipeline. It's time to make that happen, as shown here.

Listing 8.4   **Configuring -ComputerName to accept pipeline input**

```
function Get-SystemInfo {
    [CmdletBinding()]
    param(
        [Parameter(Mandatory=$True,ValueFromPipeline=$True)]
```

```
            [Alias('hostname')]
            [string[]]$ComputerName,

            [string]$ErrorLog = 'c:\retry.txt'
        )
    BEGIN {
        Write-Verbose "Error log will be $ErrorLog"
    }
    PROCESS {
        foreach ($computer in $computername) {
            Write-Verbose "Querying $computer"
            $os = Get-WmiObject -class Win32_OperatingSystem `
                            -computerName $computer
            $comp = Get-WmiObject -class Win32_ComputerSystem `
                            -computerName $computer
            $bios = Get-WmiObject -class Win32_BIOS `
                            -computerName $computer
            $props = @{'ComputerName'=$computer;
                    'OSVersion'=$os.version;
                    'SPVersion'=$os.servicepackmajorversion;
                    'BIOSSerial'=$bios.serialnumber;
                    'Manufacturer'=$comp.manufacturer;
                    'Model'=$comp.model}
            Write-Verbose "WMI queries complete"
            $obj = New-Object -TypeName PSObject -Property $props
            Write-Output $obj
        }
    }
    END {}
}
```

`'localhost','localhost' | Get-SystemInfo`

This just required a change to our [Parameter()] attribute (shown in bold) and to the last line of our script, where we're now piping two strings to the command instead of specifying the computer names on the parameter. This change will take any strings that are in the pipeline and feed them to the -ComputerName parameter. Running the script now produces this:

```
PS C:\> C:\test.ps1

Manufacturer : Parallels Software International Inc.
OSVersion    : 6.2.8250
BIOSSerial   : Parallels-D5 A7 11 48 6C 63 42 80 AB E6 90 AF C4 D3 FC DC
ComputerName : localhost
SPVersion    : 0
Model        : Parallels Virtual Platform

Manufacturer : Parallels Software International Inc.
OSVersion    : 6.2.8250
BIOSSerial   : Parallels-D5 A7 11 48 6C 63 42 80 AB E6 90 AF C4 D3 FC DC
ComputerName : localhost
SPVersion    : 0
Model        : Parallels Virtual Platform
```

Awesome—that worked perfectly. It's kind of neat to see how PowerShell is running this. We'll make a minor change, shown in the following listing. We're just going to add some more verbose output. Also note that we're adding a line to the end of the script, so that we can test the function in pipeline input mode as well as in parameter mode.

Listing 8.5   Testing both modes of the tool

```
function Get-SystemInfo {
    [CmdletBinding()]
    param(
        [Parameter(Mandatory=$True,ValueFromPipeline=$True)]
        [Alias('hostname')]
        [string[]]$ComputerName,

        [string]$ErrorLog = 'c:\retry.txt'
    )
    BEGIN {
        Write-Verbose "Error log will be $ErrorLog"
    }
    PROCESS {
        Write-Verbose "Beginning PROCESS block"
        foreach ($computer in $computername) {
            Write-Verbose "Querying $computer"
            $os = Get-WmiObject -class Win32_OperatingSystem `
                            -computerName $computer
            $comp = Get-WmiObject -class Win32_ComputerSystem `
                            -computerName $computer
            $bios = Get-WmiObject -class Win32_BIOS `
                            -computerName $computer
            $props = @{'ComputerName'=$computer;
                        'OSVersion'=$os.version;
                        'SPVersion'=$os.servicepackmajorversion;
                        'BIOSSerial'=$bios.serialnumber;
                        'Manufacturer'=$comp.manufacturer;
                        'Model'=$comp.model}
            Write-Verbose "WMI queries complete"
            $obj = New-Object -TypeName PSObject -Property $props
            Write-Output $obj
        }
    }
    END {}
}

Write-Host "---- PIPELINE MODE ----"
'localhost','localhost' | Get-SystemInfo -Verbose

Write-Host "---- PARAM    MODE ----"
Get-SystemInfo -ComputerName localhost,localhost -Verbose
```

Here's the output. Note that we don't normally encourage the use of `Write-Host` (Don's had some creative things to say about it, to say the least), but in this case we're using it purely to make the output more illustrative in this book. First up is the output from pipeline mode:

```
--- PIPELINE MODE ----
VERBOSE: Error log will be c:\retry.txt
VERBOSE: Beginning PROCESS block
VERBOSE: Querying localhost
VERBOSE: WMI queries complete
```

```
Manufacturer : Parallels Software International Inc.
OSVersion    : 6.2.8250
BIOSSerial   : Parallels-D5 A7 11 48 6C 63 42 80 AB E6 90 AF C4 D3 FC DC
ComputerName : localhost
SPVersion    : 0
Model        : Parallels Virtual Platform

VERBOSE: Beginning PROCESS block
VERBOSE: Querying localhost
VERBOSE: WMI queries complete
Manufacturer : Parallels Software International Inc.
OSVersion    : 6.2.8250
BIOSSerial   : Parallels-D5 A7 11 48 6C 63 42 80 AB E6 90 AF C4 D3 FC DC
ComputerName : localhost
SPVersion    : 0
Model        : Parallels Virtual Platform
```

Here you can see that we entered the PROCESS block twice, once per computer. That squares with what we explained in previous chapters: When you pipe objects to a tool, the PROCESS block executes once for each object, and in our case the $ComputerName parameter contains only one computer name each time. Now for parameter mode:

```
---- PARAM    MODE ----
VERBOSE: Error log will be c:\retry.txt
VERBOSE: Beginning PROCESS block
VERBOSE: Querying localhost
VERBOSE: WMI queries complete
Manufacturer : Parallels Software International Inc.
OSVersion    : 6.2.8250
BIOSSerial   : Parallels-D5 A7 11 48 6C 63 42 80 AB E6 90 AF C4 D3 FC DC
ComputerName : localhost
SPVersion    : 0
Model        : Parallels Virtual Platform

VERBOSE: Querying localhost
VERBOSE: WMI queries complete
Manufacturer : Parallels Software International Inc.
OSVersion    : 6.2.8250
BIOSSerial   : Parallels-D5 A7 11 48 6C 63 42 80 AB E6 90 AF C4 D3 FC DC
ComputerName : localhost
SPVersion    : 0
Model        : Parallels Virtual Platform
```

This time we only entered the PROCESS block once, and $ComputerName contained both names. The ForEach loop took care of spinning through them one at a time so that we could work with them individually.

8.5 *Parameter validation*

Because our script uses WMI, it has a potential downside, related to the fact that we're making three WMI queries and doing so against each computer, one at a time, in sequence. Simply put, this could take a long time to query a lot of computers! To help keep that from happening, we're going to add a validation attribute so that PowerShell will only accept 1 to 10 computer names. The following listing contains the change.

Listing 8.6   Adding a validation attribute to −ComputerName

```
function Get-SystemInfo {
    [CmdletBinding()]
    param(
        [Parameter(Mandatory=$True,ValueFromPipeline=$True)]
        [ValidateCount(1,10)]
        [Alias('hostname')]
        [string[]]$ComputerName,

        [string]$ErrorLog = 'c:\retry.txt'
    )
    BEGIN {
        Write-Verbose "Error log will be $ErrorLog"
    }
    PROCESS {
        Write-Verbose "Beginning PROCESS block"
        foreach ($computer in $computername) {
            Write-Verbose "Querying $computer"
            $os = Get-WmiObject -class Win32_OperatingSystem `
                                -computerName $computer
            $comp = Get-WmiObject -class Win32_ComputerSystem `
                                -computerName $computer
            $bios = Get-WmiObject -class Win32_BIOS `
                                -computerName $computer
            $props = @{'ComputerName'=$computer;
                        'OSVersion'=$os.version;
                        'SPVersion'=$os.servicepackmajorversion;
                        'BIOSSerial'=$bios.serialnumber;
                        'Manufacturer'=$comp.manufacturer;
                        'Model'=$comp.model}
            Write-Verbose "WMI queries complete"
            $obj = New-Object -TypeName PSObject -Property $props
            Write-Output $obj
        }
    }
    END {}
}

Get-SystemInfo -ComputerName one,two,three,four,five,
                    six,seven,eight,nine,ten,eleven
```

NOTE That last line in the script will run exactly as typed. Because we ended the second-to-last line with a comma (after the value five), PowerShell will look for the command to continue on the second line. It's a cool trick!

Here's what happens when we run that script:

```
PS C:\> C:\test.ps1
Get-SystemInfo : Cannot validate argument on parameter 'ComputerName'. The
number of supplied arguments (11) exceeds the
maximum number of allowed arguments (10). Specify less than 10
arguments and then try the command again.
At C:\test.ps1:38 char:30
+ Get-SystemInfo -ComputerName
one,two,three,four,five,six,seven,eight,nine,ten,el ...
```

```
+
~~~~~~~~~~~~~~~~~~~~~~~~~~~~~~~~~~~~~~~~~~~~~~~~~~~~~~~~~~~
    + CategoryInfo          : InvalidData: (:) [Get-SystemInfo],
    ParameterBindingValidationException
    + FullyQualifiedErrorId : ParameterArgumentValidationError,Get-SystemInfo
```

That's the error we expected. We highlighted the relevant text in bold for your
convenience.

There are actually a bunch of other validation attributes that PowerShell understands: Run `help about_functions_advanced_parameters` in the shell to learn all
about them.

8.6   Adding a switch parameter

You know, it occurs to us that we might not always want an error log file. Even though
we haven't actually implemented the creation of that log, we'd like a way to be able to
turn it on or off, kind of like we can turn the verbose output on or off. Check out the
next listing.

Listing 8.7   Adding a switch parameter

```
function Get-SystemInfo {
    [CmdletBinding()]
    param(
        [Parameter(Mandatory=$True,ValueFromPipeline=$True)]
        [ValidateCount(1,10)]
        [Alias('hostname')]
        [string[]]$ComputerName,

        [string]$ErrorLog = 'c:\retry.txt',

        [switch]$LogErrors
    )
    BEGIN {
        Write-Verbose "Error log will be $ErrorLog"
    }
    PROCESS {
        Write-Verbose "Beginning PROCESS block"
        foreach ($computer in $computername) {
            Write-Verbose "Querying $computer"
            $os = Get-WmiObject -class Win32_OperatingSystem `
                            -computerName $computer
            $comp = Get-WmiObject -class Win32_ComputerSystem `
                            -computerName $computer
            $bios = Get-WmiObject -class Win32_BIOS `
                            -computerName $computer
            $props = @{'ComputerName'=$computer;
                    'OSVersion'=$os.version;
                    'SPVersion'=$os.servicepackmajorversion;
                    'BIOSSerial'=$bios.serialnumber;
                    'Manufacturer'=$comp.manufacturer;
                    'Model'=$comp.model}
            Write-Verbose "WMI queries complete"
            $obj = New-Object -TypeName PSObject -Property $props
```

```
            Write-Output $obj
        }
    }
    END {}
}

Get-SystemInfo -ComputerName localhost
```

Not much has changed here: We added a comma after the $ErrorLog parameter, because we're now adding a third parameter after it within the Param() block. The new parameter, which users will see as -LogErrors, has been declared as the type [switch]. PowerShell will automatically populate the $LogErrors variable with True if the command is run with -LogErrors and populate it with False if the command is run without the parameter. So the default now will be to not log errors, and someone can add -LogErrors if they want the log.

8.7   *Parameter help*

The last thing we're going to do is add some parameter help. This will help folks understand what each parameter is meant to do, especially the -ComputerName parameter, which is something they may be prompted for. To revisit an earlier example, here's what the prompt looks like for the -ComputerName parameter:

```
cmdlet Get-SystemInfo at command pipeline position 1
Supply values for the following parameters:
ComputerName[0]: localhost
ComputerName[1]:
```

Take a look at this listing, where we've made another minor change.

Listing 8.8   Adding parameter help

```
function Get-SystemInfo {
    [CmdletBinding()]
    param(
        [Parameter(Mandatory=$True,
                   ValueFromPipeline=$True,
                   HelpMessage="Computer name or IP address")]
        [ValidateCount(1,10)]
        [Alias('hostname')]
        [string[]]$ComputerName,

        [string]$ErrorLog = 'c:\retry.txt',

        [switch]$LogErrors
    )
    BEGIN {
        Write-Verbose "Error log will be $ErrorLog"
    }
    PROCESS {
        Write-Verbose "Beginning PROCESS block"
        foreach ($computer in $computername) {
            Write-Verbose "Querying $computer"
            $os = Get-WmiObject -class Win32_OperatingSystem `
```

```
                              -computerName $computer
        $comp = Get-WmiObject -class Win32_ComputerSystem `
                              -computerName $computer
        $bios = Get-WmiObject -class Win32_BIOS `
                              -computerName $computer
        $props = @{'ComputerName'=$computer;
                   'OSVersion'=$os.version;
                   'SPVersion'=$os.servicepackmajorversion;
                   'BIOSSerial'=$bios.serialnumber;
                   'Manufacturer'=$comp.manufacturer;
                   'Model'=$comp.model}
        Write-Verbose "WMI queries complete"
        $obj = New-Object -TypeName PSObject -Property $props
        Write-Output $obj
      }
    }
    END {}
}
```

Get-SystemInfo

This new help message, which is part of the [Parameter()] attribute, can now be displayed by the shell when it prompts for that parameter. Because the other two parameters won't ever be prompted, we didn't bother creating a help message for them. Also note that we broke up the formatting of the [Parameter()] attribute. Because that thing gets longer and longer, putting each little setting on its own line makes it easier to read—and helps it fit into this book! Because the first two settings have a comma after them, we can hit Enter after the comma and continue the attribute on the next line.

8.8 Coming up next

Our tool is starting to look and feel a lot like a "real" PowerShell command, which is making us more and more aware of the ways in which it *doesn't* yet behave like an actual cmdlet. For example, anyone who has learned to use PowerShell effectively knows to use the shell's help system, but our function doesn't yet provide very good help output. We want to fix that, and it's what we'll be addressing in the next chapter.

8.9 Labs

In this chapter we're going to build on the functions you created in the last chapter using the concepts you hopefully picked up today. As you work through these labs, add verbose messages to display key steps or progress information.

8.9.1 Lab A

Modify your advanced function from chapter 7, Lab A, to accept pipeline input for the –ComputerName parameter. Also, add verbose input that will display the name of each computer contacted. Include code to verify that the –ComputerName parameter will not accept a null or empty value. Test the function by adding 'localhost' | <function-name> -verbose to the end of your script. The output should look something like this:

```
VERBOSE: Starting Get-Computerdata
VERBOSE: Getting data from localhost
VERBOSE: Win32_Computersystem
VERBOSE: Win32_Bios
VERBOSE: Win32_OperatingSystem

Workgroup                 :
Manufacturer              : innotek GmbH
Computername              : CLIENT2
Version                   : 6.1.7601
Model                     : VirtualBox
AdminPassword             : NA
ServicePackMajorVersion   : 1
SerialNumber              : 0

VERBOSE: Ending Get-Computerdata
```

8.9.2   *Lab B*

Modify your advanced function from chapter 7, Lab B, to accept pipeline input for the –ComputerName parameter. Add verbose output that will display the name of each computer contacted. Ensure that the –ComputerName parameter will not accept a null or empty value. Test the function by adding 'localhost' | <function-name> -verbose to the end of your script. The output should look something like this:

```
VERBOSE: Starting Get-VolumeInfo
VERBOSE: Getting volume data from localhost
VERBOSE: Procssing volume \\?\Volume{8130d5f3-8e9b-11de-b460-806e6f6e6963}\
```

FreeSpace	Drive	Computername	Size
0.07	\\?\Volume{8130d5f3...	CLIENT2	0.10

```
VERBOSE: Procssing volume C:\Temp\
```

| 9.78 | C:\Temp\ | CLIENT2 | 10.00 |

```
VERBOSE: Procssing volume C:\
```

| 2.72 | C:\ | CLIENT2 | 19.90 |

```
VERBOSE: Procssing volume D:\
```

| 2.72 | D:\ | CLIENT2 | 4.00 |

```
VERBOSE: Ending Get-VolumeInfo
```

8.9.3   *Lab C*

Modify your advanced function from Lab C in chapter 7 to accept pipeline input for the –ComputerName parameter. Add verbose output that will display the name of each computer contacted and the name of each service queried. Ensure that the –ComputerName parameter will not accept a null or empty value. Test the function by running 'localhost' | <function-name> -verbose. The output for two services should look something like this:

```
VERBOSE: Starting Get-ServiceInfo
VERBOSE: Getting services from localhost
VERBOSE: Processing service AudioEndpointBuilder

Computername : CLIENT2
ThreadCount  : 13
```

```
ProcessName   : svchost.exe
Name          : AudioEndpointBuilder
VMSize        : 172224512
PeakPageFile  : 83112
Displayname   : Windows Audio Endpoint Builder
```

8.9.4 Standalone lab

Use this script as your starting point.

> **Listing 8.9 Standalone script**

```
function Get-SystemInfo {
    [CmdletBinding()]
    param(
        [string[]]$ComputerName
    )
    PROCESS {
        foreach ($computer in $computerName) {
            $os = Get-WmiObject -class Win32_OperatingSystem `
                                -computerName $computer
            $cs = Get-WmiObject -class Win32_ComputerSystem `
                                -computerName $computer
            $props = @{'ComputerName'=$computer;
                   'LastBootTime'=($os.ConvertToDateTime($os.LastBootupTime));
                   'OSVersion'=$os.version;
                   'Manufacturer'=$cs.manufacturer;
                   'Model'=$cs.model}
            $obj = New-Object -TypeName PSObject -Property $props
            Write-Output $obj
        }
    }
}
```

Modify this function to accept pipeline input for the –ComputerName parameter. Add verbose output that will display the name of each computer contacted. Ensure that the –ComputerName parameter will not accept a null or empty value. Test the script by adding this line to the end of the script file:

```
'localhost','localhost' | Get-SystemInfo -verbose
```

The output should look something like this:

```
VERBOSE: Getting WMI data from localhost

Model         : VirtualBox
ComputerName  : localhost
Manufacturer  : innotek GmbH
LastBootTime  : 6/19/2012 8:55:34 AM
OSVersion     : 6.1.7601
```

> **NOTE** Labs A, B, and C for chapters 7 through 14 build on what was accomplished in previous chapters. If you haven't finished a lab from a previous chapter, please do so. Then check your results with sample solutions on MoreLunches.com before proceeding to the next lab in the sequence.

Writing help 9

You'll notice in this book that each progressive chapter (through at least chapter 14) will make your tools progressively better and better. You could just take what you've learned to this point and stop, knowing that you have a functional, useful, and well-designed tool. But why stop now when it's just getting fun?

We're going to start focusing more and more on making your tools look, feel, smell, and taste (imagine that) more and more like a "real" PowerShell cmdlet. One way to do that is to have your tools include help that looks just like the help for PowerShell's native cmdlets.

9.1   *Comment-based help*

Right now, if we try to ask the help system for assistance with our `Get-SystemInfo` function, we'll get something like this:

```
NAME
    Get-SystemInfo

SYNTAX
    Get-SystemInfo [-ComputerName] <string[]> [[-ErrorLog] <string>]
    [-LogErrors]
    [<CommonParameters>]

ALIASES
    None

REMARKS
    Get-Help cannot find the Help files for this cmdlet on this computer.
    It is
    displaying only partial help.
        -- To download and install Help files for the module that includes
           this
    cmdlet, use Update-Help.
```

Not so helpful, really. In fact, it's downright wrong, because despite what it says, running `Update-Help` won't do anything to give our function better-looking, more-complete help. Fortunately, there's an easy fix, shown in the following listing.

Listing 9.1 Adding comment-based help to our function

```
function Get-SystemInfo {

<#
.SYNOPSIS
Retrieves key system version and model information
from one to ten computers.
.DESCRIPTION
Get-SystemInfo uses Windows Management Instrumentation
(WMI) to retrieve information from one or more computers.
Specify computers by name or by IP address.
.PARAMETER ComputerName
One or more computer names or IP addresses, up to a maximum
of 10.
.PARAMETER LogErrors
Specify this switch to create a text log file of computers
that could not be queried.
.PARAMETER ErrorLog
When used with -LogErrors, specifies the file path and name
to which failed computer names will be written. Defaults to
C:\Retry.txt.
.EXAMPLE
 Get-Content names.txt | Get-SystemInfo
.EXAMPLE
 Get-SystemInfo -ComputerName SERVER1,SERVER2
#>
    [CmdletBinding()]
    param(
        [Parameter(Mandatory=$True,
                   ValueFromPipeline=$True,
                   HelpMessage="Computer name or IP address")]
        [ValidateCount(1,10)]
        [Alias('hostname')]
        [string[]]$ComputerName,

        [string]$ErrorLog = 'c:\retry.txt',

        [switch]$LogErrors
    )
    BEGIN {
        Write-Verbose "Error log will be $ErrorLog"
    }
    PROCESS {
        Write-Verbose "Beginning PROCESS block"
        foreach ($computer in $computername) {
            Write-Verbose "Querying $computer"
            $os = Get-WmiObject -class Win32_OperatingSystem `
                            -computerName $computer
            $comp = Get-WmiObject -class Win32_ComputerSystem `
                            -computerName $computer
```

```
              $bios = Get-WmiObject -class Win32_BIOS `
                                     -computerName $computer
              $props = @{'ComputerName'=$computer;
                         'OSVersion'=$os.version;
                         'SPVersion'=$os.servicepackmajorversion;
                         'BIOSSerial'=$bios.serialnumber;
                         'Manufacturer'=$comp.manufacturer;
                         'Model'=$comp.model}
              Write-Verbose "WMI queries complete"
              $obj = New-Object -TypeName PSObject -Property $props
              Write-Output $obj
          }
      }
      END {}
}
help Get-SystemInfo -full
```

> **NOTE**   We added a last line to this script that will attempt to display help for
> `Get-SystemInfo`. This will let you test by running the script in the ISE.

We have a few things to point out:

- What we've added is called *comment-based help*, and you can read more about it
  by running `help about_comment_based_help` in the shell. We prefer to put the
  help immediately after our function's name but before the `[CmdletBinding()]`
  attribute, which is one of a couple of valid locations for the help and is the easiest location to not mess up.
- The help text is contained between <# and #>, which are PowerShell's *block comment* characters.
- The comment-based help is broken into sections, each of which starts with a
  specific keyword. The keywords needn't be in all uppercase as we've typed
  them, although that is the preferred style. The keywords all start with a period
  in the first column.
- Notice that the `.PARAMETER` section is included for each parameter the function
  offers, and the `.PARAMETER` keyword is followed by the parameter's name.
- The `.EXAMPLE` sections aren't numbered, but as you'll see in a moment, Power-
  Shell will sequentially number them for us.

We're big believers in documenting scripts, and this comment-based help serves to
document this script quite well. Unlike code comments, comment-based help isn't just
for someone reading the script! It also works for someone who is using our tool,
because when they ask for help they get a standard-looking PowerShell help display:

```
NAME
    Get-SystemInfo

SYNOPSIS
    Retrieves key system version and model information
    from one to ten computers.

SYNTAX
```

```
Get-SystemInfo [-ComputerName] <String[]> [[-ErrorLog] <String>] [-
LogErrors]
[<CommonParameters>]
```

DESCRIPTION
    Get-SystemInfo uses Windows Management Instrumentation
    (WMI) to retrieve information from one or more computers.
    Specify computers by name or by IP address.

PARAMETERS
    -ComputerName <String[]>
        One or more computer names or IP addresses, up to a maximum
        of 10.

Required?	true
Position?	1
Default value	
Accept pipeline input?	true (ByValue)
Accept wildcard characters?	false

    -ErrorLog <String>
        When used with -LogErrors, specifies the file path and name
        to which failed computer names will be written. Defaults to
        C:\Retry.txt.

Required?	false
Position?	2
Default value	c:\retry.txt
Accept pipeline input?	false
Accept wildcard characters?	false

    -LogErrors [<SwitchParameter>]
        Specify this switch to create a text log file of computers
        that could not be queried.

Required?	false
Position?	named
Default value	False
Accept pipeline input?	false
Accept wildcard characters?	false

    <CommonParameters>
        This cmdlet supports the common parameters: Verbose, Debug,
        ErrorAction, ErrorVariable, WarningAction, WarningVariable,
        OutBuffer and OutVariable. For more information, see
        about_CommonParameters (http://go.microsoft.com/fwlink/
    ?LinkID=113216).

INPUTS

OUTPUTS

    ------------------------ EXAMPLE 1 -------------------------

    C:\PS>Get-Content names.txt | Get-SystemInfo

    ------------------------ EXAMPLE 2 -------------------------

    C:\PS>Get-SystemInfo -ComputerName SERVER1,SERVER2

Now c'mon, tell us that isn't cool! Our examples are all broken out and numbered, the parameter help is all formatted, and it even picked up on our `-ComputerName` parameter's ability to accept input from the pipeline `ByValue`! This is, in the words of a PowerShell enthusiast friend of ours, $GREAT! The help system even word-wrapped our help to properly fit the screen and added the little `C:\PS>` prompt to our examples! Sorry—we know we're gushing, but this is just an incredibly neat feature. Our suggestion is that you document every one of your functions this way, so that they're documented both for other scripters and for the folks who will use them.

> **TRY IT NOW** You'll notice that some sections of the help display, like `INPUT` and `OUTPUT`, are empty. See if you can read `about_comment_based_help` and figure out how to get those sections to contain information.

Above and beyond

If you're happy putting your comment-based help where we did—at the top of the function but inside the function—then you can skip this sidebar.

It's also legal to put the comment-based help just before the function keyword, or "just above the function." For the first function in your script file, however, make sure there is no more than one blank line between the end of the comment-based help block and the function keyword. Also, there must be at least two blank lines between the start of the script and the first line of the comment-based help. Otherwise, the help will be interpreted as being for the script rather than for the function.

It's also legal to put the comment-based help at the very end of the function, after all of the function's code but before the function's closing curly bracket }. We think that's a silly place to put it, because it forces another scripter to have to scroll to the end of a function to figure out what it's supposed to be doing.

These rules are *exactly* why we put the comment-based help where we did: It's easier, as we mentioned, to not mess things up that way!

9.2   *XML-based help*

Our honest preference is to use comment-based help—but that's because we only speak English. The one downside to comment-based help is that it doesn't support multilingual help. You can type your comment-based help in English or German or any other language, but you have to pick just one language. Using XML-based help, on the other hand, lets you provide help in multiple languages. PowerShell automatically picks the language based on Windows' own configuration. This is how PowerShell's native commands provide their help.

> **APOLOGIES IN ADVANCE** We hate doing this, but honestly XML-based help isn't something you're going to use in conjunction with a script. You'd mainly only use it in conjunction with a module, which is just a way of packaging a script and several supporting files, like the XML-based help. We won't get to modules until chapter 13, but we're going to talk about XML-based help now. The fact is that most folks (other than major software vendors like Microsoft) won't use it, because it's a lot more hassle than comment-based help.

PowerShell's native help system uses an XML format called MAML, which is a bit of a bear to work with and is mostly not very well documented. On the plus side, this help is contained in an external file, which helps to keep your functions a bit shorter and more readable by moving the help out of those sometimes-lengthy comments.

There are a couple of ways to make working with MAML a bit easier:

- Use Microsoft InfoPath, along with an InfoPath template to create a help file from your script.

  You'll find details and the template in a blog post at http://blogs.technet .com/b/jamesone/archive/2009/07/24/powershell-on-line-help-a-change-you -should-make-for-v2-3-and-how-to-author-maml-help-files-for-powershell.aspx.

  Note that you can't use the file that's created by InfoPath; you have to make a minor adjustment to it in order for PowerShell to use the file properly. That blog post explains what you'll need to do.

- Download http://blogs.msdn.com/b/powershell/archive/2011/02/24/cmdlet-help-editor-v2-0-with-module-support.aspx, which is a cmdlet help editor. This tool lets you copy and paste the bits of your help (synopsis, description, and so forth) and produces a ready-to-use MAML file. We think this is a bit easier to use, but it's a pretty cumbersome, manual process.

Each XML file contains the help for a single language. You then have to create the proper folder structure in which to place the files. Assume that you've created US English help and German help, all for a module named Test.psm1 (if you were to save our existing Test.ps1 file as test.psm1, within the folder structure we're about to show you, it would magically become a "script module"). Your help file folder structure has to start in the same folder where your script module resides. Here's the folder structure:

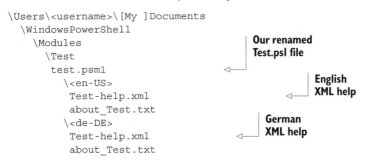

```
\Users\<username>\[My ]Documents
  \WindowsPowerShell
    \Modules
      \Test
       test.psm1
         \<en-US>
          Test-help.xml
          about_Test.txt
         \<de-DE>
          Test-help.xml
          about_Test.txt
```

Our renamed
Test.psl file

**English
XML help**

**German
XML help**

NOTE This folder structure needs to go in your My Documents folder, not in your Public Documents folder, which can be hard to distinguish on Windows Vista and later, because they're both part of the Documents Library. So be careful. Also, the WindowsPowerShell folder and everything under it doesn't exist by default—you have to create all of it yourself.

The English help goes under the <en-US> folder, while the German help goes under <de-DE>—those two folder names reflect the internal culture codes that Windows uses to identify a language (such as en or de) and its regional variants (such as US or, for British English, UK).

TIP You can find a complete list of culture codes and their corresponding languages at http://msdn.microsoft.com/en-us/library/ee825488(v=CS.20).aspx.

Notice that we've also specified an about topic for the entire module, which is just a plain text file. That file has to have the filename about_<moduleName>.txt, where <moduleName> is the exact name of your module—Test in this example. We've also provided an XML file in each language, which contains help for the individual functions. Those XML files are created using the PowerShell Help Editor tool (or Info-Path, if you prefer). You can add as many languages as you want, provided each is included in a folder with the proper culture name.

NOTE One thing you should know is that many international PowerShell users actually use a US English version of Windows, so their default help language is en-US. Some folks at Microsoft tell us that, although the company provides PowerShell help in more than a dozen languages, the en-US ones are the most-often used. Apparently there have been errors in some of the non-English files that went undetected for months because people don't use those files. So before you dive into the work of translating help files into languages other than US English, you might check with the folks who will be using that help to find out what language(s) they want.

The XML-based help definitely requires a bit more effort. It's worth it if you have (or want to write) extensive help that makes comment-based help unwieldy, or if you want to provide help in multiple languages for a given script.

9.3 Coming up next

Okay, our Get-SystemInfo has had an -ErrorLog parameter for a few chapters now, and we recently added -LogErrors on top of that. It's time to stop putting off the task of actually making those do something, so error handling will be the topic of our next chapter.

9.4 Labs

These labs will build on what you've already created, applying new concepts from this chapter.

9.4.1 Lab A

Add comment-based help to your advanced function from Lab A in chapter 8. Include at least a synopsis, description, and help for the -ComputerName parameter. Test your help by adding help <function-name> to the end of your script.

9.4.2 Lab B

Add comment-based help to your advanced function from Lab B in chapter 8. Include at least a synopsis, description, and help for the -ComputerName parameter. Test your help by adding help <function-name> to the end of your script.

9.4.3   Lab C

Add comment-based help to your advanced function from Lab C in chapter 8. Include at least a synopsis, description, and help for the –ComputerName parameter. Test your help by adding `help <function-name>` to the end of your script.

9.4.4   Standalone lab

Using the script in the following listing, add comment-based help.

Listing 9.2   Standalone lab starting point

```
function Get-SystemInfo {
    [CmdletBinding()]
    param(
        [Parameter(Mandatory=$True,ValueFromPipeline=$True)]
        [ValidateNotNullOrEmpty()]
        [string[]]$ComputerName
    )
    PROCESS {
        foreach ($computer in $computerName) {
            Write-Verbose "Getting WMI data from $computer"
            $os = Get-WmiObject -class Win32_OperatingSystem
    ➥ -computerName $computer
            $cs = Get-WmiObject -class Win32_ComputerSystem
    ➥ -computerName $computer
            $props = @{'ComputerName'=$computer;
                        'LastBootTime'=
    ➥ ($os.ConvertToDateTime($os.LastBootupTime));
                        'OSVersion'=$os.version;
                        'Manufacturer'=$cs.manufacturer;
                        'Model'=$cs.model
                }
            $obj = New-Object -TypeName PSObject -Property $props
            Write-Output $obj
        }
    }
}
```

Include at least a synopsis, description, and help for the –ComputerName parameter. Test your help by adding `help <function-name>` to the end of your script.

> **NOTE** Labs A, B, and C for chapters 7 through 14 build on what was accomplished in previous chapters. If you haven't finished a lab from a previous chapter, please do so. Then check your results with sample solutions on MoreLunches.com before proceeding to the next lab in the sequence.

Error handling

10

The Get-SystemInfo function we wrote earlier was designed from the outset to log the names of computers it failed to reach. In this chapter, we'll make that happen, through a set of techniques collectively known as *error handling*.

10.1 It's all about the action

Whenever a PowerShell command—be it a native cmdlet or a function you write—encounters a non-terminating error, it asks PowerShell what to do. PowerShell looks at a built-in variable, $ErrorActionPreference, to see what it should do.

Before we dive into that, let's talk about this *non-terminating error* thing. It's any error that presents a problem, but one from which the command can recover and continue. "Hey, this computer was unreachable, but if you want, I can continue trying with the next computer in the list." That's different than a *terminating error*, which means everything will stop completely.

So what does $ErrorActionPreference do? It can be set to one of four values:

- Continue—This is the default, and it says, "Hey, if you can keep going, go for it, but display an error message to let me know what happened." It looks like this:

```
PS C:\> $ErrorActionPreference = 'Continue'

PS C:\> Get-WmiObject -class Win32_BIOS -ComputerName
NOTONLINE,localhost
Get-WmiObject : The RPC server is unavailable. (Exception from
HRESULT: 0x800706BA)
At line:1 char:1
+ Get-WmiObject -class Win32_BIOS -ComputerName NOTONLINE,localhost
+ ~~~~~~~~~~~~~~~~~~~~~~~~~~~~~~~~~~~~~~~~~~~~~~~~~~~~~~~~~~~~~~~~~~~~~
    + CategoryInfo          : InvalidOperation: (:) [Get-WmiObject],
COMException
```

```
    + FullyQualifiedErrorId :
GetWMICOMException,Microsoft.PowerShell.Commands.Get
   WmiObjectCommand

SMBIOSBIOSVersion : 7.0.15094.749908
Manufacturer      : Parallels Software International Inc.
Name              : Default System BIOS
SerialNumber      : Parallels-D5 A7 11 48 6C 63 42 80 AB E6 90 AF C4 D3
FC DC
Version           : PRLS   - 1
```

- SilentlyContinue—This is the setting you wish your kids had: "Keep going, don't talk about it, don't display any error messages—just shut up and get on with it." It looks like this:

```
PS C:\> $ErrorActionPreference = 'SilentlyContinue'

PS C:\> Get-WmiObject -class Win32_BIOS -ComputerName
NOTONLINE,localhost

SMBIOSBIOSVersion : 7.0.15094.749908
Manufacturer      : Parallels Software International Inc.
Name              : Default System BIOS
SerialNumber      : Parallels-D5 A7 11 48 6C 63 42 80 AB E6 90 AF C4 D3
FC DC
Version           : PRLS   - 1
```

- Stop—This turns the non-terminating error into a terminating exception, meaning the command stops. By default, that'll also display an error message. Here's what happens:

```
PS C:\> $ErrorActionPreference = 'Stop'

PS C:\> Get-WmiObject -class Win32_BIOS -ComputerName
NOTONLINE,localhost
Get-WmiObject : The RPC server is unavailable. (Exception from HRESULT:
0x800706BA)
At line:1 char:1
+ Get-WmiObject -class Win32_BIOS -ComputerName NOTONLINE,localhost
+ ~~~~~~~~~~~~~~~~~~~~~~~~~~~~~~~~~~~~~~~~~~~~~~~~~~~~~~~~~~~~~~~~~~~~~
    + CategoryInfo          : InvalidOperation: (:) [Get-WmiObject],
COMException
    + FullyQualifiedErrorId :
GetWMICOMException,Microsoft.PowerShell.Commands.Get
   WmiObjectCommand
```

- Inquire—"Ask me what to do." Literally, with a prompt. This is almost never the right answer, but it can sometimes be useful in troubleshooting situations. It looks like this:

```
PS C:\> $ErrorActionPreference = 'Inquire'
PS C:\> Get-WmiObject -Class Win32_BIOS -ComputerName
NOTONLINE,localhost

Confirm
The RPC server is unavailable. (Exception from HRESULT: 0x800706BA)
[Y] Yes  [A] Yes to All  [H] Halt Command  [S] Suspend  [?] Help
(default is "Y"):
```

Now, let's be crystal clear about something: You should not be modifying $ErrorActionPreference in most cases. One of the things that bugs us the most is getting a script from someone and seeing $ErrorActionPreference= 'SilentlyContinue' right at the top. What, exactly, are they trying to hide? Sure, maybe there's some command that causes an error, and they're comfortable just hiding that error, but their approach is hiding every error the script might produce! That might well be useful information, and hiding it might feel better (no ugly red text on the screen!), but it doesn't help you get the script working.

What's needed is a way to tell a specific command that you want it to take some behavior other than the default when an error occurs.

10.2 *Setting the error action*

And you can do exactly that. It's hard to realize, but every command—even the ones you write yourself—support a set of common parameters. You'll see <CommonParameters> listed in the syntax help for every command, and if you run help about _common_parameters, you can see a list of them all. The one that concerns us right now is -ErrorAction, which can be abbreviated as -EA. The parameter accepts the same four values as $ErrorActionPreference: Continue, SilentlyContinue, Stop, and Inquire. The trick is that, unlike $ErrorActionPreference, -ErrorAction affects only that single command. You can suppress errors for just the one command you *expect* to cause them, while leaving everything else able to raise any *unexpected* errors that come up.

But SilentlyContinue isn't going to be our focus. Instead, we're going to be using Stop a lot. That's because the terminating exception produced by Stop is something we can trap, enabling us to handle the error ourselves rather than just getting the default error message.

10.3 *Saving the error*

Another common parameter is -ErrorVariable, or -EV. This lets you specify a variable name (remember, the variable name doesn't include a dollar sign), and any error produced by the command will be stored in that variable so that you can examine it and take whatever action you like. Here's how it works:

```
PS C:\> Get-WmiObject -Class Win32_BIOS -ComputerName NOTONLINE -EV err -EA
    SilentlyContinue

PS C:\> $err
Get-WmiObject : The RPC server is unavailable. (Exception from HRESULT:
    0x800706BA)
At line:1 char:1
+ Get-WmiObject -Class Win32_BIOS -ComputerName NOTONLINE -EV err -EA
    SilentlyCont
...
+
~~~~~~~~~~~~~~~~~~~~~~~~~~~~~~~~~~~~~~~~~~~~~~~~~~~~~~~~~~~~~~~~~~~~~~~~~~~~~~~~~~~
~~~~~
    + CategoryInfo          : InvalidOperation: (:) [Get-WmiObject],
 COMException
```

```
    + FullyQualifiedErrorId :
GetWMICOMException,Microsoft.PowerShell.Commands.Get
    WmiObjectCommand
```

You have to be really careful with –ErrorVariable. For example, consider this:

```
PS C:\> $x = 'fred'

PS C:\> Gwmi Win32_BIOS -ErrorVariable $x
```

The error isn't in $x. The error is in $fred. You see, we told –ErrorVariable to *access the contents of x*—that's what the $ means in front of a variable name. So –ErrorVariable looked inside x, found fred, and created a variable $fred. There's no problem with using this technique if that's what you intended, but if you intended for the error to go into $x, then you can see how this would be confusing. If that was our intent, then the command should have looked like this:

```
PS C:\> Gwmi Win32_BIOS -ErrorVariable x
```

Be careful when you're providing that variable name.

10.4 *Error handling v1: Trap*

We're going to briefly cover this error-handling construct, because you may well run across it in someone's script that you've found on the internet. If you don't think that'll ever happen, then skip to the next section, because we don't think you'll be writing any new commands using this construct.

The construct's name is Trap. Essentially, it works like this: When a command causes a terminating error (which you can trigger by using –ErrorAction Stop), PowerShell scans *backward* in the *current scope* to see if a Trap construct exists. Read that carefully: It won't scan ahead in the scope, which means you have to define your Trap before you think the error will occur. As a result, Traps tend to occur at the top of the script file. When PowerShell finds a Trap, it runs whatever code is inside.

Scope plays an important role with Trap, and it can become very complex—which is a big part of why people don't use it so much anymore. For example, say you're in a function and an error occurs. PowerShell will look inside the function for a Trap. If it doesn't find one, PowerShell exits the function, goes up one level (let's say the function is inside a script, so we're now in the script's scope), and looks for a Trap there. If it finds one, it'll execute it.

At the end of the Trap, you can execute one of two commands: Break or Continue. Break exits the current scope, passing the original error up to the parent scope. That's kind of like saying, "I couldn't handle this error, so I'm handing it off to you, and I'm finished." Continue will resume execution *in the same scope*, on the command *following* the one that caused the error.

Confused? Yeah, us too. This is really hard to follow. What's worse is that the Trap itself has its own scope—so it's tricky to modify variables or anything within the Trap, because doing so just (by default) creates new items inside the Trap itself, without affecting the Trap's parent scope.

We're not going to explore this construct any further. If you need to learn more about it in order to translate some old script you've found, run `help about_trap` in the shell; we recommend sticking with newer techniques in any new tools you write.

10.5 *Error Handling v2+: Try...Catch...Finally*

Introduced in PowerShell v2, this is the real way to do error handling. All the cool kids are doing it, because it's easier and much more like the error handling found in traditional programming languages. It's called `Try...Catch...Finally`, and we're going to slap it into our `Get-SystemInfo` function to show you how it works. Check out this listing.

Listing 10.1 Adding `Try...Catch` to our function

```
function Get-SystemInfo {
<#
.SYNOPSIS
Retrieves key system version and model information
from one to ten computers.
.DESCRIPTION
Get-SystemInfo uses Windows Management Instrumentation
(WMI) to retrieve information from one or more computers.
Specify computers by name or by IP address.
.PARAMETER ComputerName
One or more computer names or IP addresses, up to a maximum
of 10.
.PARAMETER LogErrors
Specify this switch to create a text log file of computers
that could not be queried.
.PARAMETER ErrorLog
When used with -LogErrors, specifies the file path and name
to which failed computer names will be written. Defaults to
C:\Retry.txt.
.EXAMPLE
 Get-Content names.txt | Get-SystemInfo
.EXAMPLE
 Get-SystemInfo -ComputerName SERVER1,SERVER2
#>
    [CmdletBinding()]
    param(
        [Parameter(Mandatory=$True,
                   ValueFromPipeline=$True,
                   HelpMessage="Computer name or IP address")]
        [ValidateCount(1,10)]
        [Alias('hostname')]
        [string[]]$ComputerName,

        [string]$ErrorLog = 'c:\retry.txt',

        [switch]$LogErrors
    )
    BEGIN {
        Write-Verbose "Error log will be $ErrorLog"
    }
```

```
PROCESS {
    Write-Verbose "Beginning PROCESS block"
    foreach ($computer in $computername) {
        Write-Verbose "Querying $computer"
        Try {
            $os = Get-WmiObject -class Win32_OperatingSystem `
                                -computerName $computer `
                                -erroraction Stop
        } Catch {
            if ($LogErrors) {
                $computer | Out-File $ErrorLog -Append
            }
        }
        $comp = Get-WmiObject -class Win32_ComputerSystem `
                              -computerName $computer
        $bios = Get-WmiObject -class Win32_BIOS `
                              -computerName $computer
        $props = @{'ComputerName'=$computer;
                   'OSVersion'=$os.version;
                   'SPVersion'=$os.servicepackmajorversion;
                   'BIOSSerial'=$bios.serialnumber;
                   'Manufacturer'=$comp.manufacturer;
                   'Model'=$comp.model}
        Write-Verbose "WMI queries complete"
        $obj = New-Object -TypeName PSObject -Property $props
        Write-Output $obj
    }
}
END {}
}

Get-SystemInfo -computername NOTONLINE
```

So what have we done?

- We added -ErrorAction Stop to the command that we expect to cause an error, Get-WmiObject.
- We surrounded the error-causing command in a Try{} construct.
- We created a Catch{} construct, which will be executed if a terminating exception occurs anywhere within the Try{} construct. Notice that we check the $LogErrors variable, which is our -LogErrors switch parameter, to see if we're supposed to be logging errors. If we are, we append the failed computer name to whatever file is specified in $ErrorLog.
- We didn't include a Finally{} construct, because it's optional. But had we chosen to do so, its contents would have executed whether or not an error occurred within the Try{} construct.
- You have the option of including multiple Catch{} constructs. If you do, each one identifies one or more exceptions for that particular Catch{} block. You can define different error handling for different exceptions. Read about_try _catch_finally in the shell for examples of multiple Catch{} blocks.

We've not quite finished with our error handling. Right now, our function is only checking for errors on the first `Get-WmiObject` command. If that fails, shouldn't we just skip the remaining ones? After all, they're just as likely to fail, right? Look at the next listing.

Listing 10.2   Finishing off the error handling

```
function Get-SystemInfo {
<#
.SYNOPSIS
Retrieves key system version and model information
from one to ten computers.
.DESCRIPTION
Get-SystemInfo uses Windows Management Instrumentation
(WMI) to retrieve information from one or more computers.
Specify computers by name or by IP address.
.PARAMETER ComputerName
One or more computer names or IP addresses, up to a maximum
of 10.
.PARAMETER LogErrors
Specify this switch to create a text log file of computers
that could not be queried.
.PARAMETER ErrorLog
When used with -LogErrors, specifies the file path and name
to which failed computer names will be written. Defaults to
C:\Retry.txt.
.EXAMPLE
 Get-Content names.txt | Get-SystemInfo
.EXAMPLE
 Get-SystemInfo -ComputerName SERVER1,SERVER2
#>
    [CmdletBinding()]
    param(
        [Parameter(Mandatory=$True,
                   ValueFromPipeline=$True,
                   HelpMessage="Computer name or IP address")]
        [ValidateCount(1,10)]
        [Alias('hostname')]
        [string[]]$ComputerName,

        [string]$ErrorLog = 'c:\retry.txt',

        [switch]$LogErrors
    )
    BEGIN {
        Write-Verbose "Error log will be $ErrorLog"
    }
    PROCESS {
        Write-Verbose "Beginning PROCESS block"
        foreach ($computer in $computername) {
            Write-Verbose "Querying $computer"
            Try {
                $everything_ok = $true
                $os = Get-WmiObject -class Win32_OperatingSystem `
                                    -computerName $computer `
```

```
                                -erroraction Stop
        } Catch {
            $everything_ok = $false
            if ($LogErrors) {
                $computer | Out-File $ErrorLog -Append
            }
        }

        if ($everything_ok) {
            $comp = Get-WmiObject -class Win32_ComputerSystem `
                                -computerName $computer
            $bios = Get-WmiObject -class Win32_BIOS `
                                -computerName $computer
            $props = @{'ComputerName'=$computer;
                    'OSVersion'=$os.version;
                    'SPVersion'=$os.servicepackmajorversion;
                    'BIOSSerial'=$bios.serialnumber;
                    'Manufacturer'=$comp.manufacturer;
                    'Model'=$comp.model}
            Write-Verbose "WMI queries complete"
            $obj = New-Object -TypeName PSObject -Property $props
            Write-Output $obj
        }
    }
  }
  END {}
}

Get-SystemInfo -computername NOTONLINE -logerrors
```

We put the new stuff in boldface in listing 10.2. Basically, before running the first Get-WmiObject command, we created a new variable, $everything_ok, and set it to $True. We're optimistic guys. If that command causes an error, $everything_ok gets set to $False whether we're going to log the error or not. Then, we only execute the rest of the function if $everything_ok is still $True.

TRY IT NOW The proof is in the execution, so make sure you can run this script (be sure to include the -LogErrors parameter, as we did in the last line of the script) with a bad computer name and have that computer name show up in the log file.

10.6 *Providing some visuals*

One problem we have with our error handling is that we're no longer displaying a useful error message to whoever is running our script. They might not, for example, even remember or realize where the error log file is! So let's make one final change, in the following listing, that displays a warning (which is less severe than an error) to the user.

> **Listing 10.3 Adding a warning message**

```
function Get-SystemInfo {
<#
.SYNOPSIS
Retrieves key system version and model information
```

```
from one to ten computers.
.DESCRIPTION
Get-SystemInfo uses Windows Management Instrumentation
(WMI) to retrieve information from one or more computers.
Specify computers by name or by IP address.
.PARAMETER ComputerName
One or more computer names or IP addresses, up to a maximum
of 10.
.PARAMETER LogErrors
Specify this switch to create a text log file of computers
that could not be queried.
.PARAMETER ErrorLog
When used with -LogErrors, specifies the file path and name
to which failed computer names will be written. Defaults to
C:\Retry.txt.
.EXAMPLE
 Get-Content names.txt | Get-SystemInfo
.EXAMPLE
 Get-SystemInfo -ComputerName SERVER1,SERVER2
#>
    [CmdletBinding()]
    param(
        [Parameter(Mandatory=$True,
                   ValueFromPipeline=$True,
                   HelpMessage="Computer name or IP address")]
        [ValidateCount(1,10)]
        [Alias('hostname')]
        [string[]]$ComputerName,

        [string]$ErrorLog = 'c:\retry.txt',

        [switch]$LogErrors
    )
    BEGIN {
        Write-Verbose "Error log will be $ErrorLog"
    }
    PROCESS {
        Write-Verbose "Beginning PROCESS block"
        foreach ($computer in $computername) {
            Write-Verbose "Querying $computer"
            Try {
                $everything_ok = $true
                $os = Get-WmiObject -class Win32_OperatingSystem `
                                    -computerName $computer `
                                    -erroraction Stop
            } Catch {
                $everything_ok = $false
                Write-Warning "$computer failed"
                if ($LogErrors) {
                    $computer | Out-File $ErrorLog -Append
                    Write-Warning "Logged to $ErrorLog"
                }
            }

            if ($everything_ok) {
                $comp = Get-WmiObject -class Win32_ComputerSystem `
```

```
                               -computerName $computer
            $bios = Get-WmiObject -class Win32_BIOS `
                               -computerName $computer
            $props = @{'ComputerName'=$computer;
                       'OSVersion'=$os.version;
                       'SPVersion'=$os.servicepackmajorversion;
                       'BIOSSerial'=$bios.serialnumber;
                       'Manufacturer'=$comp.manufacturer;
                       'Model'=$comp.model}
            Write-Verbose "WMI queries complete"
            $obj = New-Object -TypeName PSObject -Property $props
            Write-Output $obj
        }
      }
    }
    END {}
}

Get-SystemInfo -ComputerName NOTONLINE -LogErrors
```

Just a couple of calls to `Write-Warning` make the output of our script much more useful:

```
PS C:\> C:\test.ps1
WARNING: NOTONLINE failed
WARNING: Logged to c:\retry.txt
```

> **TIP** The exception object is passed to the `Catch` block as `$_` so you can capture a lot of information from it. One thing Jeff often includes in his `Catch` blocks is a line like this: `Write-Warning $_.Exception.Message` so that the user can see the error message without the exception. If you use the common `-errorvariable`, you can also pass that. But the variable is the exception, so you could do this, assuming an `errorrvariable` of err: `Write-Warning $err.message`.

10.7 Coming up next

We're starting to make these tools complex enough that there are bound to be bugs, and we need to show you how to squash those as efficiently as possible. So in the next chapter, we're going to take a quick break from building `Get-SystemInfo` (and your lab functions) and focus on debugging.

10.8 Labs

You are going to continue with the functions you've been building the last few chapters. The next step is to begin incorporating some error handling using `Try...Catch...Finally`. If you haven't done so, take a few minutes to read the help content on `Try...Catch...Finally`. For any changes you make, don't forget to update your comment-based help.

10.8.1 Lab A

Using Lab A from chapter 9, add a `-ErrorLog` parameter to your advanced function, which accepts a filename for an error log and defaults to C:\Errors.txt. When the function is run with this parameter, failed computer names should be appended to the error log file.

Next, if the first WMI query fails, the function should output nothing for that computer and should not attempt a second or third WMI query. Write an error to the pipeline containing each failed computer name.

Test all of this by adding this line `<function-name>` -ComputerName localhost, NOTONLINE -verbose to the end of your script. A portion of the output should look something like this:

```
VERBOSE: Starting Get-Computerdata
VERBOSE: Getting data from localhost
VERBOSE: Win32_Computersystem
VERBOSE: Win32_Bios
VERBOSE: Win32_OperatingSystem

Workgroup                 :
Manufacturer              : innotek GmbH
Computername              : CLIENT2
Version                   : 6.1.7601
SerialNumber              : 0
Model                     : VirtualBox
AdminPassword             : NA
ServicePackMajorVersion : 1

VERBOSE: Getting data from notonline
VERBOSE: Win32_Computersystem
Get-Computerdata : Failed getting system information from notonline. The RPC
    server is
unavailable. (Exception from HRESULT: 0x800706BA)
At S:\Toolmaking\Ch10-LabA.ps1:115 char:40
+ 'localhost','notonline','localhost' | Get-Computerdata -logerrors -verbose
+                                        ~~~~~~~~~~~~~~~~~~~~~~~~~~~~~~~~~~~~~
    + CategoryInfo          : NotSpecified: (:) [Write-Error],
      WriteErrorException
    + FullyQualifiedErrorId :
      Microsoft.PowerShell.Commands.WriteErrorException,Get-Comp
    uterData

VERBOSE: Getting data from localhost
```

10.8.2 *Lab B*

Using Lab B from chapter 9, add a -ErrorLog parameter to your advanced function, which accepts a filename for an error log and defaults to C:\Errors.txt. When the function is run with this parameter, failed computer names should be appended to the error log file.

Test all of this by adding this line `<function-name>` -ComputerName localhost, NOTONLINE -verbose to the end of your script. A portion of the output should look something like this:

```
VERBOSE: Starting Get-VolumeInfo
VERBOSE: Getting data from localhost
```

FreeSpace	Drive	Computername	Size
---------	-----	------------	----
0.07	\\?\Volume{8130d5f3...	CLIENT2	0.10
9.78	C:\Temp\	CLIENT2	10.00
2.72	C:\	CLIENT2	19.90
2.72	D:\	CLIENT2	4.00

```
VERBOSE: Getting data from NotOnline
Get-VolumeInfo : Failed to get volume information from NotOnline. The RPC
    server is
unavailable. (Exception from HRESULT: 0x800706BA)
At S:\Toolmaking\Ch10-LabB.ps1:96 char:27
+ 'localhost','NotOnline' | Get-VolumeInfo -Verbose -logerrors
+                           ~~~~~~~~~~~~~~~~~~~~~~~~~~~~~~~~~~~~
    + CategoryInfo          : NotSpecified: (:) [Write-Error],
    WriteErrorException
    + FullyQualifiedErrorId :
    Microsoft.PowerShell.Commands.WriteErrorException,Get-Volu
  meInfo

VERBOSE: Logging errors to C:\Errors.txt
VERBOSE: Ending Get-VolumeInfo
```

10.8.3 *Lab C*

Using Lab C from chapter 9, add a -LogErrors switch parameter to your advanced function. Also add a -ErrorFile parameter, which accepts a filename for an error log and defaults to C:\Errors.txt. When the function is run with the -LogErrors parameter, failed computer names should be appended to the error log file. Also, if -LogErrors is used, the log file should be deleted at the start of the function if it exists, so that each time the command starts with a fresh log file.

Test all of this by adding this line <function-name> -ComputerName localhost, NOTONLINE -verbose -logerrors to the end of your script. A portion of the output should look something like this:

```
VERBOSE: Processing service wuauserv
VERBOSE: Getting process for wuauserv
Computername : CLIENT2
ThreadCount  : 45
ProcessName  : svchost.exe
Name         : wuauserv
VMSize       : 499363840
PeakPageFile : 247680
Displayname  : Windows Update

VERBOSE: Getting services from NOTOnline
Get-ServiceInfo : Failed to get service data from NOTOnline. The RPC server is
unavailable. (Exception from HRESULT: 0x800706BA)
At S:\Toolmaking\Ch10-LabC.ps1:109 char:39
+ "localhost","NOTOnline","localhost" | Get-ServiceInfo -logerrors -verbose
+                                       ~~~~~~~~~~~~~~~~~~~~~~~~~~~~~~~~~~~~
    + CategoryInfo          : NotSpecified: (:) [Write-Error],
    WriteErrorException
    + FullyQualifiedErrorId :
    Microsoft.PowerShell.Commands.WriteErrorException,Get-Serv
  iceInfo
```

```
VERBOSE: Logging errors to C:\Errors.txt
VERBOSE: Getting services from localhost
VERBOSE: Processing service AudioEndpointBuilder
VERBOSE: Getting process for AudioEndpointBuilder
```

10.8.4   *Standalone lab*

Use the code in the following listing as a starting point.

Listing 10.4   Standalone lab starting point

```
Function Get-SystemInfo {

<#
.SYNOPSIS
Gets critical system info from one or more computers.
.DESCRIPTION
This command uses WMI, and can accept computer names, CNAME aliases,
and IP addresses. WMI must be enabled and you must run this
with admin rights for any remote computer.
.PARAMETER Computername
One or more names or IP addresses to query.
.EXAMPLE
Get-SystemInfo -computername localhost
#>
    [CmdletBinding()]
    param(
        [Parameter(Mandatory=$True,ValueFromPipeline=$True)]
        [ValidateNotNullOrEmpty()]
        [string[]]$ComputerName
    )
    PROCESS {
        foreach ($computer in $computerName) {
            WWrite-Verbose "Getting WMI data from $computer"
            $os = Get-WmiObject -class Win32_OperatingSystem
   ➥ -computerName $computer
            $cs = Get-WmiObject -class Win32_ComputerSystem
   ➥ -computerName $computer
            $props = @{'ComputerName'=$computer;
                       'LastBootTime'=
➥ ($os.ConvertToDateTime($os.LastBootupTime));
                       'OSVersion'=$os.version;
                       'Manufacturer'=$cs.manufacturer;
                       'Model'=$cs.model
                                }
            $obj = New-Object -TypeName PSObject -Property $props
            Write-Output $obj
        }
    }
}
```

Add a –LogErrors switch to this advanced function. When the function is run with
this switch, failed computer names should be logged to C:\Errors.txt. This file should
be deleted at the start of the function each time it is run, so that it starts out fresh each
time. If the first WMI query fails, the function should output nothing for that

computer and should not attempt a second WMI query. Write an error to the pipeline containing each failed computer name.

Test your script by adding this line to the end of your script.

```
Get-SystemInfo -computername localhost,NOTONLINE,localhost -logerrors
```

A portion of the output should look something like this:

```
Model        : VirtualBox
ComputerName : localhost
Manufacturer : innotek GmbH
LastBootTime : 6/19/2012 8:55:34 AM
OSVersion    : 6.1.7601

Get-SystemInfo : NOTONLINE failed
At S:\Toolmaking\Ch10-Standalone.ps1:51 char:1
+ Get-SystemInfo -computername localhost,NOTONLINE,localhost -logerrors
+ ~~~~~~~~~~~~~~~~~~~~~~~~~~~~~~~~~~~~~~~~~~~~~~~~~~~~~~~~~~~~~~~~~~~~~~~~
    + CategoryInfo          : NotSpecified: (:) [Write-Error],
    WriteErrorException
    + FullyQualifiedErrorId :
    Microsoft.PowerShell.Commands.WriteErrorException,Get-Syst
  emInfo

Model        : VirtualBox
ComputerName : localhost
Manufacturer : innotek GmbH
LastBootTime : 6/19/2012 8:55:34 AM
OSVersion    : 6.1.7601
```

NOTE Labs A, B, and C for chapters 7 through 14 build on what was accomplished in previous chapters. If you haven't finished a lab from a previous chapter, please do so. Then check your results with sample solutions on MoreLunches.com before proceeding to the next lab in the sequence.

Debugging techniques 11

Debugging can be one of the most frustrating parts of toolmaking, and we feel it's often because folks don't have a consistent, methodical approach to debugging. That's what we're going to offer you in this chapter. We'll even make a promise: If you follow our recommendations, you'll find debugging to be infinitely less frustrating. We'll even walk you through some real-life debugging examples to help drive home the point.

11.1 Two types of bugs

We feel that the entire universe of software bugs, at least the PowerShell universe, essentially comes down to one of two types: typos and logic errors.

Typos are straightforward enough: They're what happen when you type something wrong. Maybe it's a command name. Maybe you mistype a variable name. Maybe you forgot a closing quotation mark or curly bracket. Whatever the cause, typos are relatively easy to prevent (we'll offer some tips shortly) and to solve, at least compared to their more sinister cousin, logic errors.

When a script has a logic error, it may run without actually displaying any error messages, or any errors it does produce seem unrelated or vague. Either way, the script doesn't do what you want it to do. We find that, in the end, logic errors come down to one single, straightforward cause: You (or whoever wrote the script) made a wrong assumption. Perhaps you assumed a command would output "True" when in fact it outputs an entire object full of data; maybe you assumed a variable contained a string value when in fact it contained a number. Whatever the cause, bad assumptions are at the root of almost every logic error. The bulk of this chapter will focus on how to validate and correct those assumptions and expectations.

11.2   Solving typos

Typos are fixable. They're even easy to catch up front—especially if you're formatting your scripts carefully. Yeah, we told you back in the beginning of this book that the formatting thing would keep surfacing, and we're really going to pound it in now.

We don't want to make this a big chapter on typos, though, so let's stick with this short list of tips:

- Get to know your script editing software, whether it's the PowerShell ISE or something else. Get used to its colors, its error indicators, its display options, and so forth. Half the time, typos like unclosed quotes and brackets reveal themselves in not-normal coloring and other artifacts, making them pretty easy to catch if you're paying attention.
- Format your scripts neatly. Indent code within curly brackets {} and parentheses (), and put the closing bracket (or parentheses) at the same indent level as the line that opened the construct.
- Read error messages. Honestly, PowerShell does its best to tell you what it's upset about. Consider this command and its resulting error, where PowerShell is making it clear that it doesn't understand the misspelled parameter name (we've boldfaced it for you) and even telling you the exact character position (13) where the problem exists. It even, in its character-based way, underlined the part it had a problem with (also in our boldfacing)!

```
PS C:\> Get-Service -conputername localhost -Name s*
Get-Service : A parameter cannot be found that matches parameter name
'conputername'.
At line:1 char:13
+ Get-Service -conputername localhost -Name s*
+             ~~~~~~~~~~~~~
    + CategoryInfo          : InvalidArgument: (:) [Get-Service],
    ParameterBinding
  Exception
    + FullyQualifiedErrorId :
    NamedParameterNotFound,Microsoft.PowerShell.Commands
  .GetServiceCommand
```

We know, every time the screen fills with red text, we curl into a ball and go back to high school English class, where red ink was a bad, bad thing. But relax, take a breath, and read what PowerShell is trying to tell you. Typo solved.

11.3   The real trick to debugging: expectations

As we mentioned earlier, assumptions and expectations are at the heart of the trickier errors and bugs that you'll find. Before you can begin debugging, you therefore *have to have an expectation* for what each line of your script will do, and you have to be able to *validate* those expectations. When you find the place where your expectation differs from reality, then you've found your bug. But you can't debug without first sitting down and thinking about what the script is supposed to do—or at least what you think it's supposed to do.

This is exactly where most folks go wrong. The idea of sitting down and poring over a script, line by line, seems inefficient, boring, and frustrating. So they'll just jump right in and start making changes. That way, in our experience, leads to madness. We've watched students pound away at a broken script for hours, painfully making change after change that doesn't help. Yes, it can seem inefficient to try to read through a script and document your expectations (although when you become more experienced, you'll do a lot of it in your head and it'll go faster). But our way of debugging is far more efficient than the "just try stuff and see what happens" approach. Our way results in a better understanding of the script, and a faster fix time, than just randomly trying stuff.

Let's start with a simple example that doesn't even use a script but rather uses a simple, three-command one-liner:

```
PS C:\>
Get-CimInstance -class Win32_LogicalDisk `
                -filter "drivetype='fixed'" |
Select -Property DeviceID,Size |
Sort -Property FreeSpace

Get-CimInstance : INVALID_QUERY
At line:2 char:1
+ Get-CimInstance -class Win32_LogicalDisk `
+ ~~~~~~~~~~~~~~~~~~~~~~~~~~~~~~~~~~~~~~~~~~~~
    + CategoryInfo          : InvalidArgument: (:) [Get-CimInstance],
      CimException
    + FullyQualifiedErrorId :
      MiClientApiError_InvalidQuery,Microsoft.Management.I
    nfrastructure.CimCmdlets.GetCimInstanceCommand
```

Oh look, an error message. It's telling us (we boldfaced the bit we're looking at) that the problem is with the Get-CimInstance command. We had an expectation about something that was wrong. Let's examine just that portion of our command. In fact, heck with that—let's run *just* that portion. We've been typing this in the PowerShell ISE, so we can just highlight the portion that represents the first command, right-click it, and select Run Selection (or press F8) to run just that command. Notice, as shown in figure 11.1, that we were careful not to highlight the pipe character after the first command. This ensures that PowerShell runs just the first command and that the shell doesn't expect anything afterward.

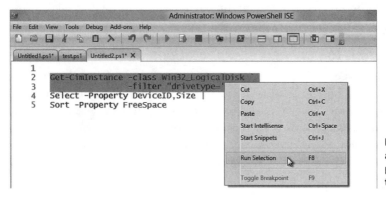

Figure 11.1 Highlight a portion of code and press F8 to run just that portion.

Here's our result:

```
PS C:\> Get-CimInstance -class Win32_LogicalDisk `
               -filter "drivetype='fixed'"
Get-CimInstance : INVALID_QUERY
At line:1 char:1
+ Get-CimInstance -class Win32_LogicalDisk `
+ ~~~~~~~~~~~~~~~~~~~~~~~~~~~~~~~~~~~~~~~~~~~~~
    + CategoryInfo          : InvalidArgument: (:) [Get-CimInstance],
    CimException
    + FullyQualifiedErrorId :
    MiClientApiError_InvalidQuery,Microsoft.Management.I
   nfrastructure.CimCmdlets.GetCimInstanceCommand
```

Same error—so the problem is definitely with this command. Our standard approach in this instance is to back off a little. This means that we'll take away a bit of the command, if possible, to reduce complexity and see if we can find what we're doing wrong. Look, there are only two parameters on this command—we've clearly typed one wrong. So let's just get rid of one, if possible:

```
PS C:\> Get-CimInstance -class Win32_LogicalDisk

DeviceID    DriveType VolumeName      Size         FreeSpace
--------    --------- ----------      ----         ---------
A:          2
C:          3                         68717375488 58424459264
D:          5         HB1_CCPA_X64F... 3583707136  0
```

Ah. That worked (although we truncated the output a bit to make it fit on the page in this book). The problem was our -Filter parameter. Looking at the output of the successful command, we can see that the DriveType property contains numbers—2, 3, or 5 in our case. That's not what we expected—we thought it would be something like "fixed," which is what was in our query. Assumption corrected. Let's fix our command and try again:

```
PS C:\>
Get-CimInstance -class Win32_LogicalDisk `
               -filter "drivetype=3" |
Select -Property DeviceID,Size |
Sort -Property FreeSpace

DeviceID                                           Size
--------                                           ----
C:                                                 68717375488
```

Well, that's better. Although...maybe not. Our computer has only one fixed drive (drive type 3), so we can't be sure our Sort command is working. Let's remove the drive type filter, so that we get more drives in the output, so that we can make sure Sort is working. It's bad to assume Sort is working when you have only one object in the output!

```
Get-CimInstance -class Win32_LogicalDisk |
Select -Property DeviceID,Size |
Sort -Property FreeSpace
```

```
DeviceID                                                    Size
--------                                                    ----
D:                                                          3583707136
C:                                                          68717375488
A:
```

Um, wait—we're sorting by FreeSpace, but that isn't even shown in the output. So we can't tell if it's working. In fact, we may have done something stupid here. Our Select command is only choosing the DeviceID and Size properties—its output probably doesn't even have a FreeSpace to sort on! Let's test this by backing off a bit and removing the Sort command and then seeing what Select is producing:

```
Get-CimInstance -class Win32_LogicalDisk |
Select -Property DeviceID,Size |
Get-Member

    TypeName: Selected.Microsoft.Management.Infrastructure.CimInstance

Name         MemberType   Definition
----         ----------   ----------
Equals       Method       bool Equals(System.Object obj)
GetHashCode  Method       int GetHashCode()
GetType      Method       type GetType()
ToString     Method       string ToString()
DeviceID     NoteProperty System.String DeviceID=A:
Size         NoteProperty Size=null
```

That's what we thought. As shown by Get-Member, our Sort command is trying to sort on a property that, at that point in the pipeline, doesn't exist. Dumb mistake on our part, but backing off one command and examining the output with Get-Member helped us confirm the suspicion. Isn't it irritating that PowerShell didn't throw an error when we tried to sort on something that didn't exist at the time? But that's what it does. Now we know that we should maybe move our Sort command to earlier in the pipeline, or just do away with it entirely, or have Select include the sort property in its output. Any of those would fix the problem.

The point of this example is that assumptions are what lead to bugs. Verifying and validating data, often by running just fragments of your script, backing off a little bit, and so forth can help you correct your assumptions and fix the bug. Let's work through a quick example of how to develop expectations: Take a look at listing 11.1.

TRY IT NOW   We haven't made any changes to this script, which one of our colleagues provided to us, other than to remove identifying names and proprietary information. We encourage you to follow along in this expectation-documentation process. Keep in mind that we're not positioning this script as one that follows best practices—far from it—but it's a realistic example!

Listing 11.1   A script we found

```
$data = import-csv c:\data.csv
$totalqty = 0
$totalsold = 0
$totalbought = 0
foreach ($line in $data) {
```

```
if ($line.transaction -eq 'buy') {
    # buy transaction (we sold)
    $totalqty -= $line.qty
    $totalsold = $line.total } else {
    # sell transaction (we bought)
    $totalqty += $line.qty
    $totalbought = $line.total }
"totalqty,totalbought,totalsold,totalamt" | out-file c:\summary.csv
"$totalqty,$totalbought,$totalsold,$($totalbought-$totalsold)" |
 out-file c:\summary.csv -append
```

This script is intended to process a CSV file, which is output by another application. The following listing shows a sample of the CSV file data.

<hr/>

Listing 11.2 Sample CSV data for listing 11.1

```
"name,transaction,qty,amount,total"
"ctgannon,buy,4,3.00,12.00"
"gshields,sell,1200,1.00,1200.00"
"tevans,sell,8,9.00,72.00"
```

We aren't going to run the script. First of all, the formatting is atrocious. We have to fix that first—no way around it. The next listing is the revised script, and right away we can see a problem. Can you spot it?

<hr/>

Listing 11.3 The reformatted script

```
$data = import-csv c:\data.csv
$totalqty = 0
$totalsold = 0
$totalbought = 0
foreach ($line in $data) {
    if ($line.transaction -eq 'buy') {
        # buy transaction (we sold)
        $totalqty -= $line.qty
        $totalsold = $line.total
    } else {
        # sell transaction (we bought)
        $totalqty += $line.qty
        $totalbought = $line.total
    }
"totalqty,totalbought,totalsold,totalamt" | out-file c:\summary.csv
"$totalqty,$totalbought,$totalsold,$($totalbought-$totalsold)" |
    out-file c:\summary.csv –append
```

If you're reading carefully, you'll notice that the ForEach construct's closing curly bracket is missing. The following listing shows the fixed script—this kind of error is a lot easier to notice when you're properly formatting your script.

<hr/>

Listing 11.4 Fixing the script's typo

```
$data = import-csv c:\data.csv
$totalqty = 0
$totalsold = 0
```

```
$totalbought = 0
foreach ($line in $data) {
    if ($line.transaction -eq 'buy') {
        # buy transaction (we sold)
        $totalqty -= $line.qty
        $totalsold = $line.total
    } else {
        # sell transaction (we bought)
        $totalqty += $line.qty
        $totalbought = $line.total
    }
}
"totalqty,totalbought,totalsold,totalamt" | out-file c:\summary.csv
"$totalqty,$totalbought,$totalsold,$($totalbought-$totalsold)" |
    out-file c:\summary.csv -append
```

> **DON'T TRY IT NOW**   Don't run this script yet. We know it's buggy—that's kind
> of the whole point of this exercise. We'll run in a second to see what it does!

Now let's start documenting our expectations. We aren't even going to run the
script—this is about our expectations, based on what we're seeing.

```
$data = import-csv c:\data.csv
$totalqty = 0
$totalsold = 0
$totalbought = 0
```

These first four lines seem to be importing a CSV file (we gave you a sample of what
that looks like). Our expectation is that each line in the CSV becomes an object, and
each column of the CSV becomes a property of that object. Using our sample data,
there should be three objects with five properties each. The remaining three lines
seem to be initializing some variables, setting their values to zero—a great idea, given
PowerShell's scope rules.

```
foreach ($line in $data) {
}
```

The ForEach construct should enumerate through those three objects, so that the
$line variable contains one object at a time.

```
if ($line.transaction -eq 'buy') {
        # buy transaction (we sold)
        $totalqty -= $line.qty
        $totalsold = $line.total
    } else {
        # sell transaction (we bought)
        $totalqty += $line.qty
        $totalbought = $line.total
    }
```

The If construct is checking the Transaction property of each object (that is, the
Transaction column from the CSV file). If it's "buy," there's one set of actions, and if
it isn't, there's another set. This raises a small red flag with us: If the CSV is guaranteed

to only contain "buy" and "sell" as our sample does, then just using an `Else` block is fine. Normally, if we expect specific values like "buy" and "sell," we'd rather see an `ElseIf` block that explicitly tests for "sell," or if there were several values perhaps a `Switch` statement. As is, if the CSV file contains something aberrant like "swap" in the `Transaction` column, it'll be treated as a "sell," which could cause problems. We'll let this slide for now.

Apart from that, the code looks straightforward: We're incrementing some variables based on the contents of the `Qty` and `Total` columns of the CSV file. The script's last two lines are

```
"totalqty,totalbought,totalsold,totalamt" | out-file c:\summary.csv
"$totalqty,$totalbought,$totalsold,$($totalbought-$totalsold)" |
    out-file c:\summary.csv -append
```

This outputs two lines to a new CSV file, with the first line acting as column headers and the second line using those variables to produce a single data line for the CSV file. Let's test that theory by running the script:

```
PS C:\> C:\debug.ps1

PS C:\> gc .\summary.csv
totalqty,totalbought,totalsold,totalamt
0,,0,0
```

So we ran the script (which we'd saved as C:\debug.ps1) and then displayed the contents of c:\summary.csv. All zeros and a blank column. Awesome. Well, we knew the script was broken—let's learn how to fix it.

11.4 Dealing with logic errors: trace code

One great technique for dealing with logic errors is to add *trace code* to your script. This lets you output some internal details about what your script is seeing and dealing with, enabling you to validate those assumptions (assuming you've made some—and if you haven't, you're not ready to debug).

Most programming languages provide a way of adding trace code; PowerShell does so in a way that means you don't have to go back later and remove, or comment out, the trace code commands. It's super convenient! We tend to add the trace code, which is implemented by using `Write-Debug`, as we write a new script. We tend to assume we're going to mess up, and adding the debug code at the outset makes debugging quicker. And to be perfectly honest, we've started relying on the trace code to act as inline comments for our scripts, rather than actual comments. The next listing shows our script with trace code added.

Listing 11.5 Adding trace code to our buggy script

```
[CmdletBinding()]
param()
$data = import-csv c:\data.csv
Write-Debug "Imported CSV data"

$totalqty = 0
```

```
$totalsold = 0
$totalbought = 0
foreach ($line in $data) {
    if ($line.transaction -eq 'buy') {

        Write-Debug "ENDED BUY transaction (we sold)"
        $totalqty -= $line.qty
        $totalsold = $line.total

    } else {

        $totalqty += $line.qty
        $totalbought = $line.total
        Write-Debug "ENDED SELL transaction (we bought)"

    }
}

Write-Debug "OUTPUT: $totalqty,$totalbought,$totalsold,
➥ $($totalbought-$totalsold)"

"totalqty,totalbought,totalsold,totalamt" | out-file c:\summary.csv
"$totalqty,$totalbought,$totalsold,$($totalbought-$totalsold)" |
    out-file c:\summary.csv -append
```

> **TIP**   If you're typing in a script like this, make sure you save it before trying to
> run it. Some things, like the [CmdletBinding()] attribute, will only work if
> your script is being run from a file on disk.

Some notes about what we did:

- In order to make this truly useful, we added [CmdletBinding()] and a blank
  Param() block to the top of the script. Those two elements have to go
  together—you can't have [CmdletBinding()] without a Param(). We'll show
  you in a second why [CmdletBinding()] is so awesome here.
- We added a Write-Debug after each major decision or operation the script
  took, giving us a chance to follow the script's logic.
- Because the ultimate output of this is a CSV file (which kind of violates our rule
  of breaking tools into input, functional, or output, but hey—it's what we were
  given to debug), we added a Write-Debug that lets us preview the output.

Let's run the script again. This time, we'll add the -Debug switch (which is enabled by
[CmdletBinding()]) to make the output of Write-Debug visible:

> **TRY IT NOW**   We're going to run this in the normal PowerShell console, which
> we like a bit better for debugging. Its messages—which you'll see in the fol-
> lowing output—are text prompts, whereas the ISE uses pop-up dialogs that we
> find a bit distracting.

```
PS C:\> .\debug.ps1 -Debug
DEBUG: Imported CSV data

Confirm
Continue with this operation?
[Y] Yes  [A] Yes to All  [H] Halt Command  [S] Suspend  [?] Help
(default is "Y"):
```

When PowerShell hit that first `Write-Debug`, it displayed its message and then paused the script. From here, we have some choices. We're going to select S for "Suspend."

```
Confirm
Continue with this operation?
[Y] Yes  [A] Yes to All  [H] Halt Command  [S] Suspend  [?] Help
(default is "Y"):s
PS C:\>> $data

name,transaction,qty,amount,total
--------------------------------
ctgannon,buy,4,3.00,12.00
gshields,sell,1200,1.00,1200.00
tevans,sell,8,9.00,72.00
```

Notice that the PowerShell prompt changed to >> instead of >, indicating that we're in debug mode. We take the opportunity to see what actually went into the `$data` variable—and it wasn't what we expected. Remember, we said that we expected `$data` to contain three objects of five properties each—but it appears to just be a bunch of text.

> **NOTE** If you've done anything to modify your PowerShell prompt (numerous third-party add-ins do so), you may not see the same output we're seeing. We recommend running PowerShell without any add-ins to restore the original debug prompt, if needed.

While still in debug mode, we'll pipe `$data` to `Get-Member` to see what's in that variable:

```
PS C:\>> $data | gm

    TypeName: System.Management.Automation.PSCustomObject

Name                              MemberType   Definition
----                              ----------   ----------
Equals                            Method       bool Equals(System.Objec...
GetHashCode                       Method       int GetHashCode()
GetType                           Method       type GetType()
ToString                          Method       string ToString()
name,transaction,qty,amount,total NoteProperty System.String name,trans...
```

Well, it isn't a string—it's an object with a property called name,transaction,qty, amount,total. Weird and not what we expected. That's one property, not five. We can't expect the rest of the script to work, which is probably why we got that weird output the first time we ran it.

Reviewing the CSV file, the problem seems to be the quotation marks. Within quotation marks, the CSV file format ignores commas, meaning the entire file is being taken as a single property. Let's fix that, with the revised sample shown here.

Listing 11.6   Correcting the sample data

```
name,transaction,qty,amount,total
ctgannon,buy,4,3.00,12.00
gshields,sell,1200,1.00,1200.00
tevans,sell,8,9.00,72.00
```

It would be legal to include each field in quotes—for example, `"name"`, `"transaction"`,`"qty"`,`"amount"`,`"total"`—but since none of our values contain commas, we can also eliminate the quotes entirely, which is faster. All of this is a potential problem, because this data is allegedly being output by another application. That application, therefore, has a bug, because it's writing out illegal CSV files. We'll let that application's developer deal with their problems, though, and continue debugging our script.

We're still at the debug prompt. Let's exit, kill the script, and run it again.

```
PS C:\>> exit

Confirm
Continue with this operation?
[Y] Yes  [A] Yes to All  [H] Halt Command  [S] Suspend  [?] Help
(default is "Y"):h
Write-Debug : Command execution stopped because the user selected the
Halt option.
At C:\debug.ps1:4 char:1
+ Write-Debug "Imported CSV data"
+ ~~~~~~~~~~~~~~~~~~~~~~~~~~~~~~~~
    + CategoryInfo          : OperationStopped: (:) [Write-Debug], Parent
   ContainsErrorRecordException
    + FullyQualifiedErrorId : ActionPreferenceStop,Microsoft.PowerShell.C
   ommands.WriteDebugCommand

PS C:\> .\debug.ps1 -Debug
DEBUG: Imported CSV data

Confirm
Continue with this operation?
[Y] Yes  [A] Yes to All  [H] Halt Command  [S] Suspend  [?] Help
(default is "Y"):s
PS C:\>> $data

name        : ctgannon
transaction : buy
qty         : 4
amount      : 3.00
total       : 12.00

name        : gshields
transaction : sell
qty         : 1200
amount      : 1.00
total       : 1200.00

name        : tevans
transaction : sell
qty         : 8
amount      : 9.00
total       : 72.00
```

Ah, much more what we were expecting: three objects of five properties each. Excellent. Let's allow the script to continue:

```
PS C:\>> exit

Confirm
Continue with this operation?
[Y] Yes  [A] Yes to All  [H] Halt Command  [S] Suspend  [?] Help
(default is "Y"):y
DEBUG: ENDED BUY transaction (we sold)

Confirm
Continue with this operation?
[Y] Yes  [A] Yes to All  [H] Halt Command  [S] Suspend  [?] Help
(default is "Y"):y
DEBUG: ENDED SELL transaction (we bought)

Confirm
Continue with this operation?
[Y] Yes  [A] Yes to All  [H] Halt Command  [S] Suspend  [?] Help
(default is "Y"):y
DEBUG: ENDED SELL transaction (we bought)

Confirm
Continue with this operation?
[Y] Yes  [A] Yes to All  [H] Halt Command  [S] Suspend  [?] Help
(default is "Y"):y
DEBUG: OUTPUT: 1204,72.00,12.00,60

Confirm
Continue with this operation?
[Y] Yes  [A] Yes to All  [H] Halt Command  [S] Suspend  [?] Help
(default is "Y"):
```

It properly recognized each of the three transactions, but we're having a bit of a problem with the proposed line of output. By our math, columns 2 and 3 shouldn't be 72 and 12, but rather 1272 and 12. So we have another problem. Tell you what: Let's kill the script again, and debug the rest of it using a different technique:

```
Confirm
Continue with this operation?
[Y] Yes  [A] Yes to All  [H] Halt Command  [S] Suspend  [?] Help
(default is "Y"):h
Write-Debug : Command execution stopped because the user selected the
Halt option.
At C:\debug.ps1:25 char:1
+ Write-Debug "OUTPUT:
$totalqty,$totalbought,$totalsold,$($totalbought-$totalsold ...
+ ~~~~~~~~~~~~~~~~~~~~~~~~~~~~~~~~~~~~~~~~~~~~~~~~~~~~~~~~~~~~~~~~~~~~~~~~~~~~
~~~~~~~~
    + CategoryInfo          : OperationStopped: (:) [Write-Debug], Parent
    ContainsErrorRecordException
    + FullyQualifiedErrorId : ActionPreferenceStop,Microsoft.PowerShell.C
    ommands.WriteDebugCommand
```

11.5 *Dealing with logic errors: breakpoints*

Technically, Write-Debug acts as a sort of permanent, manually inserted breakpoint in your script. When the shell hits Write-Debug, it pauses your script and lets you investigate things. PowerShell also supports a more dynamic form of breakpoint, called a PSBreakpoint.

You create a PSBreakpoint by running `Set-PSBreakpoint`. Using parameters of that command, you tell PowerShell what script the breakpoint goes with (it's based on the path and filename, so the breakpoint will only work so long as the script stays in the same spot) and what you want the breakpoint to trigger on. Your choices include the following:

- Stopping on a particular line or line/character position, which is similar to sticking a `Write-Debug` in the script
- Stopping when a particular command is run
- Stopping when a particular variable is read, written, or either

NOTE   Technically, you don't have to tie anything but a line/character breakpoint to a script file. The other kinds of breakpoints can also operate globally within the shell.

Keep in mind that breakpoints are dynamic: Close your shell, and they go away. You're not actually doing anything to your script but rather are asking PowerShell to remember what to do. You can also set line-based breakpoints in the ISE: Just move to the line where you want a breakpoint and press F9. Because at this point we're having trouble with our `$totalbought` and `$totalsold` variables, we'll set breakpoints on those:

```
PS C:\> Set-PSBreakpoint -Script C:\debug.ps1 -Variable totalbought,totalso
ld -Mode ReadWrite

  ID Script            Line Command        Variable        Action
  -- ------            ---- -------        --------        ------
   0 debug.ps1                             totalbought
   1 debug.ps1                             totalsold
```

Boom, two new breakpoints. Let's run the script, omitting the –Debug parameter so that our `Write-Debug` statements don't kick in:

```
PS C:\> .\debug.ps1
Entering debug mode. Use h or ? for help.

Hit Variable breakpoint on 'C:\debug.ps1:$totalsold' (ReadWrite access)

At C:\debug.ps1:7 char:1
+ $totalsold = 0
+ ~~~~~~~~~~~~~~
[DBG]: PS C:\>>
```

First breakpoint! This is where you realize that having a printout of your script, including line numbers, would be helpful. We stopped on line 7, which sets `$totalsold` to zero. We'll run `Exit` to continue running the script:

```
Hit Variable breakpoint on 'C:\debug.ps1:$totalbought' (ReadWrite access)

At C:\debug.ps1:8 char:1
+ $totalbought = 0
```

```
+   ~~~~~~~~~~~~~~~~~~
[DBG]: PS C:\>> exit
Hit Variable breakpoint on 'C:\debug.ps1:$totalsold' (ReadWrite access)

At C:\debug.ps1:14 char:9
+         $totalsold = $line.total
+         ~~~~~~~~~~~~~~~~~~~~~~~~~
[DBG]: PS C:\>>
```

Okay, line 14 is where we first modify $totalsold. Let's see what $line.total contains:

```
[DBG]: PS C:\>> $line.total
12.00
[DBG]: PS C:\>> exit
Hit Variable breakpoint on 'C:\debug.ps1:$totalbought' (ReadWrite access)

At C:\debug.ps1:19 char:9
+         $totalbought = $line.total
+         ~~~~~~~~~~~~~~~~~~~~~~~~~~~
```

12 is what we expected, so we ran Exit again. Now we've modified $totalbought, so the script paused again. Let's see what's in $line.total:

```
[DBG]: PS C:\>> $line.total
1200.00
[DBG]: PS C:\>> exit
Hit Variable breakpoint on 'C:\debug.ps1:$totalbought' (ReadWrite access)

At C:\debug.ps1:19 char:9
+         $totalbought = $line.total
+         ~~~~~~~~~~~~~~~~~~~~~~~~~~~
```

Okay, again, 1200 is right on track. We continued, so let's now look at $line.total and $totalbought again:

```
[DBG]: PS C:\>> $line.total
72.00
[DBG]: PS C:\>> $totalbought
72.00
[DBG]: PS C:\>>
```

Wait, wait, wait. $totalbought should contain 1200+72, which is 1272, but it only contains 72. Back to the code:

```
        $totalbought = $line.total
```

And there's the problem. We're not adding $line.total to what's in $totalbought; we're setting $totalbought to whatever's in $line.total. So the old value is being wiped out. The same thing is happening in $totalsold, just above it in the script. Let's make some fixes, as shown in the following listing.

Listing 11.7 Fixing the bugs

```
[CmdletBinding()]
param()
$data = import-csv c:\data.csv
Write-Debug "Imported CSV data"
```

```
$totalqty = 0
$totalsold = 0
$totalbought = 0
foreach ($line in $data) {
    if ($line.transaction -eq 'buy') {

        Write-Debug "ENDED BUY transaction (we sold)"
        $totalqty -= $line.qty
        $totalsold += $line.total

    } else {

        $totalqty += $line.qty
        $totalbought += $line.total
        Write-Debug "ENDED SELL transaction (we bought)"

    }
}

Write-Debug "OUTPUT: $totalqty,$totalbought,$totalsold,$($totalbought-
    $totalsold)"

"totalqty,totalbought,totalsold,totalamt" | out-file c:\summary.csv
"$totalqty,$totalbought,$totalsold,$($totalbought-$totalsold)" |
    out-file c:\summary.csv –append
```

Now let's clear the breakpoints and run it again:

```
PS C:\> Get-PSBreakpoint | Remove-PSBreakpoint
PS C:\> .\debug.ps1
PS C:\> gc .\summary.csv
totalqty,totalbought,totalsold,totalamt
1204,1272,12,1260
PS C:\>
```

Huzzah! It worked! Debugging complete!

11.6 *Seriously, have expectations*

You can see that this would all have been impossible if we hadn't developed some expectations: what we thought variables would contain, what we thought the output would be (we admit to pulling out a calculator to add 1200 and 72, but there's no reason to be embarrassed about that, is there?), and so on. We used tools to compare those expectations to what really happened—and each time we found a difference, we knew to dive back into the code to find the problem.

This is the simple fact about debugging: With no expectations, you're out in the cold. Have expectations, and the tools in PowerShell will let you validate them and find the bugs.

11.7 *Coming up next*

In the next chapter, we're going to return to our running Get-SystemInfo example, where we have it producing great output—but not attractive-looking output. Commands like Get-Service produce a really nicely formatted table by default, and we'd like our command to do the same. In the next chapter, we'll work on that.

11.8 *Lab*

We're sure you'll have plenty of practice debugging your own scripts. But we want to reinforce some of the concepts from this chapter and get you used to following a procedure. Never try to debug a script simply by staring at it, hoping the error will jump out at you. It might, but more than likely it may not be the only one. Follow our guidelines to identify bugs. Fix one thing at a time. If it doesn't resolve the problem, change it back and repeat the process.

The functions listed here are broken and buggy. We've numbered each line for reference purposes; the numbers are not part of the actual function. How would you debug them? Revise them into working solutions. Remember, you'll need to dot source the script each time you make a change. We recommend testing in the regular PowerShell console.

The function in the next listing is supposed to display some properties of running services sorted by the service account.

Listing 11.8   A broken function

```
1  Function Get-ServiceInfo {
2  [cmdletbinding()]
3  Param([string]$Computername)
4  $services=Get-WmiObject -Class Win32_Services -filter "state='Running" `
     -computername $computernam
5  Write-Host "Found ($services.count) on $computername" -Foreground Green
6  $sevices | sort -Property startname,name  Select -property `
   startname,name,startmode,computername
7  }
```

The function in listing 11.9 is a bit more involved. It's designed to get recent event log entries for a specified log on a specified computer. Events are sorted by the event source and added to a log file. The filename is based on the date, computer name, and event source. At the end, the function displays a directory listing of the logs. Hint: Clean up the formatting first.

Listing 11.9   Buggy export function

```
01  Function Export-EventLogSource {
02
03  [cmdletbinding()]
04  Param (
05  [Parameter(Position=0,Mandatory=$True,Helpmessage="Enter a
      computername",ValueFromPipeline=$True)]
06  [string]$Computername,
07  [Parameter(Position=1,Mandatory=$True,Helpmessage="Enter a classic event
      log name like System")]
08  [string]$Log,
09  [int]$Newest=100
10  )
11  Begin {
12  Write-Verbose "Starting export event source function"
```

```
13  #the date format is case-sensitive"
14  $datestring=Get-Date -Format "yyyyMMdd"
15  $logpath=Join-path -Path "C:\Work" -ChildPath $datestring
16  if (! (Test-Path -path $logpath) {
17  Write-Verbose "Creating $logpath"
18  mkdir $logpath
19  }
20  Write-Verbose "Logging results to $logpath"
21  }
22  Process {
23  Write-Verbose "Getting newest $newest $log event log entries from
     $computername"
24  Try {
25  Write-Host $computername.ToUpper -ForegroundColor Green
26  $logs=Get-EventLog -LogName $log -Newest $Newest -Computer $Computer -
     ErrorAction Stop
27  if ($logs) {
28  Write-Verbose "Sorting $($logs.count) entries"
29  $log | sort Source | foreach {
30  $logfile=Join-Path -Path $logpath -ChildPath "$computername-
     $($_.Source).txt"
31  $_ | Format-List TimeWritten,MachineName,EventID,EntryType,Message |
32  Out-File -FilePath $logfile -append
33
34  #clear variables for next time
35  Remove-Variable -Name logs,logfile
36  }
37  else {Write-Warning "No logged events found for $log on $Computername"}
38  }
39   Catch { Write-Warning $_.Exception.Message }
40  }
41  End {dir $logpath
42  Write-Verbose "Finished export event source function"
43  }
44  }
```

NOTE   You can find debugged versions of these functions and a commentary on how you might debug them at http://MoreLunches.com.

Creating custom format views

We're getting back to the script that we left off with in chapter 10, before our short diversion into the world of debugging. One thing we didn't like about that script was its output. Some folks would be tempted to put commands right into the script to fix that, but we know better. Remember: A tool should either create input for another tool, do something, or format output from another tool. Our tool is already doing something, so we can't have it start messing around with formatting the output as well. Instead, we'll get PowerShell to do that for us by creating a custom view.

12.1 The anatomy of a view

PowerShell ships with a number of views, all of which are contained in .format.ps1xml files that live within PowerShell's installation folder. You can get there by running `cd $pshome` in the shell, and we'll open DotNetTypes.format.ps1xml in Notepad (or the ISE) to view it.

> **CAUTION** Be very careful not to make any changes to the .format.ps1xml files in PowerShell's installation folder—or if you do, make sure you don't save those changes. The files are digitally signed, and even an extra space or carriage return will break them, rendering them useless to PowerShell.

There's a lot of stuff in there, but let's just start with a simple table view:

```
<View>
    <Name>System.Globalization.CultureInfo</Name>          ◁—— Name of the view
    <ViewSelectedBy>
        <TypeName>System.Globalization.CultureInfo</TypeName>    Object that
    </ViewSelectedBy>                                             uses view
```

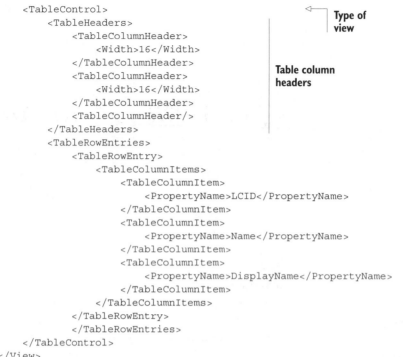

```
<TableControl>
    <TableHeaders>
        <TableColumnHeader>
            <Width>16</Width>
        </TableColumnHeader>
        <TableColumnHeader>
            <Width>16</Width>
        </TableColumnHeader>
        <TableColumnHeader/>
    </TableHeaders>
    <TableRowEntries>
        <TableRowEntry>
            <TableColumnItems>
                <TableColumnItem>
                    <PropertyName>LCID</PropertyName>
                </TableColumnItem>
                <TableColumnItem>
                    <PropertyName>Name</PropertyName>
                </TableColumnItem>
                <TableColumnItem>
                    <PropertyName>DisplayName</PropertyName>
                </TableColumnItem>
            </TableColumnItems>
        </TableRowEntry>
    </TableRowEntries>
</TableControl>
</View>
```

Here's what we'd like you to notice:

- The view is contained within the `<View>` and `</View>` XML tags. Note that all of the XML tags are case sensitive, so it's important to type accurately. We prefer to copy and paste an existing view from DotNetTypes.format.ps1xml and use that as a starting point, because doing so helps us avoid typos in the XML.

- The view has a name of its own, which is commonly just the type name that the view will apply to. The name doesn't matter much—there are a couple of ways in which the shell can use it, but they're exceedingly rare to run into.

- The view is selected by a specific type name, in this case, objects of the `System .Globalization.CultureInfo` type. So, when PowerShell needs to display that type of object, it will use this view to do so.

- This is a table view, as opposed to a list, wide, or custom view.

- There are three column headers—count those carefully. The last one is shown by the `<TableColumnHeader/>` XML tag; this represents a column where we're not providing a custom column header, width, or alignment. It's easy to miss that third column header, so make sure you see it!

- The remaining XML defines the contents of the three columns. You'll notice that each of these specifies the object property name to be displayed in the column. Because our column headers didn't include alternate names, the property names will be used at the top of each column.

This basic form is used for all views. A single XML file, as you'll see in DotNetTypes.format .ps1xml if you look in it, can contain multiple views, each for a different kind of object.

12.2 Adding a type name to output objects

Because views are triggered by the type name of the object they display, we need to ensure our script's output object has a unique type name. Right now it doesn't: The script outputs a generic type of object called PSObject. The following listing shows how we'll fix that, with a single line shown in boldface.

Listing 12.1   Adding a custom `TypeName` to the view

```
function Get-SystemInfo {
<#
.SYNOPSIS
Retrieves key system version and model information
from one to ten computers.
.DESCRIPTION
Get-SystemInfo uses Windows Management Instrumentation
(WMI) to retrieve information from one or more computers.
Specify computers by name or by IP address.
.PARAMETER ComputerName
One or more computer names or IP addresses, up to a maximum
of 10.
.PARAMETER LogErrors
Specify this switch to create a text log file of computers
that could not be queried.
.PARAMETER ErrorLog
When used with -LogErrors, specifies the file path and name
to which failed computer names will be written. Defaults to
C:\Retry.txt.
.EXAMPLE
 Get-Content names.txt | Get-SystemInfo
.EXAMPLE
 Get-SystemInfo -ComputerName SERVER1,SERVER2
#>
    [CmdletBinding()]
    param(
        [Parameter(Mandatory=$True,
                   ValueFromPipeline=$True,
                   HelpMessage="Computer name or IP address")]
        [ValidateCount(1,10)]
        [Alias('hostname')]
        [string[]]$ComputerName,

        [string]$ErrorLog = 'c:\retry.txt',

        [switch]$LogErrors
    )
    BEGIN {
        Write-Verbose "Error log will be $ErrorLog"
    }
    PROCESS {
        Write-Verbose "Beginning PROCESS block"
        foreach ($computer in $computername) {
```

```
                Write-Verbose "Querying $computer"
                Try {
                    $everything_ok = $true
                    $os = Get-WmiObject -class Win32_OperatingSystem `
                                        -computerName $computer `
                                        -erroraction Stop
                } Catch {
                    $everything_ok = $false
                    Write-Warning "$computer failed"
                    if ($LogErrors) {
                        $computer | Out-File $ErrorLog -Append
                        Write-Warning "Logged to $ErrorLog"
                    }
                }

                if ($everything_ok) {
                    $comp = Get-WmiObject -class Win32_ComputerSystem `
                                        -computerName $computer
                    $bios = Get-WmiObject -class Win32_BIOS `
                                        -computerName $computer
                    $props = @{'ComputerName'=$computer;
                               'OSVersion'=$os.version;
                               'SPVersion'=$os.servicepackmajorversion;
                               'BIOSSerial'=$bios.serialnumber;
                               'Manufacturer'=$comp.manufacturer;
                               'Model'=$comp.model}
                    Write-Verbose "WMI queries complete"
                    $obj = New-Object -TypeName PSObject -Property $props
                    $obj.PSObject.TypeNames.Insert(0,'MOL.SystemInfo')
                    Write-Output $obj
                }
            }
        }
    }
    END {}
}

Get-SystemInfo -ComputerName localhost | Get-Member
```

This is the big reason we stored our output object in a variable, $obj, in the first place—because we knew we'd be adding a custom type name to it. The Insert() method takes two arguments. The first, where we've provided zero, tells the method where to insert the new type name. Zero simply means "put this type name in the first position," making it the usable type name for our object.

The second argument is a string with the type name itself. We've used a two-part type name: MOL (which stands for "Month of Lunches") is first, and it will help set our type name apart from the others already in the .NET Framework. Think of the MOL as a kind of prefix that's unique to us. You'd want to use something unique to your organization. For example, if you worked for IBM, you might use IBM as your prefix. If you worked for IBM's Research & Development arm in Charlotte, you might use IBM.Research.Charlotte as the first part of your type name—again, just to help make sure that the complete type name is unique. SystemInfo represents, to us, the type of information this object contains.

Running our script and piping the results to `Get-Member` (which is accomplished by the last line in the script) proves that the type name has indeed been set:

```
PS C:\> C:\test.ps1

   TypeName: MOL.SystemInfo

Name          MemberType   Definition
----          ----------   ----------
Equals        Method       bool Equals(System.Object obj)
GetHashCode   Method       int GetHashCode()
GetType       Method       type GetType()
ToString      Method       string ToString()
BIOSSerial    NoteProperty System.String BIOSSerial=Parallels-48 6C 63 4...
ComputerName  NoteProperty System.String ComputerName=localhost
Manufacturer  NoteProperty System.String Manufacturer=Parallels Software ...
Model         NoteProperty System.String Model=Parallels Virtual Platform
OSVersion     NoteProperty System.String OSVersion=6.2.8250
SPVersion     NoteProperty System.UInt16 SPVersion=0
```

With the type name assigned, we can now set out to make a view. Before we do so, we'll make one change to our script: On the last line, we'll remove the `| Get-Member`, so that running the script displays the script's normal, intended output. Right now, here's what that looks like:

```
PS C:\> C:\test.ps1

Manufacturer : Parallels Software International Inc.
OSVersion    : 6.2.8250
BIOSSerial   : Parallels-D5 A7 11 48 6C 63 42 80 AB E6 90 AF C4 D3 FC DC
ComputerName : localhost
SPVersion    : 0
Model        : Parallels Virtual Platform
```

> **TRY IT NOW** Make sure you can follow along to this point and that your script is displaying this output. We won't be making further changes to the script in this chapter, so if you can get it to this point, then you should be good to go.

12.3 Making a view

We'll start with the following listing, where we've provided the basic shell for the XML file.

Listing 12.2 Basic template for an empty format file

```xml
<?xml version="1.0" encoding="utf-8" ?>
<Configuration>
    <ViewDefinitions>
    </ViewDefinitions>
</Configuration>
```

We've saved this as C:\Test.format.ps1xml. We suggest saving your view files to a short path—like C:\, or C:\Test, or something else—while you're working on the file. You'll be typing that path a lot, so keeping it short saves you time and effort. Note that the contents of our file are already showing good XML formatting practices: We're indenting each nested set of tags and making sure that each tag is closed at the proper level.

For example, the outermost tag pair is <Configuration></Configuration>. Nested fully within that is <ViewDefinitions></ViewDefinitions>, and within *that* we'll be placing our actual views.

We'll start by copying an existing table view from DotNetTypes.format.ps1xml. The new file is in the next listing.

Listing 12.3   Pasting in a starting point for our table view

```
<?xml version="1.0" encoding="utf-8" ?>
<Configuration>
    <ViewDefinitions>
        <View>
            <Name>System.Reflection.Assembly</Name>
            <ViewSelectedBy>
                <TypeName>System.Reflection.Assembly</TypeName>
            </ViewSelectedBy>
            <TableControl>
                <TableHeaders>
                    <TableColumnHeader>
                        <Label>GAC</Label>
                        <Width>6</Width>
                    </TableColumnHeader>
                    <TableColumnHeader>
                <Label>Version</Label>
                        <Width>14</Width>
                    </TableColumnHeader>
                    <TableColumnHeader/>
                </TableHeaders>
                <TableRowEntries>
                    <TableRowEntry>
                        <TableColumnItems>
                            <TableColumnItem>
<PropertyName>GlobalAssemblyCache</PropertyName>
                            </TableColumnItem>
                            <TableColumnItem>
<PropertyName>ImageRuntimeVersion</PropertyName>
                            </TableColumnItem>
                            <TableColumnItem>
                                <PropertyName>Location</PropertyName>
                            </TableColumnItem>
                        </TableColumnItems>
                    </TableRowEntry>
                </TableRowEntries>
            </TableControl>
        </View>
    </ViewDefinitions>
</Configuration>
```

We allowed our neat formatting to get a bit messed up in order to let this fit within the pages of this book. What we have here is a table with three columns. We actually want five columns:

- ComputerName
- Manufacturer, which we'll display as Mfgr in the column header and limit to 20 characters
- Model, which we'll also limit to 20 characters
- OSVersion
- SPVersion, which we'll display as SP in the column header

The following listing shows our modified table.

Listing 12.4 Modifying the pasted-in XML to meet our needs

```
<?xml version="1.0" encoding="utf-8" ?>
<Configuration>
    <ViewDefinitions>
        <View>
            <Name>MOL.SystemInfo</Name>
            <ViewSelectedBy>
                <TypeName>MOL.SystemInfo</TypeName>
            </ViewSelectedBy>
            <TableControl>
                <TableHeaders>
                    <TableColumnHeader/>                        ① Column I
                    <TableColumnHeader>
                        <Label>Mfgr</Label>                     ② Column 2
                        <Width>20</Width>
                    </TableColumnHeader>
                    <TableColumnHeader>
                        <Width>20</Width>                       ③ Column 3
                    </TableColumnHeader>
                    <TableColumnHeader/>                        ④ Column 4
                    <TableColumnHeader>
                        <Label>SP</Label>                       ⑤ Column 5
                    </TableColumnHeader>
                    <TableColumnHeader/>
                </TableHeaders>
                <TableRowEntries>
                    <TableRowEntry>
                        <TableColumnItems>
                            <TableColumnItem>
                                <PropertyName>ComputerName</PropertyName>
                            </TableColumnItem>
                            <TableColumnItem>
                                <PropertyName>Manufacturer</PropertyName>
                            </TableColumnItem>
                            <TableColumnItem>
                                <PropertyName>Model</PropertyName>
                            </TableColumnItem>
                            <TableColumnItem>
                                <Propertyname>OSVersion</Propertyname>
                            </TableColumnItem>
                            <TableColumnItem>
                                <Propertyname>SPVersion</Propertyname>
                            </TableColumnItem>
```

```
                </TableColumnItems>
              </TableRowEntry>
            </TableRowEntries>
          </TableControl>
        </View>
    </ViewDefinitions>
</Configuration>
```

Let's pay extra-close attention to the column headers:

- The first ❶ column is a `<TableColumnHeader/>` tag, which in XML is called a singleton tag. That means it doesn't come in pairs. We used this because we wanted (a) the column header to just be the property name and (b) PowerShell to calculate the best width of the column.
- The second ❷ column has both a label and a width.
- The third ❸ column has a width but no label, so the property name will be used as the column header.
- The fourth ❹ column is another singleton, meaning it'll use the property name and a best-fit width.
- The fifth ❺ column has a label but no width, meaning PowerShell will calculate the best-fit width for us.

With this saved as C:\Test.format.ps1xml, we're ready to test it.

12.4   *Loading and debugging the view*

View files have to be loaded into memory within each new shell session, which is accomplished by using `Update-FormatData`. We'll be specifying the path using the `-PrependPath` parameter; you can read the command's help to learn about other options.

```
PS C:\> Update-FormatData -PrependPath C:\test.format.ps1xml
Update-FormatData : There were errors in loading the format data file:
C:\test.format.ps1xml, Error at XPath
/Configuration/ViewDefinitions/View[1]/TableControl in file
C:\test.format.ps1xml: Header item count = 6 does not match default row
item count = 5.
C:\test.format.ps1xml, Error at XPath
/Configuration/ViewDefinitions/View[1] in file C:\test.format.ps1xml:
Missing Node from TableControl, ListControl, WideControl, CustomControl.
At line:1 char:1
+ Update-FormatData -PrependPath C:\test.format.ps1xml
+ ~~~~~~~~~~~~~~~~~~~~~~~~~~~~~~~~~~~~~~~~~~~~~~~~~~~~~~
    + CategoryInfo          : InvalidOperation: (:) [Update-FormatData],
   RuntimeException
    + FullyQualifiedErrorId : TypesXmlUpdateException,Microsoft.PowerShel
   l.Commands.UpdateFormatDataCommand
```

That's okay—errors happen sometimes. We've boldfaced the interesting part of the error, which tells us that we defined six column headers but only five column properties. Oops! Listing 12.5 shows the revised file; if you go back to listing 12.4 you can see that we had an extra `<TableColumnHeader/>` at the end of the column header list (it's on line 24 of the XML). Those singletons are hard to miss—we left it in on purpose to show you this error.

Listing 12.5 Removing the extra column header

```
<?xml version="1.0" encoding="utf-8" ?>
<Configuration>
    <ViewDefinitions>
        <View>
            <Name>MOL.SystemInfo</Name>
            <ViewSelectedBy>
                <TypeName>MOL.SystemInfo</TypeName>
            </ViewSelectedBy>
            <TableControl>
                <TableHeaders>
                    <TableColumnHeader/>
                    <TableColumnHeader>
                        <Label>Mfgr</Label>
                        <Width>20</Width>
                    </TableColumnHeader>
                    <TableColumnHeader>
                        <Width>20</Width>
                    </TableColumnHeader>
                    <TableColumnHeader/>
                    <TableColumnHeader>
                        <Label>SP</Label>
                    </TableColumnHeader>
                </TableHeaders>
                <TableRowEntries>
                    <TableRowEntry>
                        <TableColumnItems>
                            <TableColumnItem>
                                <PropertyName>ComputerName</PropertyName>
                            </TableColumnItem>
                            <TableColumnItem>
                                <PropertyName>Manufacturer</PropertyName>
                            </TableColumnItem>
                            <TableColumnItem>
                                <PropertyName>Model</PropertyName>
                            </TableColumnItem>
                            <TableColumnItem>
                                <Propertyname>OSVersion</Propertyname>
                            </TableColumnItem>
                            <TableColumnItem>
                                <Propertyname>SPVersion</Propertyname>
                            </TableColumnItem>
                        </TableColumnItems>
                    </TableRowEntry>
                </TableRowEntries>
            </TableControl>
        </View>
    </ViewDefinitions>
</Configuration>
```

Now that we've fixed the file, we can try loading it again:

```
PS C:\> Update-FormatData -PrependPath C:\test.format.ps1xml
```

No errors is good news!

Backward compatibility

In v1 and v2 of PowerShell, you have to close the shell completely in order to attempt to reload a failed view file. That was corrected in v3.

Also, v3 is less case sensitive than earlier versions. On line 38 of our XML file, we spelled one tag `<Propertyname>` instead of `<PropertyName>`, but PowerShell accepted it anyway. That wouldn't have been the case in earlier versions of the shell.

Our XML worked only because we also spelled the closing tag `</Propertyname>`. Had we not matched the case between them—had we typed `<Propertyname>` and `</PropertyName>`, for example, the XML file would have failed.

If you use the ISE to edit these XML files, its syntax checking will spot those kinds of errors, underlining them with a squiggly red underline. Pay attention to those, and let them help you spot errors before they become a problem!

12.5   Using the view

Our script is loaded into the ISE, so we'll go into its console pane and import our view file (we've been testing the view file in the normal PowerShell console, which is a separate application; in order to use the view within the ISE we have to load it there as well). Figure 12.1 shows that the file loaded without error.

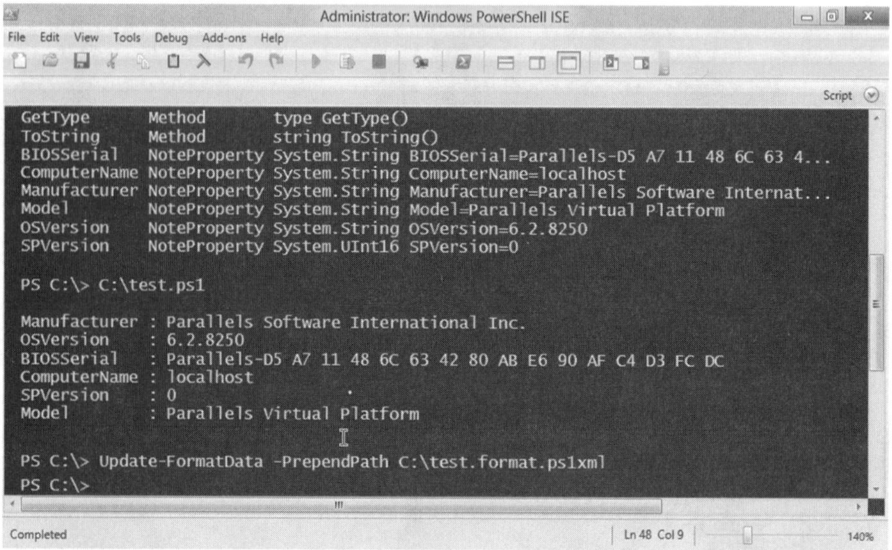

Figure 12.1   Loading the view into the ISE's runspace

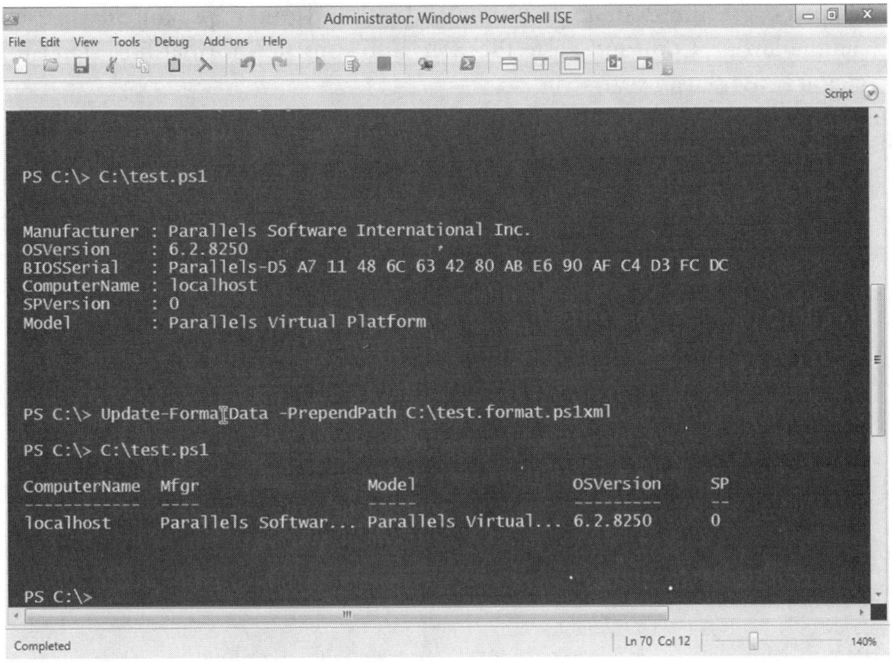

Figure 12.2 **Running our script with the new view in effect**

Now we can return to our script tab, press F9 to run it, and see if our new view took effect. Figure 12.2 shows the results.

Perfect! That's exactly what we wanted. Notice that, because we constrained the `Mfgr` and `Model` columns to 20 characters, PowerShell is truncating their contents with an ellipsis (...). That's fine; it's what we wanted. If we didn't like it, we could obviously modify the XML to provide a wider column or just remove the width directive entirely and let PowerShell calculate a best-fit width for the column.

12.6 *Coming up next*

As usual, we're ending this chapter with a problem. Specifically, we have our tool contained within a script, and if someone plans to use it, they have to also remember to manually load our custom view XML file. That's unacceptable. We also need to get our script into some kind of easily distributed form, so that people can load our tools into memory and run them as normal commands rather than having to hardcode a line to run the function at the bottom of the script.

The next chapter will solve both problems: We're going to turn our script into a module.

12.7 *Labs*

We bet you can guess what's coming. You'll be adding type information and creating custom format files for the functions you've been working on the last several chapters. Use the dotnettypes.format.ps1xml and other .ps1xml files as sources for sample layout. Copy and paste the XML into your new format file. Don't forget that tags are case sensitive.

12.7.1 *Lab A*

Modify your advanced function from Lab A in chapter 10 so that the output object has the type name MOL.ComputerSystemInfo. Then, create a custom view in a file named C:\CustomViewA.format.ps1xml. The custom view should display objects of the type MOL.ComputerSystemInfo in a list format, displaying the information in a list as indicated in your design for this lab. Go back to chapter 6 to check what the output names should be.

At the bottom of the script file, add these commands to test:

```
Update-FormatData -prepend c:\CustomViewA.format.ps1xml
<function-name> -ComputerName localhost
```

The final output should look something like the following:

```
Computername      : CLIENT2
Workgroup         :
AdminPassword     : NA
Model             : VirtualBox
Manufacturer      : innotek GmbH
BIOSSerialNumber  : 0
OSVersion         : 6.1.7601
SPVersion         : 1
```

Note that the list labels aren't exactly the same as the custom object's property names.

12.7.2 *Lab B*

Modify your advanced function Lab B from chapter 10 so that the output object has the type name MOL.DiskInfo. Then, create a custom table view in a file named C:\CustomViewB.format.ps1xml. The custom view should display objects of the type MOL.DiskInfo in a table format, displaying the information in a table as indicated in your design for this lab. Refer back to chapter 6 for a refresher. The column headers for the FreeSpace and Size properties should display FreeSpace(GB) and Size(GB), respectively.

At the bottom of the script file, add these commands to test:

```
Update-FormatData -prepend c:\CustomViewB.format.ps1xml
<function-name> -ComputerName localhost
```

The final output should look something like the following:

ComputerName	Drive	FreeSpace(GB)	Size(GB)
CLIENT2	\\?\Volume{8130d5f3-8e9b-...	0.07	0.10
CLIENT2	C:\Temp\	9.78	10.00
CLIENT2	C:\	2.72	19.90
CLIENT2	D:\	2.72	4.00

Note that the column headers are not exactly the same as the custom object's property names.

12.7.3 Lab C

Modify your advanced function Lab C from chapter 10 so that the output object has the type name `MOL.ServiceProcessInfo`. Then, create a custom view in a file named C:\CustomViewC.format.ps1xml. The custom view should display objects of the type `MOL.ServiceProcessInfo` in a table format, displaying computer name, service name, display name, process name, and process virtual size.

In addition to the table format, create a list view in the same file that displays the properties in this order:

- `ComputerName`
- `Name` (renamed as `Service`)
- `Displayname`
- `ProcessName`
- `VMSize`
- `ThreadCount`
- `PeakPageFile`

At the bottom of the script file, add these commands to test:

```
Update-FormatData –prepend c:\CustomViewC.format.ps1xml
<function-name> -ComputerName localhost
<function-name> -ComputerName localhost | Format-List
```

The final output should look something like this for the table.

```
ComputerName    Service      Displayname        ProcessName     VM
------------    -------      -----------        -----------     --
CLIENT2         AudioEndpo... Windows Audio E... svchost.exe     172208128
CLIENT2         BFE          Base Filtering ... svchost.exe     69496832
CLIENT2         BITS         Background Inte... svchost.exe     499310592
CLIENT2         Browser      Computer Browser   svchost.exe     499310592
```

And like this for the list:

```
Computername : CLIENT2
Service      : AudioEndpointBuilder
Displayname  : Windows Audio Endpoint Builder
ProcessName  : svchost.exe
VMSize       : 172208128
ThreadCount  : 13
PeakPageFile : 83112
```

Note that per the design specifications from chapter 6, not every object property is displayed by default and that some column headings are different than the actual property names.

NOTE Labs A, B, and C for chapters 7 through 13 build on what was accomplished in previous chapters. If you haven't finished a lab from a previous chapter, please do so. Then check your results with sample solutions on MoreLunches.com before proceeding to the next lab in the sequence.

Script and manifest modules

We've been building `Get-SystemInfo` for several chapters now, and we've been testing it by inserting a line, at the end of our script, that runs the function. It's time to move away from that and into something that's a bit more formal, packaged distributable for our command. We also need to find a way to get our custom view XML file to load into memory automatically when someone wants to use our tool. In this chapter, we'll accomplish both.

13.1 Introducing modules

Introduced in PowerShell v2, modules are the shell's preferred means of extension (over the original PSSnapin extension technology). Modules can, in many cases, be file copied rather than requiring packagers or installers, which makes modules easy to distribute. Best of all—from our perspective—modules can be written in script, meaning you don't need to be a C# developer to create one.

When it comes to modules, much of PowerShell's capability relies on relatively low-tech techniques. Modules must follow a specific naming and location convention in order for PowerShell to "see" them. This can really throw people for a loop in the beginning—it's tough to comprehend that PowerShell can get sensitive over things like folder names and filenames. But that's how it is.

13.1.1 Module location

In order for PowerShell to fully utilize them, modules must live in a specific location. There can actually be more then one location; the `PSModulePath` environment variable defines those permitted locations. Here are the default contents of the variable:

```
PS C:\> get-content env:\psmodulepath
C:\Users\donjones\Documents\WindowsPowerShell\Modules;C:\Windows\system32\Win
    dowsPowerShell\v1.0\Modules\
```

You can modify this environment variable—using either Windows or a Group Policy object (GPO)—to contain additional paths. Some third-party PowerShell products might also modify this variable. The variable's contents must be a semicolon-separated list of paths where modules may be stored. For this chapter, we'll start with the first default path, which is in C:\Users\<username>\Documents\WindowsPowerShell\ Modules. This path does not exist by default: You'll need to create it in order to begin using it.

> **CAUTION** In Windows Explorer, when you click the Documents library, you're actually accessing two folders: Public Documents and My Documents (or just Documents). The module path in PSModulePath refers only to the My Documents location. So if you're using Windows Explorer to create the folders in this path, be sure that you expand the Documents library and explicitly select My Documents or Documents.

We've created a handy command to create the necessary path:

```
PS C:\> New-Item -type directory -path (((get-content env:\psmodulepath)
   ➥ -split ';')[0])

    Directory: C:\Users\donjones\Documents\WindowsPowerShell

Mode              LastWriteTime     Length Name
----              -------------     ------ ----
d----         5/6/2012   8:36 PM           Modules
```

Note that this path is user specific; if you want to put your modules into a shared location that's accessible by multiple users, then it's fine to add that path to PSModulePath for those users. Doing so with a GPO would be easiest, and it's fine to put UNC paths into PSModulePath rather than having to map a network drive.

13.1.2 Module name

Module names should consist of letters, numbers, and underscores, although Microsoft-provided modules tend to be named only with letters. Don't use module names that contain spaces (it isn't technically illegal, but it makes them a bit harder to work with).

Once you've come up with a good name for your module (we're going to use MOLTools), you need to create a folder for the module. In many ways, the folder you create is the module: If you distribute this to other users, for example, it's the entire folder that you will distribute. The folder must be created in one of the paths listed in PSModulePath; if you put the module folder elsewhere, then it won't participate in numerous PowerShell features (like module autodiscovery, autoloading, updatable help, and so on).

We'll change to the allowed module path and create a folder for MOLTools:

```
PS C:\> cd .\users\donjones\Documents\WindowsPowerShell\Modules
PS C:\users\donjones\Documents\WindowsPowerShell\Modules> mkdir
cmdlet mkdir at command pipeline position 1
Supply values for the following parameters:
Path[0]: MOLTools
Path[1]:

    Directory: C:\users\donjones\Documents\WindowsPowerShell\Modules

Mode                LastWriteTime     Length Name
----                -------------     ------ ----
d----          5/6/2012   8:41 PM            MOLTools
```

We chose the name MOLTools after some serious thought. Keep in mind that PowerShell's command-naming convention allows for a prefix on the noun portion of command names. This prefix is designed to keep command names from overlapping. So, our Get-SystemInfo command should be named something like Get-MOLSystemInfo instead. The MOL stands for "Month of Lunches," and it's a noun prefix we feel is unlikely to be used by many others. That makes it private to us (although there's no way to enforce our ownership of it). Using MOL as our prefix will help ensure that our command can peacefully coexist with any Get-SystemInfo commands that someone else dreams up.

Having chosen MOL as our noun prefix, it makes sense to also include it in our module name. That way, the module name itself provides a clue as to the noun prefix used by the commands within the module.

> **TRY IT NOW** Make sure you can create a MOLTools module folder as you follow along. Also, consider the prefix that you might use for your organization's commands and modules.

13.1.3 *Module contents*

With our module folder created, we can begin adding contents to it. We want to be able to load this module by running Import-Module MOLTools or by attempting to run one of the commands within the module (Get-SystemInfo, or Get-MOLSystemInfo if we rename it). In order for that to work, we need to understand a bit about how PowerShell loads modules.

First, if a module is located in a nonstandard path (that is, a path not listed in PSModulePath), we'll always have to manually load the module. Suppose we stored the module folder in C:\MyStuff. We'd need to run Import-Module C:\MyStuff\ MOLTools in order to load the module, and PowerShell wouldn't be able to automatically load it for us.

That's why it's better to go with one of the supported module paths or to add a new supported path to the PSModulePath environment variable. That way, we can simply run Import-Module MOLTools, or just run one of the module's commands, to load the module.

When you run Import-Module, or when PowerShell attempts to automatically load a module for you, the shell looks in your module folder for one of these items, and it looks in this specific order:

1 A module manifest, which in our case would be MOLTools.psd1. Note that the filename must match the name of the module's folder, MOLTools.

2 A binary module, which in our example would be MOLTools.dll, if we were using a compiled binary, which we aren't. Again, the filename must be the complete module name plus the filename extension.

3 A script module, which for us would be MOLTools.psm1. Once again, you see that the filename must be the complete module name, exactly as the module's folder is named, plus the .psm1 filename extension.

This is the bit that really throws people. We see students put something like Test.psm1 into the \Modules\MOLTools folder, and that simply won't work. Most of PowerShell's magic is based upon the module folder being in one of the supported paths and on the module contents having the same name as that folder.

> **CAUTION** Avoid putting modules into the other predefined path, which is under C:\Windows\System32—that location is reserved for Microsoft's use.

13.2 Creating a script module

Listing 13.1 shows our current script file, which we're still calling Test.ps1. Notice that we've renamed our command to Get-MOLSystemInfo (highlighted in boldface), and we've removed the final line of the script that was being used to run the function. We're saving this as C:\Users\donjones\WindowsPowerShell\Modules\MOLTools\MOLTools.psm1—in other words, making it into a script module.

Listing 13.1 MOLTools.psm1

```
function Get-MOLSystemInfo {
<#
.SYNOPSIS
Retrieves key system version and model information
from one to ten computers.
.DESCRIPTION
Get-SystemInfo uses Windows Management Instrumentation
(WMI) to retrieve information from one or more computers.
Specify computers by name or by IP address.
.PARAMETER ComputerName
One or more computer names or IP addresses, up to a maximum
of 10.
.PARAMETER LogErrors
Specify this switch to create a text log file of computers
that could not be queried.
.PARAMETER ErrorLog
When used with -LogErrors, specifies the file path and name
to which failed computer names will be written. Defaults to
C:\Retry.txt.
.EXAMPLE
 Get-Content names.txt | Get-MOLSystemInfo
.EXAMPLE
 Get-MOLSystemInfo -ComputerName SERVER1,SERVER2
```

```
#>
[CmdletBinding()]
param(
    [Parameter(Mandatory=$True,
               ValueFromPipeline=$True,
               HelpMessage="Computer name or IP address")]
    [ValidateCount(1,10)]
    [Alias('hostname')]
    [string[]]$ComputerName,

    [string]$ErrorLog = 'c:\retry.txt',

    [switch]$LogErrors
)
BEGIN {
    Write-Verbose "Error log will be $ErrorLog"
}
PROCESS {
    Write-Verbose "Beginning PROCESS block"
    foreach ($computer in $computername) {
        Write-Verbose "Querying $computer"
        Try {
            $everything_ok = $true
            $os = Get-WmiObject -class Win32_OperatingSystem `
                                -computerName $computer `
                                -erroraction Stop
        } Catch {
            $everything_ok = $false
            Write-Warning "$computer failed"
            if ($LogErrors) {
                $computer | Out-File $ErrorLog -Append
                Write-Warning "Logged to $ErrorLog"
            }
        }

        if ($everything_ok) {
            $comp = Get-WmiObject -class Win32_ComputerSystem `
                                  -computerName $computer
            $bios = Get-WmiObject -class Win32_BIOS `
                                  -computerName $computer
            $props = @{'ComputerName'=$computer;
                       'OSVersion'=$os.version;
                       'SPVersion'=$os.servicepackmajorversion;
                       'BIOSSerial'=$bios.serialnumber;
                       'Manufacturer'=$comp.manufacturer;
                       'Model'=$comp.model}
            Write-Verbose "WMI queries complete"
            $obj = New-Object -TypeName PSObject -Property $props
            $obj.PSObject.TypeNames.Insert(0,'MOL.SystemInfo')
            Write-Output $obj
        }
    }
}
END {}
```

That's all we need to do, provided we only want the module to be visible to the currently logged-on user. Again, if we wanted the module to be shared among users, we'd have created a new path and added that to `PSModulePath`.

Running `Import-Module MOLTools` and then `Help Get-MOLSystemInfo` confirms that our module loads and works. We can then run `Get-MOLSystemInfo –computername localhost` to get the output of the command. But if you do that in a fresh shell window, you won't get the custom table view that we created in the previous chapter. Let's fix that next.

13.3 *Creating a module manifest*

A script module is intended to consist of a single .PSM1 file, and that's it. In our case, our module contents technically consist of MOLTools.psm1 and the XML view file we created in the previous chapter. A manifest would let us load both of those into memory at once, so let's create one. We'll start by copying the XML view file into our module folder:

```
PS C:\Users\donjones\Documents\WindowsPowerShell\Modules\MOLTools> copy C:\
test.format.ps1xml .\
PS C:\Users\donjones\Documents\WindowsPowerShell\Modules\MOLTools> ls


    Directory:
    C:\Users\donjones\Documents\WindowsPowerShell\Modules\MOLTools

Mode                LastWriteTime       Length Name
----                -------------       ------ ----
-a---         5/6/2012   5:52 PM          2833 MOLTools.psm1
-a---         5/6/2012   8:23 AM          2018 test.format.ps1xml
```

It seems silly to have that still named test.format.ps1xml, so let's rename it to MOLTools.format.ps1xml—that helps visually connect it to the script module file:

```
PS C:\Users\donjones\Documents\WindowsPowerShell\Modules\MOLTools> ren .\te
st.format.ps1xml MOLTools.format.ps1xml
PS C:\Users\donjones\Documents\WindowsPowerShell\Modules\MOLTools> ls


    Directory:
    C:\Users\donjones\Documents\WindowsPowerShell\Modules\MOLTools

Mode                LastWriteTime       Length Name
----                -------------       ------ ----
-a---         5/6/2012   8:23 AM          2018 MOLTools.format.ps1xml
-a---         5/6/2012   5:52 PM          2833 MOLTools.psm1
```

Now let's create a new module manifest. We're going to do so by running `NewModuleManifest` and providing the information needed using the command's parameters. Note that the module manifest filename must be MOLTools.psd1 in order for the shell to "see" the manifest.

```
PS C:\Users\donjones\Documents\WindowsPowerShell\Modules\MOLTools>
  New-ModuleManifest -Path MOLTools.psd1
                     -Author 'Don & Jeff'
        -CompanyName 'Month ofLunches'
```

```
-Copyright '(c)2012 Don Jones and Jeffery Hicks'
-Description 'Sample Module for Month of Lunches'
-FormatsToProcess .\MOLTools.format.ps1xml
-ModuleVersion 1.0
-PowerShellVersion 3.0
-RootModule .\MOLTools.psm1
```

NOTE   We've formatted this nicely to fit in the book, but you'd type it all on one line.

Aside from –Path, the –FormatsToProcess and –RootModule parameters are the really important ones. –FormatsToProcess is a comma-separated list of .format.ps1xml view files (or in our case, just the single file), and –RootModule is the "main" file in our module (in our case, our script module).

   The root module is an important concept: Only the commands in the root module will be made visible to shell users. If our script module imported other modules, by including Import-Module commands within the script file or within one of its functions, those child modules wouldn't be visible to shell users (although someone could still manually import one of those modules, if they wanted to, to see their contents).

TIP   Once you have a module manifest created, most likely a lot of it is boilerplate that you can reuse with other modules. There's nothing wrong with copying and pasting between .psd1 files and changing filenames as necessary. But you'll need to create a new GUID for each manifest, which is quite easy. Use this command in the shell to create one, [guid]::NewGuid(), and then copy and paste the result into your manifest. Any sections you don't need in the manifest you can comment out.

To test this, we're going to close the shell console and open a new one. Figure 13.1 shows that we can import the module, run the command, and get the formatted output defined in our XML view file. Success!

TRY IT NOW   Make sure you can follow along to this point and get the same results that we do.

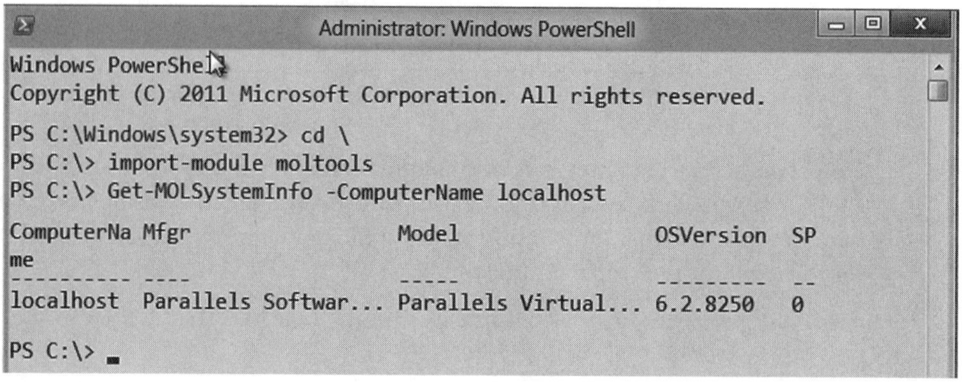

Figure 13.1   Testing the new module

13.4   *Creating a module-level setting variable*

Now that we've created a script module, we can take advantage of some other cool functionality provided by modules. For example, right now we're going to create a module variable. This will work a lot like the shell's built-in "preference" variables: The variable will be loaded into memory when the module is imported, and we'll use it to control an aspect of the module's behavior. The following listing shows the revised script file.

Listing 13.2   Adding a module-level variable to MOLTools.psm1

```
$MOLErrorLogPreference = 'c:\mol-retries.txt'          ◁──┐ Module-level
                                                          │ variable
function Get-MOLSystemInfo {
<#
.SYNOPSIS
Retrieves key system version and model information
from one to ten computers.
.DESCRIPTION
Get-SystemInfo uses Windows Management Instrumentation
(WMI) to retrieve information from one or more computers.
Specify computers by name or by IP address.
.PARAMETER ComputerName
One or more computer names or IP addresses, up to a maximum
of 10.
.PARAMETER LogErrors
Specify this switch to create a text log file of computers
that could not be queried.
.PARAMETER ErrorLog
When used with -LogErrors, specifies the file path and name
to which failed computer names will be written. Defaults to
C:\Retry.txt.
.EXAMPLE
 Get-Content names.txt | Get-MOLSystemInfo
.EXAMPLE
 Get-MOLSystemInfo -ComputerName SERVER1,SERVER2
#>
    [CmdletBinding()]
    param(
        [Parameter(Mandatory=$True,
                   ValueFromPipeline=$True,
                   HelpMessage="Computer name or IP address")]
        [ValidateCount(1,10)]
        [Alias('hostname')]
        [string[]]$ComputerName,

        [string]$ErrorLog = $MOLErrorLogPreference,          ◁──┐ Using the
                                                                │ variable
        [switch]$LogErrors
    )
    BEGIN {
        Write-Verbose "Error log will be $ErrorLog"
    }
    PROCESS {
        Write-Verbose "Beginning PROCESS block"
```

```
        foreach ($computer in $computername) {
            Write-Verbose "Querying $computer"
            Try {
                $everything_ok = $true
                $os = Get-WmiObject -class Win32_OperatingSystem `
                                    -computerName $computer `
                                    -erroraction Stop
            } Catch {
                $everything_ok = $false
                Write-Warning "$computer failed"
                if ($LogErrors) {
                    $computer | Out-File $ErrorLog -Append
                    Write-Warning "Logged to $ErrorLog"
                }
            }

            if ($everything_ok) {
                $comp = Get-WmiObject -class Win32_ComputerSystem `
                                      -computerName $computer
                $bios = Get-WmiObject -class Win32_BIOS `
                                      -computerName $computer
                $props = @{'ComputerName'=$computer;
                           'OSVersion'=$os.version;
                           'SPVersion'=$os.servicepackmajorversion;
                           'BIOSSerial'=$bios.serialnumber;
                           'Manufacturer'=$comp.manufacturer;
                           'Model'=$comp.model}
                Write-Verbose "WMI queries complete"
                $obj = New-Object -TypeName PSObject -Property $props
                $obj.PSObject.TypeNames.Insert(0,'MOL.SystemInfo')
                Write-Output $obj
            }
        }
    }
    END {}
}
Export-ModuleMember -Variable MOLErrorLogPreference          ⟵┐ Making the
Export-ModuleMember -Function Get-MOLSystemInfo                │ variable visible
```

What we've done is add a $MOLErrorLogPreference variable to the module. It's not
defined within one of the module's functions, so this becomes a module-level variable,
meaning it will exist in the shell's memory as soon as the module is loaded. We've
then utilized that to assign a default value to the Get-MOLSystemInfo command's
–ErrorLog parameter. This now enables a user to set $MOLErrorLogPreference to a
path and filename and have our command automatically use that as the default for the
–ErrorLog parameter.

   At the bottom of the revised script comes an important part. By default, module-
level variables are private, meaning they can only be seen by other items within the
module. Because our intent is to make the variable globally visible, we have to export
it, using the Export-ModuleMember command. As soon as we use that command,
everything in the module becomes private, meaning we also have to export our
Get-MOLSystemInfo function in order for that to be globally visible as well.

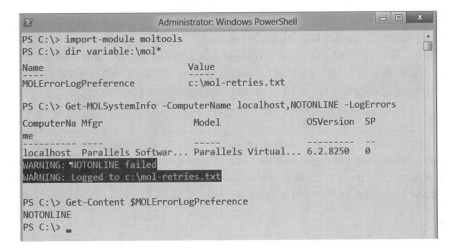

Figure 13.2 Testing the module-level variable

Figure 13.2 shows that everything is working. We start by importing the module and then checking to see that $MOLErrorLogPreference has been added to the variable drive. We then run the command, adding the –LogErrors parameter. As you can see, the filename specified in $MOLErrorLogPreference has been created and filled with the name of the failed computer.

> **NOTE** You can also create and export aliases in much the same way. Define the alias and then export it using Export-ModuleMember.

Figure 13.3 shows the real test: We removed the module and tested to make sure that $MOLErrorLogPreference was also removed from the shell. Our module is fully self-contained and can be completely loaded and unloaded on demand!

```
Administrator: Windows PowerShell
PS C:\> import-module moltools
PS C:\> dir variable:\mol*

Name                          Value
----                          -----
MOLErrorLogPreference         c:\mol-retries.txt

PS C:\> Get-MOLSystemInfo -ComputerName localhost,NOTONLINE -LogErrors

ComputerNa Mfgr               Model                OSVersion  SP
me
---------- ----               -----                ---------  --
localhost  Parallels Softwar... Parallels Virtual... 6.2.8250   0
WARNING: NOTONLINE failed
WARNING: Logged to c:\mol-retries.txt

PS C:\> Get-Content $MOLErrorLogPreference
NOTONLINE
PS C:\> remove-module moltools
PS C:\> dir variable:\mol*
PS C:\>
```

Figure 13.3 Removing the module from the shell's memory

13.5 Coming up next

We're almost finished with Get-SystemInfo—but not quite. It's a "do something" function, and we'd like to show you some examples of "input" and "output" functions. We'd also like to show you how to access databases from within a PowerShell script, and we can probably take care of all of that in the next chapter.

13.6 Lab

In this chapter you're going to assemble a module called PSHTools, from the functions and custom views that you've been working on for the last several chapters. Create a folder in the user module directory, called PSHTools. Put all of the files you will be creating in the labs into this folder.

13.6.1 Lab A

Create a single ps1xml file that contains all of the view definitions from the three existing format files. Call the file PSHTools.format.ps1xml. You'll need to be careful. Each view is defined by the <View></View> tags. These tags and everything in between should go between the <ViewDefinition></ViewDefinition> tags.

13.6.2 Lab B

Create a single module file that contains the functions from the Labs A, B, and C in chapter 12, which should be the most current version. Export all functions in the module. Be careful to copy the function only. In your module file, also define aliases for your functions and export them as well.

13.6.3 Lab C

Create a module manifest for the PSHTools module that loads the module and custom format files. Test the module following these steps:

1   Import the module.
2   Use Get-Command to view the module commands.
3   Run help for each of your aliases.
4   Run each command alias using localhost as the computer name and verify formatting.
5   Remove the module.
6   Are the commands and variables gone?

CAUTION   Once you finish these labs, please check the sample solutions at http://MoreLunches.com. Because you're going to continue building on these functions in some of the upcoming chapters, it's important that you have the correct solution (or close to it) before you continue.

Adding database access

We're going to step away briefly from the tools we've been creating and look at something you might want to add to your projects: reading and writing information from databases. For example, you may want to query a database for a list of computer names. Or perhaps you want to write the results from a function to a database. As we're going to show you, PowerShell doesn't even care what kind of database it is!

14.1 Simplifying database access

Accessing databases from PowerShell requires the use of pretty low-level .NET Framework technology. To simplify that for you, we're going to offer you a script module that bundles all the .NET stuff into a couple of PowerShell advanced functions, which should look and work a lot like a native PowerShell command. You'll need to either enter the appropriate code listings or download them from http://MoreLunches.com (find this book's name or cover image, click it, and go to the Downloads section).

14.2 Setting up your environment

First, you need to get your test environment set up properly. The techniques we're going to show you will work across any database platform for which you have .NET Framework–compatible or ODBC database drivers, but it's up to you to get those and install them. To keep things simple, we're going to work with SQL Server Express, which is a free edition of SQL Server that you can download from Microsoft. There are a variety of versions available; be sure to obtain one that's compatible with your version of the Windows operating system. Also, it's often distributed in an Express with Management Tools package, which is the one you want. The management tools provide a simple GUI that you can use to set up a test database. Sometimes the management tools (Management Studio) are a separate download, and we recommend that you install them if that's the case.

> **NOTE** We're testing with SQL Server 2012 Express with Tools on a 64-bit edition of Windows 8. SQL Server 2012 offers the normal Express install or the LocalDB install, and we chose the Express version. A full explanation of SQL Server Express and how to install it is beyond the scope of this book, but we'll at least walk you through the installation steps we took. If you're not using Windows 8, you may need to use an older version of SQL Server Express. Check the SQL Server system requirements for more information.

Here's how we installed the product:

1 We went to http://www.microsoft.com/en-us/download/details.aspx?id=29062 and downloaded ENU\x64\SQLEXPRWT_x64_ENU.exe, which is the English-language build of SQL Server 2012 Express with Tools. Microsoft may well change that URL over time, and it will eventually be superseded by later releases; visit http://download.microsoft.com to search for "SQL Express 2012" if that URL stops working.

2 We made sure that our system already had all of the listed prerequisites installed. If you don't do this, the installer will usually prompt you to download and install the necessary components, which may include a version of the .NET Framework.

3 After downloading, we double-clicked the .exe file to start the installation. Keep in mind that the steps we're following apply only to SQL Server 2012 Express; later releases, or even service pack versions, may have slightly different procedures. It isn't our goal with this book to teach you how to install SQL Server; we just want to get it up and running on your system so that you'll have something to play with.

4 We selected the option to install a new standalone installation.

5 We accepted the licensing terms and allowed the installer to check for product updates.

6 We opted to include the Database Engine Services, Management Tools, and SQL Client Connectivity. We did not include SQL Server Replication or LocalDB, although doing so shouldn't hurt, if you want to include them.

7 We installed a Names instance, named SQLExpress, with an instance ID of SQLEXPRESS. This was the default, and we kept the default installation path as well.

8 We accepted the defaults for the Service Accounts and Collation tabs.

9 We accepted the defaults for the Database Engine Configuration tabs, including Server Configuration, Data Directories, User Instances, and FILESTREAM.

10 We accepted the defaults for Error Reporting.

11 We waited a while for the installation to complete.

12 We created a folder, C:\SampleData, in which to place our sample database. We made sure that our user account had read/write permissions to the folder.

TIP You can pretty much accept the defaults and get the same installation we did. We're not claiming this is a perfect production-quality install, but it's perfect for our lab environment.

After the installation is complete, you'll need to confirm the name of your SQL Server instance. The easiest way to do that is to look at a list of running services on your computer, because that will show you all installed SQL Server instances. We ran `Get-Service`, with the following results:

```
PS C:\Windows\system32> get-service -name mssql* | select name

Name
----
MSSQL$SQLEXPRESS
```

This shows that we have a SQL Server service running with the instance ID SQLEX-PRESS (which is what we told the installer to create, so that should come as no surprise). The full name of this instance is <computername>\SQLEXPRESS, or localhost\SQLEXPRESS if you're logging in locally. You'll need to know that in order to build the correct connection string later.

For now, open SQL Server Management Studio (it should have an icon in your Start menu once the installer is complete). You'll be asked to log in, as shown in figure 14.1. We provided the instance name localhost\SQLEXPRESS and let it use our Windows credentials (which is all we told the installer we wanted to allow).

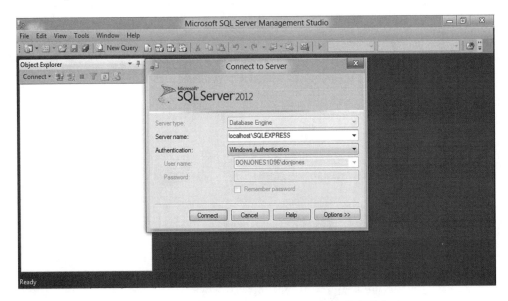

Figure 14.1 Connecting SQL Server Management Studio to our SQLEXPRESS instance

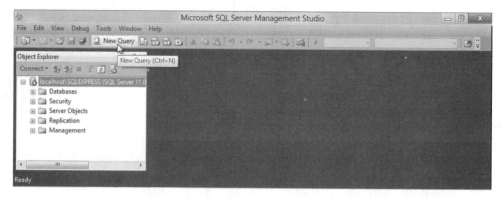

Figure 14.2   **Opening a new query window in SQL Server Management Studio**

Next, click the New Query button to open a new query window (as shown in figure 14.2). Type (or paste in, if you've downloaded this book's scripts) the code from listing 14.1 into the query window.

> **NOTE**   As a quick reminder, numbered listings in this book can be downloaded from http://MoreLunches.com. Look for this book's cover image, click it, and scroll to the Downloads section. Downloading will be a lot easier than typing them in and will ensure that you're getting a corrected version in the event that we find any bugs or make any improvements after the book is printed.

Listing 14.1   Creating a database

```
CREATE DATABASE [Inventory] ON  PRIMARY
( NAME = N'Inventory', FILENAME = N'c:\sampledata\Inventory.mdf' , SIZE =
    3096KB , FILEGROWTH = 1024KB )
 LOG ON
( NAME = N'Inventory_log', FILENAME = N'c:\sampledata\Inventory_log.ldf' ,
    SIZE = 1024KB , FILEGROWTH = 10%)
GO
USE [Inventory]
GO
SET ANSI_NULLS ON
GO
SET QUOTED_IDENTIFIER ON
GO
CREATE TABLE [dbo].[Computers](
 [computername] [nvarchar](50) NULL,
 [osversion] [nvarchar](100) NULL,
 [spversion] [nvarchar](100) NULL,
 [manufacturer] [nvarchar](100) NULL,
 [model] [nvarchar](100) NULL
) ON [PRIMARY]

GO
```

To run this after typing or pasting it in, click the ! (Execute) button in the toolbar. Make sure it runs without error.

Next, we're going to put a couple of rows of data into the database. Close the query window you were working in, and then open a new one by clicking that New Query button again. Then, enter (or paste) the code from the following listing into the query window.

Listing 14.2   Adding data to the database

```
Use [Inventory]
Go
INSERT INTO Computers (computername) VALUES ('localhost')
INSERT INTO Computers (computername) VALUES ('localhost')
INSERT INTO Computers (computername) VALUES ('not-online')
```

Once again, click ! (Execute) to run this query, and make sure it runs without error. Once it's done, you should be ready to start testing and using PowerShell.

14.3   *The database functions*

Listing 14.3 is a script module that we created to help simplify database access. We suggest saving this file on your computer as \Users\<user>\Documents\WindowsPowerShell\ Modules\MOLDatabase\MOLDatabase.psm1, where <user> is your username in Windows. This is the same folder structure where your PSHTools module, from the previous chapter, is located. Remember, the MOLDatabase folder should be at the same level as the MOLTools folder, and MOLDatabase.psm1 should go inside the MOLDatabase folder. Figure 14.3 shows what this looks like in Windows Explorer.

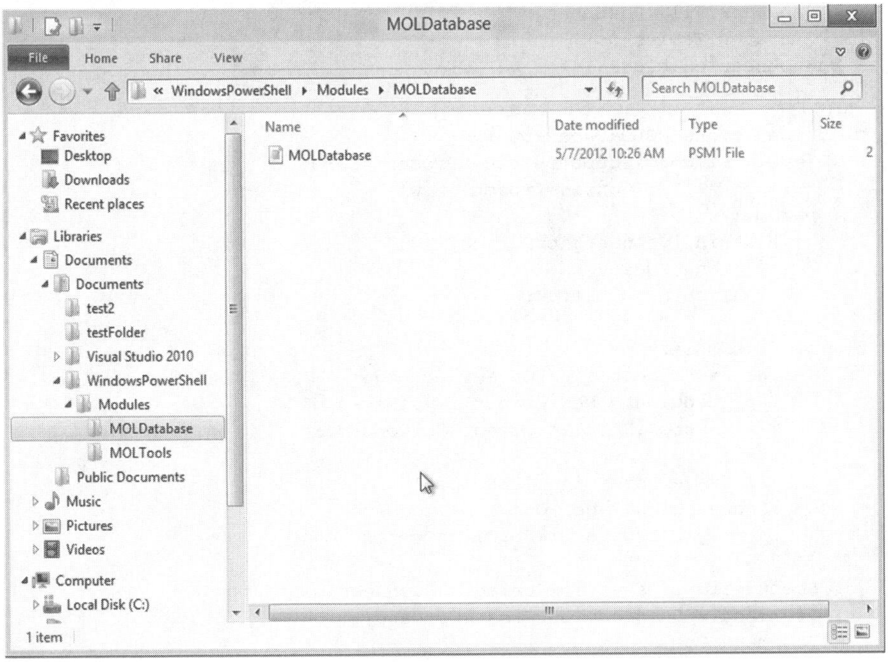

Figure 14.3   Saving the MOLDatabase module

```
function Get-MOLDatabaseData {
    [CmdletBinding()]
    param (
        [string]$connectionString,
        [string]$query,
        [switch]$isSQLServer
    )
    if ($isSQLServer) {
        Write-Verbose 'in SQL Server mode'
        $connection = New-Object -TypeName `
            System.Data.SqlClient.SqlConnection
    } else {
        Write-Verbose 'in OleDB mode'
        $connection = New-Object -TypeName `
            System.Data.OleDb.OleDbConnection
    }
    $connection.ConnectionString = $connectionString
    $command = $connection.CreateCommand()
    $command.CommandText = $query
    if ($isSQLServer) {
        $adapter = New-Object -TypeName `
        System.Data.SqlClient.SqlDataAdapter $command
    } else {
        $adapter = New-Object -TypeName `
        System.Data.OleDb.OleDbDataAdapter $command
    }
    $dataset = New-Object -TypeName System.Data.DataSet
    $adapter.Fill($dataset)
    $dataset.Tables[0]
    $connection.close()
}

function Invoke-MOLDatabaseQuery {
    [CmdletBinding(SupportsShouldProcess=$True,
                   ConfirmImpact='Low')]
    param (
        [string]$connectionString,
        [string]$query,
        [switch]$isSQLServer
    )
    if ($isSQLServer) {
        Write-Verbose 'in SQL Server mode'
        $connection = New-Object -TypeName `
            System.Data.SqlClient.SqlConnection
    } else {
        Write-Verbose 'in OleDB mode'
        $connection = New-Object -TypeName `
            System.Data.OleDb.OleDbConnection
    }
    $connection.ConnectionString = $connectionString
    $command = $connection.CreateCommand()
    $command.CommandText = $query
    if ($pscmdlet.shouldprocess($query)) {
```

```
        $connection.Open()
        $command.ExecuteNonQuery()
        $connection.close()
    }
}
```

These functions are intended to provide low-level access to a database, using a generic approach. In the next couple of sections, we'll explain what they do and how they work, and then we'll incorporate them into our running example script (the MOLTools module that you created in the previous chapter).

> **NOTE** We've provided you with these functions in the form of a module because we hope that you'll be able to use them in your own tools. Part of what we'll be showing you includes having your module load the MOLDatabase module behind the scenes, meaning you should be able to use our database functions in your own projects to simplify database access.

14.4 *About the database functions*

So let's cover a little background information on the two database functions. Get-MOLDatabaseData is to be used when you want to query information from a database; Invoke-MOLDatabaseQuery is for when you want to make changes, such as adding data, removing data, or changing data. Each supports three parameters:

- -ConnectionString—This tells PowerShell how to find the database server, what database to connect to, and how to authenticate. You can find more connection string examples at http://ConnectionStrings.com.
- -isSQLServer—Include this switch when your connection string points to a Microsoft SQL Server. Omit this string for all other database server types, and PowerShell will use OleDB instead. You'll need to make sure your connection string is OleDB compatible and that you've installed the necessary OleDB drivers to access your database. That can be MySQL, Access, Oracle, or whatever you like.
- -Query—This is the actual SQL language query that you want to run. This book isn't going to dive into detail on that language; we assume you know it already. If you'd like to learn more about the SQL language, there are numerous books and videos on the subject.

Invoke-MOLDatabaseQuery doesn't write anything to the pipeline; it just runs your query. Get-MOLDatabaseData will retrieve data and place it into the pipeline. Within the pipeline, you'll get objects with properties that correspond to the columns of the database. We're not going to dive into further detail on how the two database functions operate internally. As we said at the outset, the line in the sand for this book is the .NET Framework. These functions internally utilize the .NET Framework, and so for this book they're out of scope. The functions do, however, provide a nice wrapper around .NET, so that you can access databases without having to mess around with the raw .NET Framework stuff.

Note that `Invoke-MOLDatabaseQuery` declares support for the `-WhatIf` and `-Confirm` parameters via its `SupportsShouldProcess` attribute. We'll cover that in more detail in chapter 16. For right now, you can safely ignore it.

14.5 *Using the database functions*

Let's put the `MOLDatabase` module to use. Here's what we're going to do:

- Modify the `MOLTools` module from the previous chapter so that it internally loads the `MOLDatabase` module.
- Create a function, in `MOLTools`, that reads computer names from the database and delivers them to `Get-MOLSystemInfo`. This will be an example of an input function, which we discussed at the outset of the book.
- Create a function, in `MOLTools`, that takes the output from `Get-MOLSystemInfo` and saves that information back to the database. This will be an example of an output function, which we also discussed at the outset of the book, although in this case the output will be to a database rather than to the screen or some other visible form.

We first need to create a connection string, which we'll use throughout our new `MOLTools` functions. Referring to http://ConnectionStrings.com, the following would appear to be correct:

```
server=localhost\SQLEXPRESS;database=inventory;trusted_connection=True
```

We'll put this into a module-level variable for easy reuse, but we won't export that variable. That'll make the variable visible only to other elements within the MOL-Tools.psm1 script module file. The following listing shows the complete, new MOLTools.psm1 file.

Listing 14.4   Revised MOLTools.psm1

```
$MOLErrorLogPreference = 'c:\mol-retries.txt'
$MOLConnectionString =
     "server=localhost\SQLEXPRESS;database=inventory;trusted_connection=True"

Import-Module MOLDatabase

function Get-MOLComputerNamesFromDatabase {
<#
.SYNOPSIS
Reads computer names from the MoL sample database,
placing them into the pipeline as strings.
#>
    Get-MOLDatabaseData -connectionString $MOLConnectionString `
                        -isSQLServer `
                        -query "SELECT computername FROM computers"
}

function Set-MOLInventoryInDatabase {
<#
.SYNOPSIS
```

```
Accepts the output of Get-MOLSystemInfo and saves
the results back to the MoL sample database.
#>
    [CmdletBinding()]
    param(
        [Parameter(Mandatory=$True,
                   ValueFromPipeline=$True)]
        [object[]]$inputObject
    )
    PROCESS {
        foreach ($obj in $inputobject) {
            $query = "UPDATE computers SET
                        osversion = '$($obj.osversion)',
                        spversion = '$($obj.spversion)',
                        manufacturer = '$($obj.manufacturer)',
                        model = '$($obj.model)'
                        WHERE computername = '$($obj.computername)'"
            Write-Verbose "Query will be $query"
            Invoke-MOLDatabaseQuery -connection $MOLConnectionString `
                                    -isSQLServer `
                                    -query $query
        }
    }
}

function Get-MOLSystemInfo {
<#
.SYNOPSIS
Retrieves key system version and model information
from one to ten computers.
.DESCRIPTION
Get-SystemInfo uses Windows Management Instrumentation
(WMI) to retrieve information from one or more computers.
Specify computers by name or by IP address.
.PARAMETER ComputerName
One or more computer names or IP addresses, up to a maximum
of 10.
.PARAMETER LogErrors
Specify this switch to create a text log file of computers
that could not be queried.
.PARAMETER ErrorLog
When used with -LogErrors, specifies the file path and name
to which failed computer names will be written. Defaults to
C:\Retry.txt.
.EXAMPLE
 Get-Content names.txt | Get-MOLSystemInfo
.EXAMPLE
 Get-MOLSystemInfo -ComputerName SERVER1,SERVER2
#>
    [CmdletBinding()]
    param(
        [Parameter(Mandatory=$True,
                   ValueFromPipeline=$True,
                   ValueFromPipelineByPropertyName=$True,
                   HelpMessage="Computer name or IP address")]
```

```
            [ValidateCount(1,10)]
            [Alias('hostname')]
            [string[]]$ComputerName,

            [string]$ErrorLog = $MOLErrorLogPreference,

            [switch]$LogErrors
        )
    BEGIN {
        Write-Verbose "Error log will be $ErrorLog"
    }
    PROCESS {
        Write-Verbose "Beginning PROCESS block"
        foreach ($computer in $computername) {
            Write-Verbose "Querying $computer"
            Try {
                $everything_ok = $true
                $os = Get-WmiObject -class Win32_OperatingSystem `
                                    -computerName $computer `
                                    -erroraction Stop
            } Catch {
                $everything_ok = $false
                Write-Warning "$computer failed"
                if ($LogErrors) {
                    $computer | Out-File $ErrorLog -Append
                    Write-Warning "Logged to $ErrorLog"
                }
            }

            if ($everything_ok) {
                $comp = Get-WmiObject -class Win32_ComputerSystem `
                                    -computerName $computer
                $bios = Get-WmiObject -class Win32_BIOS `
                                    -computerName $computer
                $props = @{'ComputerName'=$computer;
                            'OSVersion'=$os.version;
                            'SPVersion'=$os.servicepackmajorversion;
                            'BIOSSerial'=$bios.serialnumber;
                            'Manufacturer'=$comp.manufacturer;
                            'Model'=$comp.model}
                Write-Verbose "WMI queries complete"
                $obj = New-Object -TypeName PSObject -Property $props
                $obj.PSObject.TypeNames.Insert(0,'MOL.SystemInfo')
                Write-Output $obj
            }
        }
    }
    END {}
}

Export-ModuleMember -Variable MOLErrorLogPreference
Export-ModuleMember -Function Get-MOLSystemInfo,
                            Get-MOLComputerNamesFromDatabase,
                            Set-MOLInventoryInDatabase
```

We need to explain what we did, but first let's test it:

```
PS C:\> remove-module mol*
PS C:\> import-module moltools
PS C:\> Get-MOLComputerNamesFromDatabase  | Get-MOLSystemInfo |
Set-MOLInventoryInDatabase
2
2
WARNING: not-online failed
```

Perfect! The 2 in the output is probably coming from our database function and is a success indicator; we could have piped that to Out-Null to suppress it, but at this stage it's nice to see something happening. So what made this work? Let's grab some snippets from MOLTools.psm1, starting with this:

```
$MOLConnectionString =
    "server=localhost\SQLEXPRESS;database=inventory;trusted_connection=True"

Import-Module MOLDatabase
```

This text at the top of the file sets our default connection string and loads the MOLDatabase module. The contents of MOLDatabase won't be visible to the shell user, because it's internal to MOLTools. Next up is our first new function:

```
function Get-MOLComputerNamesFromDatabase {
<#
.SYNOPSIS
Reads computer names from the MoL sample database,
placing them into the pipeline as strings.
#>
    Get-MOLDatabaseData -connectionString $MOLConnectionString `
                        -isSQLServer `
                        -query "SELECT computername FROM computers"
}
```

We kept this simple for illustration purposes; we should add better comment-based help to it, so feel free to expand on what we've started. This just gets all of the computer names from the database. It outputs each as an object with a ComputerName property. That's going to necessitate a minor change to Get-MOLSystemInfo's parameters:

```
        [Parameter(Mandatory=$True,
                ValueFromPipeline=$True,
                ValueFromPipelineByPropertyName=$True,
                HelpMessage="Computer name or IP address")]
        [ValidateCount(1,10)]
        [Alias('hostname')]
        [string[]]$ComputerName,
```

Here, we've added the ValueFromPipelineByParameterName attribute, enabling the function's –ComputerName parameter to accept the contents of a piped-in ComputerName property. We might, in the long run, want to remove that ValidateCount() attribute as well, because it's likely our database will eventually contain more than 10 computers.

Next is the function that saves the data back to the database:

```
function Set-MOLInventoryInDatabase {
<#
.SYNOPSIS
Accepts the output of Get-MOLSystemInfo and saves
the results back to the MoL sample database.
#>
    [CmdletBinding()]
    param(
        [Parameter(Mandatory=$True,
                   ValueFromPipeline=$True)]          Object
        [object[]]$inputObject                        change
    )
    PROCESS {
        foreach ($obj in $inputobject) {              Define a
            $query = "UPDATE computers SET            database query
                      osversion = '$($obj.osversion)',
                      spversion = '$($obj.spversion)',
                      manufacturer = '$($obj.manufacturer)',
                      model = '$($obj.model)'
                      WHERE computername = '$($obj.computername)'"
            Write-Verbose "Query will be $query"
            Invoke-MOLDatabaseQuery -connection $MOLConnectionString `
                                    -isSQLServer `
                                    -query $query           Execute the
        }                                                   database query
    }
}
```

This one is a bit more complex. You can see that we've set it to accept pipeline input of the generic type `Object`. We then construct a query that grabs the object's properties and sets them as the values of the database table's columns. We then execute the query. We've included some verbose output too, so that we can keep track of what's happening should we need to debug.

Let's see if we can't modify the function to suppress those two output lines. The next listing shows a revised MOLDatabase.psm1 file, with just one change, which we've boldfaced for you.

Listing 14.5   Revised MOLDatabase.psm1

```
function Get-MOLDatabaseData {
    [CmdletBinding()]
    param (
        [string]$connectionString,
        [string]$query,
        [switch]$isSQLServer
    )
    if ($isSQLServer) {
        Write-Verbose 'in SQL Server mode'
        $connection = New-Object -TypeName `
            System.Data.SqlClient.SqlConnection
    } else {
```

```
        Write-Verbose 'in OleDB mode'
        $connection = New-Object -TypeName `
            System.Data.OleDb.OleDbConnection
    }
    $connection.ConnectionString = $connectionString
    $command = $connection.CreateCommand()
    $command.CommandText = $query
    if ($isSQLServer) {
        $adapter = New-Object -TypeName `
        System.Data.SqlClient.SqlDataAdapter $command
    } else {
        $adapter = New-Object -TypeName `
        System.Data.OleDb.OleDbDataAdapter $command
    }
    $dataset = New-Object -TypeName System.Data.DataSet
    $adapter.Fill($dataset)
    $dataset.Tables[0]
    $connection.close()
}

function Invoke-MOLDatabaseQuery {
    [CmdletBinding(SupportsShouldProcess=$True,
                   ConfirmImpact='Low')]
    param (
        [string]$connectionString,
        [string]$query,
        [switch]$isSQLServer
    )
    if ($isSQLServer) {
        Write-Verbose 'in SQL Server mode'
        $connection = New-Object -TypeName `
            System.Data.SqlClient.SqlConnection
    } else {
        Write-Verbose 'in OleDB mode'
        $connection = New-Object -TypeName `
            System.Data.OleDb.OleDbConnection
    }
    $connection.ConnectionString = $connectionString
    $command = $connection.CreateCommand()
    $command.CommandText = $query
    if ($pscmdlet.shouldprocess($query)) {
        $connection.Open()
        $command.ExecuteNonQuery() | Out-Null
        $connection.close()
    }
}
```

Let's test again:

```
PS C:\> remove-module mol*
PS C:\> import-module moltools
PS C:\> Get-MOLComputerNamesFromDatabase | Get-MOLSystemInfo |
Set-MOLInventoryInDatabase
WARNING: not-online failed
```

Perfect! This illustrates how straightforward it is to put something together, test it, and then tweak it if you're not happy with the first results. And as you can see, with a little help from the wrapper functions in MOLDatabase, we can start working with databases pretty easily!

14.6   *Lab*

There's no lab for this chapter; your actual use of databases is going to vary greatly depending on your exact needs and the tasks that you want to complete. But the functions we've provided in this chapter should give you all of the patterns and templates you need to start using databases in your own scripts.

Interlude: creating a new tool

We're not going to teach you anything new in this chapter. Instead, we'd like to take a brief break from the learning and focus on reinforcing what you've done so far, using a different example. This chapter, then, is basically one giant lab. You'll be walking through every step of the toolmaking process (as we've covered it thus far) and creating an all-new tool for yourself.

> **NOTE** In the example Lab Answers provided at http://MoreLunches.com, we'll provide you with an example script for each section of this chapter. That way, if you get lost, you can catch up by looking at our example for that point.

15.1 Designing the tool

This chapter will require that you have a Windows 8 or Windows Server 2012 computer. You're going to design a tool that makes use of the `SmbShare` module included in those versions of Windows. Your task is to create a function named `Get-RemoteSmbShare`. It should accept one or more computer names, either on a `–ComputerName` parameter or from the pipeline, and then retrieve a list of current shared folders from each specified computer. The output must include each computer's name, the share name, description, and the path to the share.

Because the commands in the `SmbShare` module do not have `–ComputerName` parameters themselves, you'll utilize PowerShell Remoting (`Invoke-Command`). For the purposes of this lab, assume that each computer you need to query has Power-Shell Remoting enabled, with the default configuration of non-encrypted HTTP over port 5985. For testing purposes, enable Remoting on your computer by running `Enable-PSRemoting` (this must be done as an Administrator in an elevated session, and you must ensure that the command completes without error). When you test your function throughout this chapter, do so by providing "localhost" as the computer name.

15.2 Writing and testing the function

Start writing your advanced function. For now, don't include it in a module. Instead, include it in a plain .ps1 script that's saved into your C:\ directory. At the bottom of your script, after the closing } for the function, enter the following to test the function:

```
Get-RemoteSmbShare -computerName localhost,localhost
```

Because localhost is listed twice, your function's output should list each of your computer's shared folders twice.

15.3 Dressing up the parameters

Modify your Get-RemoteSmbShare function to include the following features:

- The -ComputerName parameter should be mandatory, meaning PowerShell should prompt for a value if one isn't specified.
- The -ComputerName parameter should accept input from the pipeline ByValue.
- Add -HostName as an alias for the -ComputerName parameter.
- Ensure that at least one, and no more than five, computer names are specified each time the function is run.

Add the following lines to the bottom of your script to test your additions:

```
# Section 15.3 Tests...
'localhost','localhost' | Get-RemoteSmbShare
Get-RemoteSmbShare -host localhost

# The following should prompt for a name; enter localhost
Get-RemoteSmbShare

# The following should fail with an error
Get-RemoteSmbShare -Computer one,two,three,four,five,six,seven
```

When you've finished testing your changes, remove all of the previous lines from your script.

15.4 Adding help

Add comment-based help to your Get-RemoteSmbShare function. Include at least a synopsis and description, and include help for the -ComputerName parameter. Also include at least two examples. At the bottom of your script, add the following line to test the new help:

```
Help Get-RemoteSmbShare
```

Remove that line of code from your script after testing your new help.

15.5 Handling errors

Modify your `Get-RemoteSmbShare` function to include a `-ErrorFile` parameter. This parameter should accept a single string and should default to C:\Errors.txt. Also, modify the function to catch any errors that occur while running `Invoke-Command`. When an error occurs, the function should log the failed computer name to whatever filename is specified in the `-ErrorFile` parameter. It should always append values to this file and should never attempt to delete the file. The function should also display a Warning message with the failed computer name and shouldn't attempt to create any output objects for that computer's shares. Don't forget to update your comment-based help to reflect the new parameter.

Add the following to the bottom of your script to test this new functionality:

```
Get-RemoteSmbShare -computer localhost,NOTONLINE,localhost
```

Ensure that NOTONLINE is logged to C:\Errors.txt, and then remove the previous line of code from your script.

15.6 Making a module

Incorporate your `Get-RemoteSmbShare` function into the `PSHTools` module that you created for the earlier chapters in this book. When doing so, be sure to add only the function itself to the module's .psm1 file; don't add any testing code that's in the script from previous sections of this chapter.

Open a fresh PowerShell console window and run `Import-Module PSHTools`. Run `Get-RemoteSmbShare -computer localhost` and ensure that the correct output is displayed.

15.7 Coming up next

Congratulations! You've completed the core and most important part of this book! Using the techniques you've learned to this point, you should be able to build some pretty impressive tools. In the next seven chapters, we're going to start expanding your repertoire of toolmaking tricks, showing you additional techniques. We won't always be building off of the good-old `Get-SystemInfo` function any longer, but we think you'll find plenty of cool things to work with.

Part 3

Advanced toolmaking techniques

With the toolmaking basics under your belt, you're ready to start exploring some of the other techniques and strategies that PowerShell offers. In the next few chapters, we'll explore things like workflow, pipeline input troubleshooting, and more. While none of these are intended to provide comprehensive coverage of their topics (workflow, for example, needs an entire book of its own), these chapters will get you pointed in the right direction to start using these advanced features and capabilities.

Making tools
that make changes

So far, we've been focused on tools that get information, Get-MOLSystemInfo being our running example. But you're obviously going to create tools that make changes, too. When you do so, there are a couple of extra steps that you should take in order to remain consistent with the rest of PowerShell. You've already seen a hint of this: the support for -Confirm and -WhatIf that our Invoke-MOLDatabaseQuery function included. In this chapter, we'll walk you through those details.

> **NOTE** We're going to be using some of PowerShell's CIM commands in this chapter. Those work against Windows Management Instrumentation (WMI) but only work if PowerShell Remoting has been enabled on the computer. If you're having problems using them, you can change to the older WMI command. We'll provide tips along the way for doing so.

16.1 The –Confirm and –WhatIf parameters

Look at the help for any PowerShell command that makes changes, and you're likely to see both -Confirm and -WhatIf included in the command's parameters. These parameters should be supported for any command that changes the system state in any way—even something as simple as changing a file on disk.

Fortunately, there's no need to hand-code these parameters into your tools. If you're writing an advanced function, which is more or less all we've been writing in this book, then just a little extra work can implement these two key parameters for you.

16.2   *Passthrough ShouldProcess*

We're going to create a tool called `Restart-MOLCimComputer`. Our tool will accept one or more computer names and will utilize WMI to restart them. Specifically, we're going to use the `Reboot()` method of the `Win32_OperatingSystem` class. This method accepts no parameters; it simply begins the reboot.

> **NOTE**   We're aware that a very similar `Restart-Computer` command exists natively in PowerShell. Our technique will utilize PowerShell v3's CIM cmdlet family, which utilizes the WS-MAN remoting protocol, rather than whatever black magic `Restart-Computer` uses to communicate. In addition, we needed a straightforward example, and this is what we thought of!

Anytime we start building a tool, we tend to start in the command line, running commands ad hoc to get them working. So we'll start by running this command in the PowerShell console:

```
PS C:\>Invoke-CimMethod –ClassName Win32_OperatingSystem –MethodName Reboot
    –ComputerName localhost
```

> **CAUTION**   A moment's thought will tell you that you shouldn't run this command unless you've saved all of your open files!

Switching to WMI

If this command isn't working on your system, then it's likely that PowerShell's Remoting hasn't been enabled. You can do that by running `Enable-PSRemoting` as an Administrator. Or you can switch to `Invoke-WmiMethod –Class Win32_OperatingSystem –Name Reboot –ComputerName localhost`.

You'll need to make that same substitution in listing 16.1.

A quick reboot later and we've confirmed that our command works. Now let's build a tool out of it. We're going to add the contents of listing 16.1 to our MOLTools.psm1 file, but we're just listing the additions here instead of listing the entire file contents. We're also including the last lines of MOLTools.psm1, which list the module's exported items. Notice that we've added `Restart-MOLCimComputer` to the list of exported functions.

Listing 16.1   Adding to MOLTools.psm1

```
function Restart-MOLCimComputer {
    [CmdletBinding(SupportsShouldProcess=$True,
                   ConfirmImpact='High')]
    param(
        [Parameter(Mandatory=$true,
                   ValueFromPipeline=$true)]
        [string[]]$ComputerName
    )
```

```
    PROCESS {
        ForEach ($computer in $computername) {
            Invoke-CimMethod -ClassName Win32_OperatingSystem `
                             -MethodName Reboot `
                             -ComputerName $computer
        }
    }
}

Export-ModuleMember -Variable MOLErrorLogPreference
Export-ModuleMember -Function Get-MOLSystemInfo,
                             Get-MOLComputerNamesFromDatabase,
                             Set-MOLInventoryInDatabase,
                             Restart-MOLCimComputer
```

NOTE In order to keep this example straightforward, we're not adding any error handling. In a production environment, we expect that you'd want to do that. You'd probably also want to add comment-based help and the other niceties that we've covered in the preceding chapters.

There's only one major difference between this tool and the others we've written, and that's in the [CmdletBinding()] attribute (which we've boldfaced). We've indicated that this function supports ShouldProcess, which is what enables the -WhatIf and -Confirm parameters. We've also defined a ConfirmImpact, setting it to High. We'll discuss that impact level in the next section; for now, let's test our new function.

Before we do that, look carefully at the help for Invoke-CimMethod. Notice that it too supports -WhatIf and -Confirm, which you can verify by reading its help file. We'll save our revised MOLTools.psm1 file and then go into the console. We'll remove the MOLTools module (in case it's already loaded), import it (to read in the new version), and then run our function. This will reboot the computer again, so make sure there aren't any other open, unsaved files!

```
PS C:\> remove-module moltools
Remove-Module : No modules were removed. Verify that the specification of
modules to remove is correct and those modules exist in the runspace.
At line:1 char:1
+ remove-module moltools
+ ~~~~~~~~~~~~~~~~~~~~~~~
    + CategoryInfo          : ResourceUnavailable: (:) [Remove-Module], I
   nvalidOperationException
    + FullyQualifiedErrorId : Modules_NoModulesRemoved,Microsoft.PowerShe
   ll.Commands.RemoveModuleCommand

PS C:\> import-module moltools
PS C:\> Restart-MOLCimComputer -ComputerName localhost
```

NOTE The error message tells us that the module wasn't already loaded when we tried to remove it. That's fine.

And away it goes! This confirms that our command worked. Now let's try running it with -WhatIf and -Confirm:

```
PS C:\> import-module moltools
PS C:\> Restart-MOLCimComputer -ComputerName localhost -whatif
What if: Performing operation "Invoke-CimMethod: Reboot" on Target "Win32_O
peratingSystem".
PS C:\> Restart-MOLCimComputer -ComputerName localhost -confirm

Confirm
Are you sure you want to perform this action?
Performing operation "Invoke-CimMethod: Reboot" on Target
"Win32_OperatingSystem".
[Y] Yes  [A] Yes to All  [N] No  [L] No to All  [S] Suspend  [?] Help
(default is "Y"):n
PS C:\>
```

This time, you can see the what-if output as well as the confirmation prompt. This illustrates a couple of important points:

- By specifying SupportsShouldProcess=$True in our [CmdletBinding()] attribute, we allow Restart-CimComputer to accept the -WhatIf and -Confirm parameters.
- Because our internal command, Invoke-CimMethod, already supports -WhatIf and -Confirm on its own, we don't need to do anything else. The -WhatIf or -Confirm passed to our tool is handed down to any internal commands that also support the parameters. If you examine the what-if output and the Confirm prompt, you'll see that it's actually Invoke-CimMethod that's triggering the output.

This hand-me-down effect works for all of the common parameters, including -Verbose, -Debug, and others. If someone runs your tool with one of those, they'll be passed down to any commands within your tool. So if someone runs your tool with -Verbose, every command inside the tool will also run with -Verbose, which is pretty much exactly what you'd normally want!

16.3   *Defining the impact level*

Let's circle back to the impact level. The possible values for ConfirmImpact, in the [CmdletBinding()] attribute, are Low, Medium, and High. This is a relative indication of how harmful your command might be. If you're planning to make a minor change, you specify a confirm impact of Low; if you're making a major change—like rebooting a computer—you might opt for High. There are no set rules about which level is meant for what; it's all up your judgment.

PowerShell has two built-in variables, $WhatIfPreference and $ConfirmPreference. They each work a bit differently:

- $WhatIfPreference is set to $False by default. If you change it to $True, then all commands that support -WhatIf will run as if -WhatIf was specified, even if you don't specify it. In other words, it shifts the shell into what-if mode by default. When the variable is set to $True, you can run commands with -WhatIf:$False to shut off what-if mode for just that command.

- $ConfirmPreference is set to High by default. When you run a command that supports –Confirm, the shell looks at the command's impact level. If the command's impact level is equal to or higher than the contents of $ConfirmPreference, then the –Confirm parameter is added automatically. So a command with an impact level of High should *always* result in a confirmation prompt, unless you run it with –Confirm:$False.

Reading that last bullet point, you might develop the expectation that our Restart-CimComputer command will always display a confirmation prompt. After all, we've set its ConfirmImpact to High, right? But if you recall our first test of the command, the computer rebooted without a confirmation prompt at all. What happened?

The secret is in how the hand-me-down process works. You see, Restart-CimComputer never gave the shell a chance to check the impact level. Instead, it ran Invoke-CimMethod. That command's impact level isn't set to High, so it didn't trigger the $ConfirmPreference. Your tool will only auto-trigger confirmation when it explicitly tells the shell that it's doing something that might require confirmation. That's what we'll look at next.

16.4 *Implementing ShouldProcess*

For our next tool, we're going to change a service's logon password. This is something that must be accomplished by running the Change() method of WMI's Win32_Service class. Glancing at the MSDN documentation for the class (http://msdn.microsoft.com/en-us/library/windows/desktop/aa384901(v=vs.85).aspx), we see that the Change() method accepts numerous settings. The eighth one sets the logon password, so we'll need to pass $null for the first seven parameters, so that we don't change any of them. We can omit the ninth and subsequent parameters, because we also don't want to change them. Again, we'll start by testing this in the shell—we'll modify the BITS service, because doing so won't mess up anything too severely.

> **CAUTION** BITS is certainly used in a production environment for, among other things, Windows Update. We're comfortable messing it up in our lab environment, but this isn't something you should experiment with on a live computer.

```
PS C:\> Get-WmiObject -Class Win32_Service -ComputerName Localhost -Filter
"name='BITS'" | Invoke-WmiMethod -Name Change -ArgumentList $null,$null,$nu
ll,$null,$null,$null,$null,"P@ssw0rd"
Invoke-WmiMethod : Input string was not in a correct format.
At line:1 char:84
+ Get-WmiObject -Class Win32_Service -ComputerName Localhost -Filter
"name='BITS'" ...
+ ~~~~~~~~~~~~~~~~~~~~~~~~~~~~~~~~~~~~~~~~~~~~~~~~~~~~~~~~~~~~~~~~~~~~~~~~~~
~~~~~~~~
    + CategoryInfo          : NotSpecified: (:) [Invoke-WmiMethod], Forma
   tException
    + FullyQualifiedErrorId : System.FormatException,Microsoft.PowerShell
   .Commands.InvokeWmiMethod
```

We've chosen to use the WMI command, rather than the CIM equivalent, for a specific reason: The –ArgumentList parameter of Invoke-WmiMethod can't deal with $null values. That's why we got this error message. Invoke-CimMethod accepts arguments in a different format, specifically to avoid this problem. For the moment, we're going to pretend that we're writing a tool that needs to run against older computers (such as Windows XP), so the newer CIM cmdlets aren't an option. That means that, rather than using Invoke-WmiMethod, we'll have to manually invoke the Change() method of the object. This presents a problem: Although Invoke-WmiMethod supports –WhatIf and –Confirm, an object method does not. We'll need to manually implement support for those two parameters.

The next listing shows the new function we're adding to MOLTools.psm1, along with the last couple of commands in that file, which are exporting our functions.

Listing 16.2   Adding more to MOLTools.psm1

```
function Set-MOLServicePassword {
    [CmdletBinding(SupportsShouldProcess=$True,
                   ConfirmImpact='Medium')]
    param(
        [Parameter(Mandatory=$True,
                   ValueFromPipeline=$True)]
        [string[]]$ComputerName,

        [Parameter(Mandatory=$True)]
        [string]$ServiceName,

        [Parameter(Mandatory=$True)]
        [string]$NewPassword
    )
    PROCESS {
        foreach ($computer in $computername) {
            $svcs = Get-WmiObject -ComputerName $computer `
                               -Filter "name='$servicename'" `
                               -Class Win32_Service
            foreach ($svc in $svcs) {
                if ($psCmdlet.ShouldProcess("$svc on $computer")) {
                    $svc.Change($null,
                                $null,
                                $null,
                                $null,
                                $null,
                                $null,
                                $null,
                                $NewPassword) | Out-Null
                }
            }
        }
    }
}
Export-ModuleMember -Variable MOLErrorLogPreference
Export-ModuleMember -Function Get-MOLSystemInfo,
                             Get-MOLComputerNamesFromDatabase,
                             Set-MOLInventoryInDatabase,
                             Restart-CimComputer,
                             Set-MOLServicePassword
```

NOTE   Again, we've left out things like comment-based help and error handling, just to keep this example more straightforward.

Let's test this right away. We'll start in a fresh PowerShell console, load the module, and see what happens:

```
PS C:\> Set-MOLServicePassword -ServiceName BITS -NewPassword "P@ssw0rd" -C
omputerName localhost
```

That's what we expected. We set the confirm impact to `Medium`, and we know the default value of `$ConfirmPreference` is `High`, so we weren't expecting a confirmation prompt. Now let's change that variable and try the command again:

```
PS C:\> $ConfirmPreference = "Medium"
PS C:\> Set-MOLServicePassword -ServiceName BITS -NewPassword "P@ssw0rd" -C
omputerName localhost

Confirm
Are you sure you want to perform this action?
Performing operation "Set-MOLServicePassword" on Target
"\\DONJONES1D96\root\cimv2:Win32_Service.Name="BITS" on localhost".
[Y] Yes  [A] Yes to All  [N] No  [L] No to All  [S] Suspend  [?] Help
(default is "Y"):n
PS C:\>
```

Perfect. With `$ConfirmPreference` at `Medium`, our command's impact level was equal to or higher than the variable, and so confirmation happened automatically. Now let's put the variable back to its default, and try running the command in what-if mode:

```
PS C:\> $ConfirmPreference = "High"
PS C:\> Set-MOLServicePassword -ServiceName BITS -NewPassword "P@ssw0rd" -C
omputerName localhost -WhatIf
What if: Performing operation "Set-MOLServicePassword" on Target "\\DONJONE
S1D96\root\cimv2:Win32_Service.Name="BITS" on localhost".
PS C:\>
```

Excellent. Now for confirmations:

```
PS C:\> Set-MOLServicePassword -ServiceName BITS -NewPassword "P@ssw0rd" -C
omputerName localhost -confirm

Confirm
Are you sure you want to perform this action?
Performing operation "Set-MOLServicePassword" on Target
"\\DONJONES1D96\root\cimv2:Win32_Service.Name="BITS" on localhost".
[Y] Yes  [A] Yes to All  [N] No  [L] No to All  [S] Suspend  [?] Help
(default is "Y"):n
PS C:\>
```

Wonderful! Or, as our friend Spike says, $GREAT! Now let's look at how that works. The magic is contained within a single line:

```
if ($psCmdlet.ShouldProcess("$svc on $computer")) {
```

`$psCmdlet` is a built-in object that represents the shell's cmdlet functionality for our tool. By calling its `ShouldProcess()` method, we're informing the shell that we're about to do something dangerous. We pass in a text description of whatever it is we're modifying (the target), so that the confirmation prompt and what-if output can be more informative.

> **NOTE** By referring to $svc in our target, we're displaying the complete service WMI path and name. For something a bit shorter, you might put "$($svc.name) on $computer" instead.

When ShouldProcess() executes, PowerShell does a few checks:

- If the command was run with -WhatIf, ShouldProcess() returns False, preventing the code within the If construct from executing at all. The shell displays the what-if output, using the target description passed to ShouldProcess().
- If the command was run with -Confirm, ShouldProcess() displays the confirmation prompt and returns True only if the user selects Yes or Yes to All at the prompt.
- If the command wasn't run with -Confirm, but the command's impact level is equal to or higher than $ConfirmPreference, then the shell does the confirmation prompt anyway.

So when do you need to include this If construct and the ShouldProcess() method?

- If your command is only running other commands that natively support -WhatIf and -Confirm (check their help files to be certain), you don't need the If construct or ShouldProcess(). Just include SupportsShouldProcess in your [CmdletBinding()] attribute, as we did with our Restart-MOLCimComputer function.
- If your command includes other commands that support -WhatIf and -Confirm, but you want to specify a higher impact level than those commands natively declare, then wrap those commands in the If construct that uses ShouldProcess(). In your [CmdletBinding()] attribute, include SupportsShouldProcess and your desired ConfirmImpact.
- If your command is running object methods, or commands that don't natively support -WhatIf and -Confirm, then wrap them in the If construct that uses ShouldProcess(). Your [CmdletBinding()] attribute must include SupportsShouldProcess and an impact level.

Just to make sure you're on the same page going forward, the following listing contains the complete MOLTools.psm1 file to this point.

Listing 16.3 The complete MOLTools.psm1 file

```
$MOLErrorLogPreference = 'c:\mol-retries.txt'
$MOLConnectionString =
    "server=localhost\SQLEXPRESS;database=inventory;trusted_connection=True"

Import-Module MOLDatabase

function Get-MOLComputerNamesFromDatabase {
<#
```

```
.SYNOPSIS
Reads computer names from the MoL sample database,
placing them into the pipeline as strings.
#>
    Get-MOLDatabaseData -connectionString $MOLConnectionString `
                        -isSQLServer `
                        -query "SELECT computername FROM computers"
}

function Set-MOLInventoryInDatabase {
<#
.SYNOPSIS
Accepts the output of Get-MOLSystemInfo and saves
the results back to the MoL sample database.
#>
    [CmdletBinding()]
    param(
        [Parameter(Mandatory=$True,
                   ValueFromPipeline=$True)]
        [object[]]$inputObject
    )
    PROCESS {
        foreach ($obj in $inputobject) {
            $query = "UPDATE computers SET
                        osversion = '$($obj.osversion)',
                        spversion = '$($obj.spversion)',
                        manufacturer = '$($obj.manufacturer)',
                        model = '$($obj.model)'
                        WHERE computername = '$($obj.computername)'"
            Write-Verbose "Query will be $query"
            Invoke-MOLDatabaseQuery -connection $MOLConnectionString `
                                    -isSQLServer `
                                    -query $query

        }
    }
}

function Get-MOLSystemInfo {
<#
.SYNOPSIS
Retrieves key system version and model information
from one to ten computers.
.DESCRIPTION
Get-SystemInfo uses Windows Management Instrumentation
(WMI) to retrieve information from one or more computers.
Specify computers by name or by IP address.
.PARAMETER ComputerName
One or more computer names or IP addresses, up to a maximum
of 10.
.PARAMETER LogErrors
Specify this switch to create a text log file of computers
that could not be queried.
.PARAMETER ErrorLog
When used with -LogErrors, specifies the file path and name
to which failed computer names will be written. Defaults to
C:\Retry.txt.
```

```
.EXAMPLE
Get-Content names.txt | Get-MOLSystemInfo
.EXAMPLE
Get-MOLSystemInfo -ComputerName SERVER1,SERVER2
#>
    [CmdletBinding()]
    param(
        [Parameter(Mandatory=$True,
                   ValueFromPipeline=$True,
                   ValueFromPipelineByPropertyName=$True,
                   HelpMessage="Computer name or IP address")]
        [ValidateCount(1,10)]
        [Alias('hostname')]
        [string[]]$ComputerName,

        [string]$ErrorLog = $MOLErrorLogPreference,

        [switch]$LogErrors
    )
    BEGIN {
        Write-Verbose "Error log will be $ErrorLog"
    }
    PROCESS {
        Write-Verbose "Beginning PROCESS block"
        foreach ($computer in $computername) {
            Write-Verbose "Querying $computer"
            Try {
                $everything_ok = $true
                $os = Get-WmiObject -class Win32_OperatingSystem `
                                    -computerName $computer `
                                    -erroraction Stop
            } Catch {
                $everything_ok = $false
                Write-Warning "$computer failed"
                if ($LogErrors) {
                    $computer | Out-File $ErrorLog -Append
                    Write-Warning "Logged to $ErrorLog"
                }
            }

            if ($everything_ok) {
                $comp = Get-WmiObject -class Win32_ComputerSystem `
                                      -computerName $computer
                $bios = Get-WmiObject -class Win32_BIOS `
                                      -computerName $computer
                $props = @{'ComputerName'=$computer;
                           'OSVersion'=$os.version;
                           'SPVersion'=$os.servicepackmajorversion;
                           'BIOSSerial'=$bios.serialnumber;
                           'Manufacturer'=$comp.manufacturer;
                           'Model'=$comp.model}
                Write-Verbose "WMI queries complete"
                $obj = New-Object -TypeName PSObject -Property $props
                $obj.PSObject.TypeNames.Insert(0,'MOL.SystemInfo')
                Write-Output $obj
            }
```

```
        }
    }
    END {}
}

function Restart-MOLCimComputer {
    [CmdletBinding(SupportsShouldProcess=$True,
                ConfirmImpact='High')]
    param(
        [Parameter(Mandatory=$true,
                ValueFromPipeline=$true)]
        [string[]]$ComputerName
    )
    PROCESS {
        ForEach ($computer in $computername) {
            Invoke-CimMethod -ClassName Win32_OperatingSystem `
                            -MethodName Reboot `
                            -ComputerName $computer
        }
    }
}

function Set-MOLServicePassword {
    [CmdletBinding(SupportsShouldProcess=$True,
                ConfirmImpact='Medium')]
    param(
        [Parameter(Mandatory=$True,
                ValueFromPipeline=$True)]
        [string[]]$ComputerName,

        [Parameter(Mandatory=$True)]
        [string]$ServiceName,

        [Parameter(Mandatory=$True)]
        [string]$NewPassword
    )
    PROCESS {
        foreach ($computer in $computername) {
            $svcs = Get-WmiObject -ComputerName $computer `
                                -Filter "name='$servicename'" `
                                -Class Win32_Service
            foreach ($svc in $svcs) {
                if ($psCmdlet.ShouldProcess("$svc on $computer")) {
                    $svc.Change($null,
                                $null,
                                $null,
                                $null,
                                $null,
                                $null,
                                $null,
                                $NewPassword) | Out-Null
                }
            }
        }
    }
}
```

```
Export-ModuleMember -Variable MOLErrorLogPreference
Export-ModuleMember -Function Get-MOLSystemInfo,
                              Get-MOLComputerNamesFromDatabase,
                              Set-MOLInventoryInDatabase,
                              Restart-CimComputer,
                              Set-MOLServicePassword
```

TRY IT NOW   Make sure you have this file and that you can run the commands as we've shown you in this chapter. We're going to build on this again in some upcoming chapters, so it's important to make sure you're on the same page as us.

16.5 *Lab*

In WMI, the `Win32_OperatingSystem` class has a method called `Win32Shutdown`. It accepts a single input argument, which is a number that determines if the method shuts down, powers down, reboots, and logs off the computer.

Write a function called `Set-ComputerState`. Have it accept one or more computer names on a `-ComputerName` parameter. Also provide an `-Action` parameter, which accepts only the values `LogOff`, `Restart`, `ShutDown`, or `PowerOff`. Finally, provide a `-Force` switch parameter (switch parameters don't accept a value; they're either specified or not).

When the function runs, query `Win32_OperatingSystem` from each specified computer. Don't worry about error handling at this point; assume each specified computer will be available. Be sure to implement support for the `-WhatIf` and `-Confirm` parameters, as outlined in this chapter. Based on the `-Action` specified, execute the `Win32Shutdown` method with one of the following values:

- `LogOff`—0
- `ShutDown`—1
- `Restart`—2
- `PowerOff`—8

If the `-Force` parameter is specified, add 4 to those values. So if the command was `Set-ComputerState -computername localhost -Action LogOff -Force`, then the value would be 4 (0 for `LogOff`, plus 4 for `Force`). The execution of `Win32Shutdown` is what should be wrapped in the implementing `If` block for `-WhatIf` and `-Confirm` support.

CAUTION   Be careful when testing this against localhost—be sure you've saved your work, because the function will log you off.

Creating a custom type extension

17

A few chapters back, we showed you how to create a custom formatting view for your tools' output. In this chapter, we're going to do something very similar by creating a *type extension*. Unlike views, which only affect the visual presentation of your output, a type extension can actually add functionality to objects you write to the pipeline.

17.1 The anatomy of an extension

Believe it or not, you've already seen type extensions in action. For example, run Get-Process | Get-Member, and look at the output:

```
   TypeName: System.Diagnostics.Process

Name                    MemberType     Definition
----                    ----------     ----------
Handles                 AliasProperty  Handles = Handlecount
Name                    AliasProperty  Name = ProcessName
NPM                     AliasProperty  NPM = NonpagedSystemMemorySize
PM                      AliasProperty  PM = PagedMemorySize
VM                      AliasProperty  VM = VirtualMemorySize
WS                      AliasProperty  WS = WorkingSet
__NounName              NoteProperty   System.String __NounName=Process
Company                 ScriptProperty System.Object Company {get=$t...
CPU                     ScriptProperty System.Object CPU {get=$this....
Description             ScriptProperty System.Object Description {ge...
FileVersion             ScriptProperty System.Object FileVersion {ge...
Path                    ScriptProperty System.Object Path {get=$this...
Product                 ScriptProperty System.Object Product {get=$t...
ProductVersion          ScriptProperty System.Object ProductVersion ...
```

175

We truncated the output to only show the type extensions: `AliasProperties`, `NoteProperties`, and `ScriptProperties`. Other types of extensions include `ScriptMethods` and `PropertySets`, which aren't shown here. These extensions aren't native parts of the .NET Framework's `System.Diagnostics.Process` class. If you look up that class's documentation (http://msdn.microsoft.com/en-us/library/system .diagnostics .process.aspx), you won't see `Handles` or `Description` or `FileVersion`. These properties are added by PowerShell's Extensible Type System, or ETS, because the shell is producing the objects for output. Why does the shell do this? It depends. There are several types of extension, each with a different purpose. Some of the major ones, and their purposes, are as follows:

- An `AliasProperty` provides an easier way, or a more consistent way, of referring to a native object property. For example, `Handles` is easier than `Handlecount`, and `Name` provides better across-the-shell consistency than `ProcessName`. Both of those native properties remain accessible, but the `AliasProperties` gives us an alternate way of accessing them.
- A `NoteProperty` contains a static value and is often used by PowerShell to store management information. In this example, the `NounName NoteProperty` keeps track of the noun used by the command that produced the object (`Process`). The shell might use this internally for a variety of purposes.
- A `ScriptProperty` executes PowerShell script code in order to produce a property value. For example, `Path` actually digs deep into the object's native information hierarchy to reveal a piece of information that's ordinarily buried quite deeply. A `ScriptProperty` doesn't usually access any external resources to do its job; it just reformats or reveals something that's already part of the object.
- A `ScriptMethod` is similar to a `ScriptProperty`, although sometimes it may take an action and not produce any output at all. `ScriptMethods` are a bit rarer in PowerShell's native commands, although all WMI objects include `ScriptMethods` that translate between WMI-style date values and human-readable date values.
- A `PropertySet` bundles up one or more properties that are related in some fashion. For example, run `Get-Process | Select PSResources` and you'll see different output from `Get-Process`, containing properties related to resource consumption. `PSResources` is a property set.

Type extensions are defined in XML files, much like the formatting views you worked with earlier. In PowerShell's installation folder (run `cd $pshome` to get there), you'll find Types.ps1xml, which is the main ETS file that ships with PowerShell. Be careful not to modify that file in any way (you'll break it), but do feel free to use it as a copy-and-paste template for your own extensions.

We'll focus on adding two extensions to the `MOL.SystemInfo` object that's produced by our `Get-MOLSystemInfo` function, which is in our MOLTools.psm1 file. We won't need to modify that script at all: Creating and loading the necessary ETS XML will do everything we need. We'll start with the simple template in listing 17.1, which we'll save as C:\MOLTools.ps1xml.

TIP Saving the file in C:\ lets us play with it more easily; we may have to load it over and over to get it right, so we want to make it easy to get to. We'll move it to its final location when we've finished testing.

Listing 17.1   C:\MOLTools.ps1xml

```
<?xml version="1.0" encoding="utf-8" ?>
<Types>
</Types>
```

NOTE Notice that the filename extension is .ps1xml; that's different from a view file, which should use .format.ps1xml.

Our type extensions will live within the `<Types>` and `</Types>` XML tags. We're only going to cover `ScriptProperty` and `ScriptMethod` extensions in this chapter, because they're the ones you'll use the most. You probably won't use `AliasProperty` much when you're extending your own objects (after all, because you're creating the object from scratch, you can name properties whatever you want in the first place). But you can review PowerShell's provided Types.ps1xml file to see examples of other extensions.

17.2   *Creating a script property*

Looking at the normal output of `Get-MOLSystemInfo`, we see something like this:

```
PS C:\> Get-MOLSystemInfo -ComputerName localhost | Format-List *

Manufacturer : Parallels Software International Inc.
OSVersion    : 6.2.8250
BIOSSerial   : Parallels-D5 A7 11 48 6C 63 42 80 AB E6 90 AF C4 D3 FC DC
ComputerName : localhost
SPVersion    : 0
Model        : Parallels Virtual Platform
```

That BIOS serial number is super long, at least for this computer. We'd like a version of it that omits all the spaces, to create a shorter and more concise serial number. The following listing shows what we'll add to MOLTools.ps1xml.

Listing 17.2   Our ScriptProperty type extension

```
<Type>
  <Name>MOL.SystemInfo</Name>
  <Members>
    <ScriptProperty>
      <Name>NormalizedBIOSSerial</Name>
      <GetScriptBlock>
          $this.biosserial -replace ' ',''
      </GetScriptBlock>
      </ScriptProperty>
  </Members>
</Type>
```

There are a few specifics to notice about this:

- The `<Name></Name>` tag must include the full type name of the object type that we want to extend.

- We only create one `<Type></Type>` block for a given object type. All of the extensions for that type go within the `<Members></Members>` block. You'll see what we mean by that when we add the next extension to this type.

- The `<Name></Name>` within `<ScriptProperty></ScriptProperty>` is the name of the new `ScriptProperty` extension.

- The `<GetScriptBlock></GetScriptBlock>` defines the code that will run when the property is read. Within this block, the special `$this` variable refers to the object itself, enabling us to access its other properties and methods. In this example, we're using PowerShell's `-replace` operator to replaces spaces with an empty string.

NOTE   Depending on the computer you query, you may not get a BIOS serial number that needs normalizing. In fact, you might not get a value at all! That's just the way WMI behaves. But the BIOS for this test computer offered a reasonable teaching opportunity, so we ran with it.

17.3 *Creating a script method*

Because our `MOL.SystemInfo` object represents a computer, we want to provide a quick way of pinging the computer over the network. Because that accesses external resources, we'll implement it as a `ScriptMethod` named `CanPing()`. The next listing shows our revised C:\MOLTools.ps1xml file.

> **Listing 17.3   The revised C:\MOLTools.ps1xml file**

```xml
<?xml version="1.0" encoding="utf-8" ?>
<Types>
  <Type>
    <Name>MOL.SystemInfo</Name>
    <Members>
      <ScriptProperty>
        <Name>NormalizedBIOSSerial</Name>
        <GetScriptBlock>
            $this.biosserial -replace ' ',''
        </GetScriptBlock>
      </ScriptProperty>
      <ScriptMethod>
        <Name>CanPing</Name>
        <Script>
          Test-Connection -ComputerName $this.ComputerName -Quiet
        </Script>
      </ScriptMethod>
    </Members>
  </Type>
</Types>
```

We highlighted the new `ScriptMethod` in bold. Notice that it comes between the `<Members>` and `</Members>` tag, just like the `ScriptProperty` did, because these two extensions each modify the same `MOL.SystemInfo` object. Notice that, just as with the `ScriptProperty` we created, we were able to use the `$this` variable to refer to the actual object. That gave us access to the `ComputerName` property, which is where we directed the ping.

17.4   Loading the extension

First, let's run our `Get-MOLSystemInfo` command and see what kind of object it's producing. This will be the "before" in our "before and after" test:

```
PS C:\> Get-MOLSystemInfo -ComputerName localhost | Get-Member

    TypeName: MOL.SystemInfo

Name          MemberType   Definition
----          ----------   ----------
Equals        Method       bool Equals(System.Object obj)
GetHashCode   Method       int GetHashCode()
GetType       Method       type GetType()
ToString      Method       string ToString()
BIOSSerial    NoteProperty System.String BIOSSerial=Parallels-D5 A7 11 4...
ComputerName  NoteProperty System.String ComputerName=localhost
Manufacturer  NoteProperty System.String Manufacturer=Parallels Software...
Model         NoteProperty System.String Model=Parallels Virtual Platform
OSVersion     NoteProperty System.String OSVersion=6.2.8250
SPVersion     NoteProperty System.UInt16 SPVersion=0
```

Now we'll use `Update-TypeData` to load our ETS XML file into memory. We'll use the `-PrependPath` parameter, so that our new ETS data goes into memory before whatever PowerShell has already loaded. Review the command's help for information on its other option, `-AppendPath`.

```
PS C:\> Update-TypeData -PrependPath .\MOLTools.ps1xml
```

As with most things in PowerShell, no news is good news. No error messages means that our XML parsed correctly and was loaded into the shell.

17.5   Testing the extension

Let's see what our command output looks like now:

```
PS C:\> Get-MOLSystemInfo -ComputerName localhost | Get-Member

    TypeName: MOL.SystemInfo

Name          MemberType   Definition
----          ----------   ----------
Equals        Method       bool Equals(System.Object obj)
GetHashCode   Method       int GetHashCode()
GetType       Method       type GetType()
ToString      Method       string ToString()
BIOSSerial    NoteProperty System.String BIOSSerial=Parallels-...
ComputerName  NoteProperty System.String ComputerName=localhost
Manufacturer  NoteProperty System.String Manufacturer=Parallel...
Model         NoteProperty System.String Model=Parallels Virtu...
OSVersion     NoteProperty System.String OSVersion=6.2.8250
```

```
SPVersion               NoteProperty    System.UInt16 SPVersion=0
CanPing                 ScriptMethod    System.Object CanPing();
NormalizedBIOSSerial ScriptProperty System.Object NormalizedBIOSSerial ...
```

Our two type extensions have been added! Let's try the `ScriptProperty` first:

```
PS C:\> Get-MOLSystemInfo -ComputerName localhost |
>> Select-Object -Property ComputerName,OSVersion,NormalizedBIOSSerial |
>> Format-Table -AutoSize
>>

ComputerName OSVersion NormalizedBIOSSerial
------------ --------- --------------------
localhost    6.2.8250  Parallels-D5A711486C634280ABE690AFC4D3FCDC
```

Perfect! That's exactly what we wanted in the serial number. Now let's try the `ScriptMethod`. For this, we're going to get just one object and save it in a variable, so that we can easily test the method:

```
PS C:\> $obj = Get-MOLSystemInfo -ComputerName localhost
PS C:\> $obj.CanPing()
True
```

Perfect! Now let's see how we could use that with multiple computers, to filter out those that don't respond to a ping:

```
PS C:\> Get-MOLSystemInfo -ComputerName localhost,NOTONLINE |
>> Where-Object -FilterScript { $_.CanPing() }
>>

ComputerNa Mfgr                  Model              OSVersion  SP
me
---------- ----                  -----              ---------  --
localhost  Parallels Softwar... Parallels Virtual... 6.2.8250  0
WARNING: NOTONLINE failed
```

Perfect! Although...well, let's think about this. `Get-MOLSystemInfo` itself relies on network connectivity, right? So that sort of means everything it *can* connect to will also respond to a ping, right? Well, not necessarily. A computer can respond to `Get-MOLSystemInfo`'s use of WMI but still have a local firewall blocking the ICMP ports used by ping. So we're still conducting a useful check. At the very least, it's a straightforward example of how to create a `ScriptMethod`!

17.6   *Adding the extension to a manifest*

Now let's move MOLTools.ps1xml into the folder used by the `MOLTools` module:

```
PS C:\> move .\MOLTools.ps1xml C:\Users\donjones\Documents\WindowsPowerShel
l\Modules\MOLTools
```

We need to have the type extension load at the same time that the rest of the module loads. We could use `New-ModuleManifest` to create the necessary manifest, as we did in the chapter on creating a custom format view. But we already have a manifest, so why not just modify it? The following listing shows our modified MOLTools.psd1 manifest, with our one change highlighted in bold.

Listing 17.4   Adding our ETS file to MOLTools.psd1

```
#
# Module manifest for module 'MOLTools'
#
# Generated by: Don & Jeff
#
# Generated on: 5/6/2012
#

@{

# Script module or binary module file associated with this manifest
RootModule = '.\MOLTools.psm1'

# Version number of this module.
ModuleVersion = '1.0'

# ID used to uniquely identify this module
GUID = '9b230d35-c473-4498-91a5-58f2b8c7425a'

# Author of this module
Author = 'Don & Jeff'

# Company or vendor of this module
CompanyName = 'Month of Lunches'

# Copyright statement for this module
Copyright = '(c)2012 Don Jones and Jeffery Hicks'

# Description of the functionality provided by this module
Description = 'Sample Module for Month of Lunches'

# Minimum version of the Windows PowerShell engine required by this module
PowerShellVersion = '3.0'

# Name of the Windows PowerShell host required by this module
# PowerShellHostName = ''

# Minimum version of the Windows PowerShell host required by this module
# PowerShellHostVersion = ''

# Minimum version of the .NET Framework required by this module
# DotNetFrameworkVersion = ''

# Minimum version of the common language runtime (CLR) required by this
      module
# CLRVersion = ''

# Processor architecture (None, X86, Amd64) required by this module
# ProcessorArchitecture = ''

# Modules that must be imported into the global environment prior to
      importing this module
# RequiredModules = @()

# Assemblies that must be loaded prior to importing this module
# RequiredAssemblies = @()

# Script files (.ps1) that are run in the caller's environment prior to
      importing this module
# ScriptsToProcess = @()
```

```
# Type files (.ps1xml) to be loaded when importing this module
TypesToProcess = "MOLTools.ps1xml"

# Format files (.ps1xml) to be loaded when importing this module
FormatsToProcess = 'MOLTools.format.ps1xml'

# Modules to import as nested modules of the module specified in RootModule/
    ModuleToProcess
# NestedModules = @()

# Functions to export from this module
FunctionsToExport = '*'

# Cmdlets to export from this module
CmdletsToExport = '*'

# Variables to export from this module
VariablesToExport = '*'

# Aliases to export from this module
AliasesToExport = '*'

# Commands to export from this module as Workflows
# ExportAsWorkflow = @()

# List of all modules packaged with this module
# ModuleList = @()

# List of all files packaged with this module
# FileList = @()

# Private data to pass to the module specified in RootModule/ModuleToProcess
# PrivateData = ''

# HelpInfo URI of this module
# HelpInfoURI = ''

# Default prefix for commands exported from this module. Override the default
    prefix using Import-Module -Prefix.
# DefaultCommandPrefix = ''

}
```

With this change, we can import our module and it'll load our commands, our format view, and our type extension, all at once.

17.7   *Lab*

Revisit the advanced function that you wrote for Lab A in chapters 6 through 14 of this book. Create a custom type extension for the object output by that function. Your type extension should be a ScriptMethod named CanPing(), as outlined in this chapter. Save the type extension file as PSHTools.ps1xml. Modify the PSHTools module manifest to load PSHTools.ps1xml, and then test your revised module to make sure the CanPing() method works.

18

Creating
PowerShell workflows

Workflows are an important new feature of PowerShell v3. They're an incredibly rich, complex technology that we can't possibly cover comprehensively in this chapter; they really deserve their own book. But they *are* a type of tool you can create and make great use of, so we wanted to include this chapter as an introduction to them.

18.1 Workflow overview

Workflows are a type of PowerShell command, just as cmdlets and functions are types of commands. One of the easiest ways to understand workflows is to contrast them with their closest cousin: functions.

Functions are declared with the `function` keyword, as you've seen several times in earlier chapters; workflows are declared with the `workflow` keyword. Functions are executed by PowerShell itself; workflows are translated to the .NET Framework's Windows Workflow Foundation (WF) and executed by WF external to PowerShell. Both functions and workflows execute a given set of commands in a specific sequence, but workflows—thanks to WF—include detailed logging and tracking of each and include the ability to retry steps that fail because of, for example, an intermittent network hiccup or other transitory issue. Functions do one thing at a time; workflows can do one thing at multiple times—parallel multitasking. Functions start, run, and finish; a workflow can pause, stop, and restart. If you turn off your computer in the middle of a function, the function is lost; if you do so while a workflow is running, the workflow can potentially be recovered and resumed automatically.

Table 18.1   Function or workflow

Function	Workflow
Executed by PowerShell	Executed by workflow engine
Logging and retry attempts through complicated coding	Logging and retry attempts part of the workflow engine
Single-action processing	Supports parallelism
Runs to completion	Can run, pause, and restart
Data loss possible during network problems	Data can persist during network problems
Full language set and syntax	Limited language set and syntax
Runs cmdlets	Runs activities

Table 18.1 illustrates some of the differences between a function and a workflow.

Workflows are incorporated into the shell by running `Import-Module PSWorkflow`; that module extends PowerShell to understand workflows and to execute them properly. Workflows are exposed as commands, meaning you execute them just like commands. For example, if you created a workflow named Do-Something, you'd just run `Do-Something` to execute it or run `Do-Something –AsJob` to run it in PowerShell's background job system. Executing a workflow as a job is cool, because you can then use the standard `–Job` cmdlets (like `Get-Job` and `Receive-Job`) to manage them. There are also `Suspend-Job` and `Resume-Job` commands to pause and resume a workflow job.

18.1.1 *Common parameters for workflows*

Just by using the `workflow` keyword, you give your workflow command a pretty large set of built-in common parameters. We're not going to provide an extensive list, but here are some of the more interesting ones (and you can consult PowerShell's documentation for the complete list):

- `-PSComputerName`—A list of computers to execute the workflow on
- `-PSParameterCollection`—A list of hash tables that specify different parameter values for each target computer, enabling the workflow to have variable behavior on a per-machine basis
- `-PSCredential`—The credential to be used to execute the workflow
- `-PSPersist`—Force the workflow to save (checkpoint) the workflow data and state after executing each step (we'll show you how you can also do this manually)

There are also a variety of parameters that let you specify remote connectivity options, such as `-PSPort`, `-PSUseSSL`, `-PSSessionOption`, and so on; these correspond to the similarly named parameters of Remoting commands like `Invoke-Command` and `New-PSSession`.

The values passed to these parameters are accessible as values within the workflow. For example, a workflow can access `$PSComputerName` to get the name of the computer that particular instance of the workflow is executing against right then.

18.1.2 *Activities and stateless execution*

Workflow is built around the concept of *activities*. Each PowerShell command that you run within a workflow is a single, standalone activity.

The big thing to get used to in workflow is that each command, or activity, executes entirely on its own. Because a workflow can be interrupted and later resumed, each command has to assume that it's running in a completely fresh, brand-new environment. Variables created by one command can't be used by the next command, which can get a bit weird. Workflow does support an InlineScript block, which will execute all commands inside the block within a single PowerShell session. Everything within the block is a standalone script.

Now, this isn't to say that variables don't work at all; that would be pretty pointless. For example, consider the script in the following listing (we've included this as a numbered listing so that you can run it for yourself in the PowerShell ISE, if you like).

> **Listing 18.1 Example workflow with variables**

```
Import-Module PSWorkflow

workflow Test-Workflow {

    $a = 1
    $a

    $a++
    $a

    $b = $a + 2
    $b

}

Test-Workflow
```

> **TRY IT NOW** Run this, and you should see the output 1, 2, and 4, with each number on its own line. That's the expected output, and seeing that will help you verify that workflow is operating on your system.

Now try the example in this listing.

> **Listing 18.2 Example workflow that won't work properly**

```
Import-Module PSWorkflow

workflow Test-Workflow {

    $obj = New-Object -TypeName PSObject
    $obj | Add-Member -MemberType NoteProperty `
                      -Name ExampleProperty `
                      -Value 'Hello!'
    $obj | Get-Member
}

Test-Workflow
```

This doesn't produce the intended results, in that the object in `$obj` won't have an `ExampleProperty` property containing "Hello!" That's because `Add-Member` runs in its own space, and its modification to `$obj` doesn't persist to the third command in the workflow. To make this work, we could wrap the entire set of commands as an `InlineScript`, forcing them to all execute at the same time, within a single PowerShell instance. The following listing shows this example.

Listing 18.3   Example workflow using `InlineScript`

```
Import-Module PSWorkflow

workflow Test-Workflow {

    InlineScript {
        $obj = New-Object -TypeName PSObject
        $obj | Add-Member -MemberType NoteProperty `
                          -Name ExampleProperty `
                          -Value 'Hello!'
        $obj | Get-Member
    }
}

Test-Workflow
```

> **TRY IT NOW**   Try each of these three examples and compare their results. Workflows do take a bit of getting used to, and these simple examples will help you to start understanding workflow's key differences.

18.1.3 *Persisting state*

The state of a workflow consists of its current output, the task that it's currently executing, and other information. It's important that you help workflow maintain this state, especially when kicking off a long-running command that might be executed. To do so, run the `Checkpoint-Workflow` command (or the `Persist` workflow activity). You can force this to happen after every single command is executed by running the workflow with the `-PSPersist` switch.

18.1.4 *Suspending and resuming workflows*

A workflow can suspend itself if you run `Suspend-Workflow` within the workflow. You might do this, for example, if you're about to run some high-workload command that can only be run during a maintenance window. Before running the command, you check the time, and if you're not in the window, you suspend the workflow. Someone would need to manually resume the workflow (or schedule it in Task Scheduler) by running `Resume-Job` and providing the necessary job ID.

18.1.5 *Inherently remotable*

Workflows are designed from the ground up to be remoted, which is why all workflow commands get a `-PSComputerName` parameter automatically. If you run a workflow with one or more computer names, PowerShell connects to the remote computers via

Remoting (which must be enabled) and has those computers run the workflow using their local resources. This means the remote computers must also be running Power-Shell 3.0. But the following core PowerShell commands always run locally on the machine where the workflow was initiated:

- Add-Member
- ConvertFrom-Csv, ConvertFtom-Json, ConvertFrom-StringData
- ConvertTo-Csv, ConvertTo-Html, ConvertTo-Xml
- Get-Host
- Get-Random
- Group-Object
- Measure-Object

- New-TimeSpan

- Select-Object
- Update-List
- Write-Debug, Write-Error, Write-Host, Write-Output, Write-Progress, Write-Verbose, Write-Warning

- Compare-Object
- Convert-Path

- ForEach-Object

- Get-Member
- Get-Unique
- Measure-Command
- New-PSSessionOption, New-PSTransportOption
- Out-Default, Out-Host, Out-Null, Out-String
- Sort-Object
- Where-Object

These are run locally mainly for performance reasons; if you need one of these to run on a targeted remote computer, wrap it in an InlineScript{} block.

18.1.6 *Parallelism*

Windows workflow is designed to execute tasks in parallel, and PowerShell exposes that capability through a modified ForEach scripting construct and a new Parallel construct. They work a bit differently.

With Parallel, the commands inside the construct can run in any order. Within the Parallel block, you can use the Sequence keyword to surround a set of commands that must be executed in order; that batch of commands may begin executing at any point, for example:

```
Workflow Test-Workflow {
    "This will run first"

    parallel {
        "Command 1"
        "Command 2"

        sequence {
            "Command A"
            "Command B"
        }
    }
}
```

The output here might be

```
Command 1
Command A
Command B
Command 2
```

Command B will always come after Command A, but Command A might come first, second, or last—there's no guarantee. The commands actually execute at the same time, meaning Command 1, Command 2, and the sequence may all kick off at once, which is what makes the output somewhat nondeterministic. This is useful for when you have several tasks to complete, don't care about the order in which they run, and want them to finish as quickly as possible.

The parallelized ForEach is somewhat different:

```
Workflow Test-Workflow {
    Foreach -parallel ($computer in $computerName) {
        Do-Something -computerName $computer
    }
}
```

Here, WF may launch multiple simultaneous Do-Something commands, each targeting a different computer. Execution should be roughly in whatever order the computers are stored in $ComputerName, although because of varying execution times the order of the results is nondeterministic.

18.2   *General workflow design strategy*

It's important to understand that the entire contents of the workflow get translated into WF's own language, which only understands activities. With the exception of a few commands that we'll list at the end of this chapter, Microsoft has provided WF activities that correspond to most of the core PowerShell cmdlets. That means most of PowerShell's built-in commands—the ones available before any modules have been imported—work fine.

That isn't the case with add-in modules, though. Further, because each workflow activity executes in a self-contained space, you can't even use Import-Module by itself in a workflow. You'd basically import a module, but it would then go away by the time you tried to run any of the module's commands.

The solution is to think of a workflow as a high-level task coordination mechanism. You're likely to have a number of InlineScript{} blocks within a workflow, because the contents of those blocks execute as a single unit, in a single PowerShell session. Within an InlineScript{}, you can import a module and then run its commands. Each InlineScript{} block that you include runs independently, so think of each one as a standalone script file of sorts: Each should perform whatever setup tasks are necessary for it to run successfully. You'll see an example of this approach in this chapter.

18.3 Example workflow scenario

As an example scenario, we're going to pretend we have a new in-house corporate application update that needs to be deployed. We've already taken care of getting the necessary executables deployed to our client computers, but the developers neglected to make a few critical configuration changes as part of the installer. It's up to us to make those changes. We need to do the following:

- Add an `HKEY_LOCAL_MACHINE\SOFTWARE\Company\LOBApp\Settings` registry key, adding the setting `Rebuild` with a value of `0` (zero).
- Register a new PowerShell Remoting endpoint (or session configuration) named LOBApp. There's already a local session configuration file stored on each computer that defines this endpoint's capabilities; the file should be in C:\CorpApps\LOBApp\LOBApp.psc1.
- Set the service named LOBApp to start automatically, and ensure that the service is started.
- Run `Set-LOBRebuildMode -Mode 1`—that command is located in a module named `LOBAppTools`, which is already deployed to the client computers.

None of these need to be done in any particular order. Keep in mind that the contents of our workflow are intended to be remoted, so we can assume that everything we're doing is running locally, and they'll be deployed to the remote computers and executed there.

DON'T TRY IT NOW Because we're using made-up stuff in this example, you won't be able to follow along.

18.4 Writing the workflow

Here's the workflow we might write to accomplish our example scenario.

Listing 18.4 A sample workflow

```
workflow Set-LOBAppConfiguration {

    parallel {

        InlineScript {
            New-Item -Path HKLM:\SOFTWARE\Company\LOBApp\Settings
            New-ItemProperty -Path HKLM:\SOFTWARE\Company\LOBApp\Settings `
                            -Name Rebuild `
                            -Value 0
        }

        InlineScript {
            Set-Service -Name LOBApp -StartupType Automatic
            Start-Service -Name LOBApp
        }

        InlineScript {
            Register-PSSessionConfiguration `
                -Path C:\CorpApps\LOBApp\LOBApp.psc1 `
```

```
            -Name LOBApp
    }

    InlineScript {
        Import-Module LOBAppTools
        Set-LOBRebuildMode -Mode 1
    }

  }

}
```

You can see that we've followed the general strategy of breaking each distinct task into its own `InlineScript{}` block, allowing each of those to execute independently. Each can assume it's accessing local resources, because the contents of the workflow will be remoted out to whatever machines we target. We'd run this like so:

```
PS C:\> Set-LOBAppConfiguration –PSComputerName one,two,three
```

That would run the workflow on computers named ONE, TWO, and THREE.

18.5   *Workflows vs. functions*

Workflows seem so similar to functions that it can be tempting to assume they're just a fancy kind of function. In many ways, it's safe to think of them that way, which is one of their most appealing aspects: If you already know a lot about functions, you can move that knowledge right into workflows with very little additional learning. That said, there are a few major differences. Specifically, workflows differ from functions in the following ways:

- You can't use the BEGIN, PROCESS, and END script blocks that we've been using in our advanced functions.
- You can't use subexpressions, like `$myvar = "$($service.name)"`.
- You can't access drive-qualified variables like `$env:computername`; use `Get-Content ENV:ComputerName` instead.
- Variable names may only contain letters, digits, -, and _.
- You can't execute methods of objects. This is tricky, but there's a good reason: In order to execute a method, you need a live object. If the workflow resumes from interruption, however, all you'll have is a persisted, deserialized object, which has no methods. If you create an object within an `InlineScript` block, then you can execute its methods within that block, because the block ensures that the commands all execute together.
- You can't assign values to object properties—again, doing so assumes a live object, which you won't necessarily have.
- You can't dot source scripts or use the invocation (&) operator.
- Advanced function parameter validation (like the mandatory attribute and other attributes we've used) aren't supported on workflows that are contained within other workflows. Technically, they're not allowed at all, but PowerShell fakes it for the outermost workflow.

- Positional parameters aren't permitted on commands within a workflow. This forces you to follow what you should be doing anyway and list the parameter name for every parameter you use. This means `Dir C:\` won't work, but `Dir -Path C:\` will.
- The old `Trap` error-handling statement isn't supported. Use `Try...Catch ...Finally` instead.
- The `Switch` statement doesn't work the same within a workflow; we recommend not using it at all in a workflow.
- Workflows can't use comment-based help. If you want to include help for a workflow command, you must create an external XML file in the appropriate MAML format; we won't be covering that in this book.
- Within a workflow, you can't change the value of a variable that has already been defined in a parent scope. In a normal PowerShell function, doing so creates a new local-scope variable of the same name; in workflow, you get an error. PowerShell adds a new `$workflow` scope identifier to provide access to a workflow's scope from any child scope. For example, `$workflow:myvar` will provide access to the `$myvar` variable defined in the workflow scope. This syntax is mandatory for any child scope; were one of them to try to modify `$myvar` without specifying `$workflow:myvar`, it would get an error.

NOTE This isn't a comprehensive list of things that are legal in a function but not in a workflow, but the list does cover every function-related thing we've shown you in this book (including stuff in upcoming chapters).

Most of these restrictions come from the fact that a workflow is eventually translated into an external language usable by WF, meaning a workflow can't contain anything for which there's no WF equivalent. There are also a few native PowerShell commands that can't be used inside a workflow, mainly because in most cases they make no sense:

- `Get-Alias, Export-Alias, Import-Alias, New-Alias, Set-Alias`
- `Update-FormatData`
- `Add-History, Clear-History, Get-History, Invoke-History`
- `New-PSDrive, Remove-PSDrive`
- `Set-StrictMode`
- `Start-Transcript, Stop-Transcript`
- `Remove-TypeData, Update-TypeData`
- `Clear-Variable, Get-Variable, New-Variable`

18.6 Lab

Because workflows are necessarily complex, and because we've only provided you with an overview of them in this chapter, we won't be asking you to complete a lab involving workflows.

NOTE If you'd like to learn more about PowerShell workflows, get a copy of *PowerShell in Depth: An Administrator's Guide* by Don Jones, Richard Siddaway, and Jeffery Hicks. You'll find a chapter on this feature along with many examples.

Troubleshooting
pipeline input

19

Part of what makes PowerShell so unique and powerful is its object-oriented pipeline. When you're writing tools, it's especially important that you understand how the pipeline works, how your tools can work within it and—most important of all—that you know how to troubleshoot what's happening in the pipeline. That's what this chapter will cover.

19.1 Refresher: how pipeline input works

Whenever you pipe one command to another—say, `Get-Service | Where Status -eq 'Running' | Sort Name | Export-CSV services.csv`—output is taken from one command and passed to the next. There's no magic way for that output to be passed along: PowerShell commands can accept input only via their parameters. In this example, PowerShell has to take the output of `Get-Service` and figure out which parameter of `Where-Object` can accept those objects. After `Where-Object` runs, its output goes into the pipeline, and PowerShell has to figure out which parameter of `Sort-Object` can accept that. This process of figuring out is called pipeline parameter binding.

PowerShell has two modes for pipeline parameter binding. The first mode, or Plan A, as we call it, is called ByValue. In this mode, PowerShell looks to see if the receiving command has a parameter that can accept the exact type of object that was put into the pipeline by the sending command. For example, in the command `Get-Service -Name BITS | Stop-Service`, `Get-Service` is the sending command, and it's producing objects of the type `ServiceController`. You can verify this by running `Get-Service -Name BITS | Get-Member` and looking at the first line of output. `Stop-Service` is the receiving command, and its `-InputObject` parameter is capable of accepting objects of the type `ServiceController`, from the pipeline, ByValue. The help file for `Stop-Service` confirms this capability (run `Help Stop-Service -full` and see for yourself). So the service objects are bound to the `-InputObject` parameter.

When the receiving command doesn't have a parameter capable of accepting the type of object in the pipeline ByValue, PowerShell shifts to Plan B, which is called ByPropertyName. In this mode, the type of the object doesn't matter. Rather, Power-Shell makes an inventory of the receiving command parameters that are programmed to accept pipeline input ByPropertyName (you can read the full help for a command to inventory those parameters on your own). PowerShell then looks at the objects in the pipeline and matches any properties that happen to be spelled the same as the receiving parameters.

For example, in the command `Get-Service | Stop-Process -whatIf` (which you're welcome to run, if you want to see what happens), we know that the sending command produces objects of the type `ServiceController`. The receiving command has no parameters capable of accepting that type of object, so Plan A, ByValue, is out of the question. `Stop-Process` has two parameters capable of accepting pipeline input ByPropertyName, which is Plan B. Those parameters are `-Id` and `-Name`. So PowerShell will take the `ID` property of the pipeline objects and feed their values to the `-Id` parameter. It'll also take the `Name` property of the pipeline objects and feed those values to the `-Name` parameter. As it turns out, `ServiceController` objects don't have an `ID` property, so it'll just be the `-Name` parameter that receives the values of the objects' `Name` properties.

> **NOTE** This pipeline parameter-binding process is PowerShell 101. Hopefully if you're engaged in toolmaking, you're already familiar with the basic process. If you're not, we suggest reading *Learn Windows PowerShell 3 in a Month of Lunches,* which covers the process in more depth.

Being able to think about that process in your head and predict what PowerShell will do with any given command is an important skill, because it lets you create your own combinations of commands. But what can be even better—especially for trouble-shooting—is to see it happening. Remember, most errors are the result of a bad assumption or prediction. If you have an expectation for how PowerShell will bind two commands together, then you can use what we're about to show you to confirm or correct that expectation.

19.2 Introducing Trace-Command

PowerShell's built-in `Trace-Command` cmdlet provides a number of useful diagnostic and troubleshooting capabilities, but in this chapter we're going to focus on its ability to reveal what PowerShell is doing with pipeline parameter binding. As an example, let's take this command:

```
Import-CSV computers.csv |
Get-WmiObject -class Win32_BIOS
```

Our assumption is that Computers.csv looks like this:

```
Computername
SERVER-R2
DC01
LOCALHOST
CLIENTA
```

Running the `import` command by itself results in the following:

```
PS C:\> import-csv .\computers.csv

computername
------------
SERVER-R2
DC01
LOCALHOST
CLIENTA
```

The command has produced four objects, each of which has a `ComputerName` property. Our expectation is that those properties will bind, ByPropertyName, to the `-ComputerName` parameter of `Get-WmiObject`. In this fashion, we expect it to retrieve the `Win32_BIOS` class from each of those four computers.

> **DON'T TRY IT NOW**   Don't bother running this command just yet. Our goal isn't to try it but rather to predict what it will do and then test that prediction by using a troubleshooting tool.

The basic usage format for `Trace-Command` is as follows:

```
Trace-Command -Name Parameterbinding -PSHost -Expression { }
```

Inside the expression {} block, you put whatever command you want to test. That command *will execute*, so if it's doing something dangerous, use appropriate caution. In addition to the command executing, the shell will capture and display some internals about what it's doing. So we'll run the following:

```
PS C:\> Trace-Command -name ParameterBinding -PSHost -Expression { Import-C
sv .\computers.csv | Get-WmiObject -Class Win32_BIOS }
```

19.3   *Interpreting trace-command output*

We're going to paste in a chunk of the trace output and provide an explanation for what we're seeing:

```
DEBUG: ParameterBinding Information: 0 : BIND NAMED cmd line args
[Import-Csv]
DEBUG: ParameterBinding Information: 0 : BIND POSITIONAL cmd line args
[Import-Csv]
DEBUG: ParameterBinding Information: 0 :    BIND arg [.\computers.csv] to
 parameter [Path]
```

This means that PowerShell is binding named and positional parameters. It's handling whatever parameters we've typed manually. Those always get bound first and override anything piped in that might have attached to those parameters. Here you can see that our path, .\computers.csv, is being attached to the -Path parameter:

```
DEBUG: ParameterBinding Information: 0 :          Binding collection
parameter Path: argument type [String], parameter type [System.String[]],
collection type Array, element type [System.String], no coerceElementType
DEBUG: ParameterBinding Information: 0 :          Creating array with
element type [System.String] and 1 elements
DEBUG: ParameterBinding Information: 0 :          Argument type String is
not IList, treating this as scalar
DEBUG: ParameterBinding Information: 0 :          Adding scalar element of
type String to array position 0
DEBUG: ParameterBinding Information: 0 :          Executing VALIDATION
metadata: [System.Management.Automation.ValidateNotNullOrEmptyAttribute]
DEBUG: ParameterBinding Information: 0 :          BIND arg
[System.String[]] to param [Path] SUCCESSFUL
```

The -Path parameter of Import-CSV requires an array. Because we specified only one value, PowerShell is creating an array and adding our single value to that array. The last thing it does is validate that the -Path parameter is not null, and not empty, before declaring the -Path parameter's binding successful:

```
DEBUG: ParameterBinding Information: 0 : MANDATORY PARAMETER CHECK on
cmdlet [Import-Csv]
```

The shell just checked to make sure all mandatory parameters of Import-Csv were provided. They were, or we'd have seen error messages. So we're ready to move on to the next command:

```
DEBUG: ParameterBinding Information: 0 : BIND NAMED cmd line args
[Get-WmiObject]
DEBUG: ParameterBinding Information: 0 :      BIND arg [Win32_BIOS] to
parameter [Class]
DEBUG: ParameterBinding Information: 0 :          COERCE arg to
[System.String]
DEBUG: ParameterBinding Information: 0 :             Parameter and arg
types the same, no coercion is needed.
DEBUG: ParameterBinding Information: 0 :          BIND arg [Win32_BIOS] to
param [Class] SUCCESSFUL
DEBUG: ParameterBinding Information: 0 : BIND POSITIONAL cmd line args
[Get-WmiObject]
DEBUG: ParameterBinding Information: 0 : MANDATORY PARAMETER CHECK on
cmdlet [Get-WmiObject]
```

All of that was for Get-WmiObject. Here, the -Class parameters wants a String, which is what we gave it, so PowerShell acknowledges that no data type conversion (coercion) is necessary. We've provided all of the mandatory parameters, so we're cleared for takeoff.

```
DEBUG: ParameterBinding Information: 0 : CALLING BeginProcessing
DEBUG: ParameterBinding Information: 0 : CALLING BeginProcessing
```

Those two lines indicate that we're starting to run the cmdlets:

```
DEBUG: ParameterBinding Information: 0 : BIND PIPELINE object to
parameters: [Get-WmiObject]
DEBUG: ParameterBinding Information: 0 :     PIPELINE object TYPE =
[System.Management.Automation.PSCustomObject]
```

This is the key bit of the process. Here, PowerShell is saying, "Okay, Import-Csv produces objects of the type PSCustomObject. Those are in the pipeline, so we need to bind them to the next command, which is Get-WmiObject."

```
DEBUG: ParameterBinding Information: 0 :     RESTORING pipeline
parameter's original values
DEBUG: ParameterBinding Information: 0 : BIND PIPELINE object to
parameters: [Out-Default]
```

You'll almost always see Out-Default in the trace code, because it's hardcoded, behind the scenes, at the end of every pipeline. Even though we didn't explicitly type it, it's there and PowerShell has to deal with it.

```
DEBUG: ParameterBinding Information: 0 :     PIPELINE object TYPE =
[System.Management.Automation.ErrorRecord]
DEBUG: ParameterBinding Information: 0 :     RESTORING pipeline
parameter's original values
DEBUG: ParameterBinding Information: 0 :     Parameter [InputObject]
PIPELINE INPUT ValueFromPipeline NO COERCION
DEBUG: ParameterBinding Information: 0 :     BIND arg [The input object
cannot be bound to any parameters for the command either because the
command does not take pipeline input or the input and its properties do
not match any of the parameters that take pipeline input.] to parameter
[InputObject]
```

This isn't good. It means PowerShell couldn't find any parameters of Get-WmiObject that could accept our pipeline objects, either ByValue or ByPropertyName. Our command is failing. Much of the rest of the trace output is just PowerShell dealing with the error and preparing an error record for our display.

So what went wrong? Take a look at the full help for Get-WmiObject. No parameter accepts an object of the type PSCustomObject, so Plan A, ByValue, fails. That leaves it trying to attach the ComputerName property to the –ComputerName parameter, which is unfortunately not programmed, in this case, to accept pipeline input. So the command failed. Had we read the help thoroughly ahead of time, we probably could have predicted that!

Let's run a second command through the process—this time, one that should work, so that you can see what a successful binding looks like. We'll use a similar command but one whose –computerName parameter is wired up for pipeline input:

```
PS C:\> Trace-Command -name ParameterBinding -PSHost -Expression { Import-C
sv .\computers.csv | Get-Service -Name * }
DEBUG: ParameterBinding Information: 0 : BIND NAMED cmd line args
[Import-Csv]
DEBUG: ParameterBinding Information: 0 : BIND POSITIONAL cmd line args
[Import-Csv]
DEBUG: ParameterBinding Information: 0 :     BIND arg [.\computers.csv] to
 parameter [Path]
```

Once again, we've started by binding the filename to the -Path parameter of
Import-Csv:

```
DEBUG: ParameterBinding Information: 0 :          Binding collection
parameter Path: argument type [String], parameter type [System.String[]],
collection type Array, element type [System.String], no coerceElementType
DEBUG: ParameterBinding Information: 0 :          Creating array with
element type [System.String] and 1 elements
DEBUG: ParameterBinding Information: 0 :          Argument type String is
not IList, treating this as scalar
DEBUG: ParameterBinding Information: 0 :          Adding scalar element of
type String to array position 0
DEBUG: ParameterBinding Information: 0 :          Executing VALIDATION
metadata: [System.Management.Automation.ValidateNotNullOrEmptyAttribute]
DEBUG: ParameterBinding Information: 0 :          BIND arg
[System.String[]] to param [Path] SUCCESSFUL
DEBUG: ParameterBinding Information: 0 : MANDATORY PARAMETER CHECK on
cmdlet [Import-Csv]
```

PowerShell created a single-item array, validated it, and ensured we provided all mandatory parameters.

```
DEBUG: ParameterBinding Information: 0 : BIND NAMED cmd line args
[Get-Service]
DEBUG: ParameterBinding Information: 0 :     BIND arg [*] to parameter
[Name]
DEBUG: ParameterBinding Information: 0 :          COERCE arg to
[System.String[]]
DEBUG: ParameterBinding Information: 0 :          Trying to convert
argument value from System.String to System.String[]
DEBUG: ParameterBinding Information: 0 :          ENCODING arg into
collection
DEBUG: ParameterBinding Information: 0 :          Binding collection
parameter Name: argument type [String], parameter type [System.String[]],
collection type Array, element type [System.String], coerceElementType
DEBUG: ParameterBinding Information: 0 :          Creating array with
element type [System.String] and 1 elements
DEBUG: ParameterBinding Information: 0 :          Argument type String
is not IList, treating this as scalar
DEBUG: ParameterBinding Information: 0 :          COERCE arg to
[System.String]
DEBUG: ParameterBinding Information: 0 :          Parameter and arg
 types the same, no coercion is needed.
DEBUG: ParameterBinding Information: 0 :          Adding scalar element
 of type String to array position 0
DEBUG: ParameterBinding Information: 0 :          BIND arg
[System.String[]] to param [Name] SUCCESSFUL
DEBUG: ParameterBinding Information: 0 : BIND POSITIONAL cmd line args
[Get-Service]
DEBUG: ParameterBinding Information: 0 : MANDATORY PARAMETER CHECK on
cmdlet [Get-Service]
```

The -Name parameter of Get-Service also needs an array, so we can see PowerShell
creating a single-item array from our value of *. Keep in mind that, to this point, the

cmdlets haven't actually executed; this is just the setup. PowerShell can't do pipeline parameter binding until it sees what the first command outputs.

```
DEBUG: ParameterBinding Information: 0 : CALLING BeginProcessing
DEBUG: ParameterBinding Information: 0 : CALLING BeginProcessing
DEBUG: ParameterBinding Information: 0 : BIND PIPELINE object to
parameters: [Get-Service]
DEBUG: ParameterBinding Information: 0 :     PIPELINE object TYPE =
[System.Management.Automation.PSCustomObject]
DEBUG: ParameterBinding Information: 0 :     RESTORING pipeline
parameter's original values
```

Now we're executing commands, and PowerShell knows that it needs to bind our CSV objects to something on Get-Service.

```
DEBUG: ParameterBinding Information: 0 :     Parameter [ComputerName]
PIPELINE INPUT ValueFromPipelineByPropertyName NO COERCION
DEBUG: ParameterBinding Information: 0 :     BIND arg [SERVER-R2] to
parameter [ComputerName]
```

PowerShell has chosen the –ComputerName parameter, and it sees that no data coercion is needed. So our first value, SERVER-R2, is being attached to the –ComputerName parameter.

```
DEBUG: ParameterBinding Information: 0 :           Binding collection
parameter ComputerName: argument type [String], parameter type
[System.String[]], collection type Array, element type [System.String], no
 coerceElementType
DEBUG: ParameterBinding Information: 0 :           Creating array with
element type [System.String] and 1 elements
DEBUG: ParameterBinding Information: 0 :           Argument type String is
not IList, treating this as scalar
DEBUG: ParameterBinding Information: 0 :           Adding scalar element of
type String to array position 0
DEBUG: ParameterBinding Information: 0 :           Executing VALIDATION
metadata: [System.Management.Automation.ValidateNotNullOrEmptyAttribute]
DEBUG: ParameterBinding Information: 0 :           BIND arg
[System.String[]] to param [ComputerName] SUCCESSFUL
DEBUG: ParameterBinding Information: 0 : MANDATORY PARAMETER CHECK on
cmdlet [Get-Service]
```

Once again, an array is expected, so the shell creates a single-item array from our SERVER-R2 value, checks its validation rules on the parameter, and ensures we've provided all the mandatory parameters for the command:

```
DEBUG: ParameterBinding Information: 0 : BIND PIPELINE object to
parameters: [Out-Default]
DEBUG: ParameterBinding Information: 0 :     PIPELINE object TYPE =
[System.Management.Automation.ErrorRecord]
DEBUG: ParameterBinding Information: 0 :     RESTORING pipeline
parameter's original values
DEBUG: ParameterBinding Information: 0 :     Parameter [InputObject]
PIPELINE INPUT ValueFromPipeline NO COERCION
DEBUG: ParameterBinding Information: 0 :     BIND arg [Cannot open Service
 Control Manager on computer 'SERVER-R2'. This operation might require
```

```
other privileges.] to parameter [InputObject]
DEBUG: ParameterBinding Information: 0 :         BIND arg [Cannot open
Service Control Manager on computer 'SERVER-R2'. This operation might
require other privileges.] to param [InputObject] SUCCESSFUL
DEBUG: ParameterBinding Information: 0 : MANDATORY PARAMETER CHECK on
cmdlet [Out-Default]
```

What you're seeing here is an error record being sent to `Out-Default`, because the `Get-Service` command couldn't contact the Service Control Manager on SERVER-R2. That's okay; the command is working, but that computer might not be online or might be behind a firewall. The remaining trace output is more or less a repetition of the previous, with the remaining values from our CSV file. At the end, we see the command's error regarding SERVER-R2:

```
Get-Service : Cannot open Service Control Manager on computer
'SERVER-R2'. This operation might require other privileges.
At line:1 char:89
+ ... omputers.csv | Get-Service -Name * }
+                    ~~~~~~~~~~~~~~~~~~~~
    + CategoryInfo          : NotSpecified: (:) [Get-Service], InvalidOpe
   rationException
    + FullyQualifiedErrorId : System.InvalidOperationException,Microsoft.
   PowerShell.Commands.GetServiceCommand

PS C:\>
```

And now you know how to troubleshoot pipeline parameter binding: Using `Trace-Command`, you can see what data is going to which parameters, helping you validate your expectations. But if you didn't have any expectations, you can't troubleshoot. It's still important (as we explained in the chapter on debugging) to have an understanding of what should be happening, so that you can spot the problem when things don't happen that way.

19.4   Lab

Create a text file named C:\Computers.csv. In it, place the following content:

```
ComputerName
LOCALHOST
NOTONLINE
```

Be sure there are no extra blank lines at the end of the file. Then, consider the following command:

```
Import-CSV C:\Computers.txt | Invoke-Command –Script { Get-Service }
```

The help file for `Invoke-Command` indicates that its –ComputerName parameter accepts pipeline input ByValue. Therefore, our expectation is that the computer names in the CSV file will be fed to the –ComputerName parameter. But if you run the command, that isn't what happens. Troubleshoot this command using the techniques described in this chapter, and determine where the computer names from the CSV file are being bound.

Using object hierarchies for complex output

Way back in chapter 7, we showed you how to create custom objects to use as the output of your functions. To this point, the objects you've created have essentially been flat, meaning they could be easily represented in a flat data file structure such as a CSV file or in an Excel spreadsheet or in a simple table. That's because your objects, to this point, have represented only a single entity, such as a computer system. In this chapter, we're going to show you how to work with more complex objects that include multiple entities in a single, hierarchical object.

20.1 When a hierarchy might be necessary

Typically, a single object should represent one single kind of thing. That might be a computer system, a disk drive, a user, or a file. The properties of those objects should directly relate to the entity that the object represents. For example, if you're creating an object to represent a computer system, then it might have properties such as these:

- Computer name
- Operating system version
- BIOS serial number
- Manufacturer name

A computer object like that wouldn't usually contain much information about the computer's disk drives. That's because the disk drives are their own entity. They're usually removable from the computer system, and the properties of a disk drive have little or nothing to do with the computer system itself. A disk drive has a size, which doesn't change when it's moved to a different computer system or when it's removed from any computer altogether.

But there's obviously a relationship between computers and disk drives, right? A computer system usually *contains* disk drives. Windows Explorer shows this relationship in a tree view, as shown in figure 20.1.

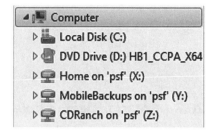

In PowerShell, you can represent that relationship using an *object hierarchy*. Such a hierarchy might be needed anytime you want to combine information about many distinct yet related entities into a single output object.

Figure 20.1   Windows Explorer uses a tree view to illustrate the relationship between a computer and its disk drives.

20.2   Hierarchies and CSV: not a good idea

Before we show you how to create and manipulate these object hierarchies, we want to caution you against outputting them to a CSV file. For example, try running this command in PowerShell:

```
Get-Service | Export-CSV services.csv
```

TRY IT NOW   Go ahead and run this for yourself; the output is worth looking at, and it's a bit more than we're able to completely share in the pages of this book.

Opening the Services.csv file in Notepad looks something like figure 20.2. What you're seeing is what happens when PowerShell has to convert a hierarchy of objects into a flat-file format like CSV. For example, you'll see that the second column of this CSV file is `RequiredServices`, which lists the services each service depends on. But the data rows for that column show `System.ServiceProcess.ServiceController[]`, which is Power-Shell's way of saying, "What should go here is a bunch of `ServiceController` objects, but this file format doesn't let me show child objects."

```
                         services.csv - Notepad                    _ □ x
File  Edit  Format  View  Help
#TYPE System.ServiceProcess.ServiceController
"Name","RequiredServices","CanPauseAndContinue","CanSh
"AeLookupSvc","System.ServiceProcess.ServiceController
"ALG","System.ServiceProcess.ServiceController[]","Fal
"AllUserInstallAgent","System.ServiceProcess.ServiceCo
"AppIDSvc","System.ServiceProcess.ServiceController[]"
"Appinfo","System.ServiceProcess.ServiceController[]",
"AppMgmt","System.ServiceProcess.ServiceController[]",
"AudioEndpointBuilder","System.ServiceProcess.ServiceC
"Audiosrv","System.ServiceProcess.ServiceController[]"
"AxInstSV","System.ServiceProcess.ServiceController[]"
"BDESVC","System.ServiceProcess.ServiceController[]","
"BFE","System.ServiceProcess.ServiceController[]","Fal
"BITS","System.ServiceProcess.ServiceController[]","Fa
"BrokerInfrastructure","System.ServiceProcess.ServiceC
"Browser","System.ServiceProcess.ServiceController[]",
"bthserv","System.ServiceProcess.ServiceController[]",
"CertPropSvc","System.ServiceProcess.ServiceController
"COMSysApp","System.ServiceProcess.ServiceController[]
"CryptSvc","System.ServiceProcess.ServiceController[]"
"CscService","System.ServiceProcess.ServiceController[
```

Figure 20.2   Looking at object hierarchies in a CSV file

The CliXML format used by `Export-CliXML` and `Import-CliXML` is much better at representing object hierarchies. Try exporting a list of services to CliXML and looking at the result in Windows Notepad. Anytime you see an object type name followed by `[]`, such as `ServiceController[]`, PowerShell is letting you know, "I'd like to display multiple subobjects here, but I can't."

20.3   *Creating nested objects*

Let's walk through a complete example. We're going to create a function named `Get-DetailedSystemInfo`. We want the main, top-level object to contain the computer name and the version numbers for both the operating system and its service pack. Each object will also contain a `Disks` property, which will list additional information for each local, fixed disk installed in the computer. The following listing shows the completed script file, which includes a line at the end to run the function.

Listing 20.1   Example of creating an object hierarchy

```
function Get-DetailedSystemInfo {
    [CmdletBinding()]
    param(
        [Parameter(Mandatory=$True)][string[]]$computerName
    )
    PROCESS {
        foreach ($computer in $computerName) {
            $params = @{computerName=$computer;
                        class='Win32_OperatingSystem'}          ❶ Get OS info
            $os = Get-WmiObject @params

            $params = @{computerName=$computer;
                        class='Win32_LogicalDisk';              ❷ Get disk info
                        filter='drivetype=3'}
            $disks = Get-WmiObject @params
                                                        ❸ Empty
            $diskobjs = @()                                array for disks
            foreach ($disk in $disks) {
                $diskprops = @{Drive=$disk.DeviceID;         Create disk
                               Size=$disk.size;            ❹ object
                               Free=$disk.freespace}
                $diskobj = new-object -Type PSObject -Property $diskprops
                $diskobjs += $diskobj
            }                                              Add disk
                                                        ❺ to array
            $mainprops = @{ComputerName=$computer;
                           Disks=$diskobjs;                 Create top-
                           OSVersion=$os.version;        ❻ level object
                           SPVersion=$os.servicepackmajorversion}
            $mainobject = New-Object -Type PSObject -Property $mainprops
            Write-Output $mainobject
        }
    }
}

Get-DetailedSystemInfo -computerName localhost,DONJONES1D96
```

Within the PROCESS block of this function, we start by ❶ creating a hashtable containing the parameters for our first Get-WmiObject call and then executing that call. This technique is called *splatting*, and it can make it visually easier to add several parameters to a single command. Next, ❷ we do the same thing with the Get-WmiObject call that's retrieving our disk information.

We take the time to create an empty array ❸, named $diskobjs. We'll use this later. Because each computer we query might well have several disks installed, we use a ForEach loop to go through each one. For each one, ❹ we assemble a hashtable of the properties we want to save for each of those disks. We then create a new object having those properties and ❺ add that object to our $diskobjs array.

Once all of the disk objects have been created and saved into the $diskobjs array, ❻ we create the top-level output object. We define its properties, one of which is Disks, to which we assign our $diskobjs array. We then output the main object. The output of the script, run against two computers, looks like this:

```
ComputerName        SPVersion Disks                   OSVersion
------------        --------- -----                   ---------
localhost                   0 {@{Drive=C:; Free=52... 6.2.8250
DONJONES1D96                0 {@{Drive=C:; Free=52... 6.2.8250
```

Now, we'll replace the last line in the script

```
Get-DetailedSystemInfo -computerName localhost,DONJONES1D96
```

with this:

```
Get-DetailedSystemInfo -computerName localhost |
Select-Object -ExpandProperty Disks
```

This queries only one computer, but it's asking the shell to expand the Disks property. Remember, that property can contain multiple subobjects, each of which represents a single disk that's installed in the computer. The results look something like this:

```
Drive               Free                    Size
-----               ----                    ----
C:                  52591726592             68717375488
E:                  75673727263             94746282712
```

> **NOTE** We've used the term *disks* a bit liberally; we're really querying *logical disks*, which Windows also calls *partitions*.

This has been a good example of why, when, and how you'd use object hierarchies.

20.4 Working with nested objects

Whether you create your own object hierarchies or merely have some that were output from existing commands, you need to know how to work with them effectively. There are four main techniques:

- Use `Select-Object` to expand a property that contains subobjects, enabling you to see the individual subobjects.
- Use `Format-Custom` to expand the entire object hierarchy.
- Use a `ForEach` loop.
- Use PowerShell's array syntax to work with individual subobjects.

To illustrate each of these techniques, we'll use `Get-Service`. The objects produced by this command have several properties that are child objects (which we've also been calling nested objects or subobjects). Those properties include `ServicesDependedOn` (also known as `RequiredServices`) and `DependentServices`.

20.4.1 *Using Select-Object to expand child objects*

The `-ExpandProperty` parameter of `Select-Object` can expand the content of a single property. When given a property that contains a single value, such as a string, the parameter returns that value. When given a property that contains subobjects, the parameter returns those subobjects.

```
PS C:\> Get-service | select -ExpandProperty ServicesDependedOn

Status    Name             DisplayName
------    ----             -----------
Running   RPCSS            Remote Procedure Call (RPC)
Running   RpcSs            Remote Procedure Call (RPC)
Running   CryptSvc         Cryptographic Services
Stopped   AppID            AppID Driver
Running   RpcSs            Remote Procedure Call (RPC)
Running   ProfSvc          User Profile Service
Stopped   MMCSS            Multimedia Class Scheduler
Running   RpcSs            Remote Procedure Call (RPC)
Running   AudioEndpointBu... Windows Audio Endpoint Builder
Running   rpcss            Remote Procedure Call (RPC)
Running   RpcSs            Remote Procedure Call (RPC)
Running   WfpLwfs          WFP LightWeight Filters
Running   RpcSs            Remote Procedure Call (RPC)
Running   EventSystem      COM+ Event System
```

We've truncated this output, but it's showing you every "service depended on" for every service on the system. You'll notice some repetition, such as the Remote Procedure Call service, because that service is depended upon by several other services. This technique is often most useful when you're working with only a single top-level object:

```
PS C:\> Get-service -Name BITS | select -ExpandProperty ServicesDependedOn

Status    Name             DisplayName
------    ----             -----------
Running   RpcSs            Remote Procedure Call (RPC)
Running   EventSystem      COM+ Event System
```

Here, we've retrieved only a single service, BITS, so we can more clearly see the services that it depends on: `RpcSs` and `EventSystem`.

20.4.2 *Using Format-Custom to expand an object hierarchy*

The Format-Custom command, which when used with an object for which there is no predefined view, will expand the object's entire hierarchy:

```
PS C:\> get-service | format-custom -Property *

class ServiceController
{
  Name = AllUserInstallAgent
  RequiredServices =
    [
      class ServiceController
      {
        Status = Running
        Name = RPCSS
        DisplayName = Remote Procedure Call (RPC)
      }
    ]

  CanPauseAndContinue = False
  CanShutdown = False
  CanStop = False
  DisplayName = Windows All-User Install Agent
  DependentServices =
    [
    ]

  MachineName = .
  ServiceName = AllUserInstallAgent
  ServicesDependedOn =
    [
      class ServiceController
      {
        Status = Running
        Name = RPCSS
        DisplayName = Remote Procedure Call (RPC)
      }
    ]

  ServiceHandle =
    class SafeServiceHandle
    {
      IsInvalid = False
      IsClosed = False
    }
  Status = Stopped
  ServiceType = Win32ShareProcess
  Site =
  Container =
}

class ServiceController
{
  Name = AppIDSvc
  RequiredServices =
    [
```

```
      class ServiceController
      {
        Status = Running
        Name = RpcSs
        DisplayName = Remote Procedure Call (RPC)
      }
      class ServiceController
      {
        Status = Running
        Name = CryptSvc
        DisplayName = Cryptographic Services
      }
      class ServiceController
      {
        Status = Stopped
        Name = AppID
        DisplayName = AppID Driver
      }
    ]

CanPauseAndContinue = False
CanShutdown = False
CanStop = False
DisplayName = Application Identity
DependentServices =
  [
  ]

MachineName = .
ServiceName = AppIDSvc
ServicesDependedOn =
  [
    class ServiceController
    {
      Status = Running
      Name = RpcSs
      DisplayName = Remote Procedure Call (RPC)
    }
    class ServiceController
    {
      Status = Running
      Name = CryptSvc
      DisplayName = Cryptographic Services
    }
    class ServiceController
    {
      Status = Stopped
      Name = AppID
      DisplayName = AppID Driver
    }
  ]

ServiceHandle =
  class SafeServiceHandle
  {
    IsInvalid = False
```

```
        IsClosed = False
    }
  Status = Stopped
  ServiceType = Win32ShareProcess
  Site =
  Container =
}
```

In this listing, you can see that each service has been expanded, and both the ServicesDependedOn (also shown as RequiredServices) and DependentServices properties have been expanded to show their subobjects. You can also see that the ServiceHandle property contains subobjects of the type SafeServiceHandle and that those subobjects each have two properties. We've shown only two services here to save room, but it's a good illustration of how Format-Custom can be used.

20.4.3 *Using a ForEach loop to enumerate subobjects*

ForEach loops are a perfect way to enumerate objects, and nested ForEach loops let you recursively work with subobjects, for example:

```
$services = Get-Service
foreach ($main_service in $services) {
    Write "  $($main_service.name) depends on:"
    foreach ($sub_service in $main_service.requiredservices) {

        Write "`t $($sub_service.name)"
    }
}
```

Here's a portion of the output from that short script:

```
AeLookupSvc depends on:
ALG depends on:
AllUserInstallAgent depends on:
    RPCSS
AppIDSvc depends on:
    CryptSvc
    AppID
    RpcSs
Appinfo depends on:
    RpcSs
    ProfSvc
AppMgmt depends on:
AudioEndpointBuilder depends on:
Audiosrv depends on:
    AudioEndpointBuilder
    MMCSS
    RpcSs
AxInstSV depends on:
    rpcss
BDESVC depends on:
BFE depends on:
    RpcSs
    WfpLwfs
```

```
BITS depends on:
   RpcSs
   EventSystem
BrokerInfrastructure depends on:
   DcomLaunch
   RpcEptMapper
   RpcSs
Browser depends on:
   LanmanWorkstation
   LanmanServer
```

How you structure your loops will depend on how you plan to use the information, but as you can see, you get a great deal of fine control over how you enumerate the object hierarchy.

20.4.4   *Using PowerShell's array syntax to access individual subobjects*

Finally, you can access individual subobjects and their properties by using Power-Shell's array notation syntax:

```
PS C:\> $services = get-service

PS C:\> $services[4].requiredservices[0].name
RpcSs

PS C:\>
```

Here, we pulled a list of all services into $services. We then accessed the fifth service (index number 4), its RequiredServices property, the first required service (index number 0), and that service's Name property, which turned out to be RpcSS.

20.5   *Lab*

Create a new function in your existing PSHTools module. Name the new function Get-ComputerVolumeInfo. This function's output will include some information that your other functions already produce, but this particular function is going to combine them all into a single, hierarchical object.

This function should accept one or more computer names on a –ComputerName parameter. Don't worry about error handling at this time. The output of this function should be a custom object with the following properties:

- ComputerName
- OSVersion (Version from Win32_OperatingSystem)
- SPVersion (ServicePackMajorVersion from Win32_OperatingSystem)
- LocalDisks (all instances of Win32_LogicalDisk having a DriveType of 3)
- Services (all instances of Win32_Service)
- Processes (all instances of Win32_ProcessS)

The function will therefore be making at least four WMI queries to each specified computer.

Globalizing a function

PowerShell v2 introduced a *data language* element for the shell, designed to help separate text from the functional code of a script or command. By separating text, you can make it easier to swap out alternate versions of that text. Separating text is referred to as *globalizing*, a process of making your script ready for localization. *Localization* lets you swap out your original language text strings for an alternate language—or multiple languages. We'll acknowledge up front that this is a fairly specialized feature and that few administrators will typically use it. We're including it to help ensure that this book is as complete as possible, but we'll keep it brief. You can find additional help in two of PowerShell's help files: `about_script_internationalization` and `about_data_sections`.

21.1 Introduction to globalization

Globalization (or *internationalization*, a term some prefer) is implemented through several specific features in PowerShell:

- A data section, which we'll discuss next, that contains all of the text strings intended for display or other output.
- Two built-in variables, `$PSCulture` and `$PSUICulture`, that store the name of the user interface language in use by the current system. This lets you detect the language that the current user is utilizing in Windows. `$PSCulture` contains the language used for regional settings such as date, time, and currency formats, whereas `$PSUICulture` contains the language for user interface elements such as menus and text strings.
- `ConvertFrom-StringData`, a cmdlet that converts text strings into a hash table, which makes it easier to import a batch of strings in a specific language

and then utilize them from within your script. By varying the batch that you import, you can dynamically vary what your script outputs.

- The .psd1 file type, which in addition to being used for module manifests can also be used to store language-specific strings. You provide a single .psd1 file for each language you want to support.
- `Import-LocalizedData`, a cmdlet that imports translated text strings for a specific language into a script.

We figure the best way to show you all of this is to dive into a sample project and explain as we go, so that's what we'll do. We're going to start with a script that's functionally simple. Shown in listing 21.1, it includes several `Write-Verbose` statements that output strings of text. We're going to focus on those for our internationalization efforts. For our examples, we're using Google Translate to produce non-English text strings; we hope any native speakers of our chosen languages will forgive any translation errors!

Listing 21.1 Our starting point, Global.psm1

```
function Get-OSInfo {
    [CmdletBinding()]
    param(
        [Parameter(Mandatory=$True,ValueFromPipeline=$True)]
        [string[]]$computerName
    )
    BEGIN {
        Write-Verbose "Starting Get-OSInfo"
    }
    PROCESS {
        ForEach ($computer in $computername) {
            try {
                $connected = $True
                Write-Verbose "Attempting $computer"
                $os = Get-WmiObject -ComputerName $computer `
                                    -class Win32_OperatingSystem `
                                    -EA Stop
            } catch {
                $connected = $false
                Write-Verbose "Connection to $computer failed"
            }
            if ($connected) {
                Write-Verbose "Connection to $computer succeeded"
                $cs = Get-WmiObject -ComputerName $computer `
                                    -class Win32_ComputerSystem
                $props = @{ComputerName=$computer;
                           OSVersion=$os.version;
                           Manufacturer=$cs.manufacturer;
                           Model=$cs.model}
                $obj = New-Object -TypeName PSObject -Property $props
                Write-Output $obj
            }
        }
    }
```

```
    }
    END {
        Write-Verbose "Ending Get-OSInfo"
    }
}
```

NOTE We've used the backtick (`) character in this code listing so that longer lines could be broken into multiple physical lines. If you're typing this in, be sure to include the backtick character, and make sure it's the very last thing on the line—it can't be followed by any spaces or tabs. We don't think it's the prettiest way to type code, but it makes it easier to fit it within the constraints of the printed page.

We've saved this script as \Documents\WindowsPowerShell\Modules\Global\Global .psm1. That enabled us to load it into the console by running `Import-Module global` and to test it by then running `Get-OSInfo -computername localhost`. If you're going to follow along, make sure that you can successfully complete those steps before continuing.

21.2 *PowerShell's data language*

Currently, our script has hardcoded strings—primarily the `Write-Verbose` statements, which we're going to address, but also the output object's property names. We could also localize the property names, but we're not going to. Generally speaking, even Microsoft doesn't translate those, because other bits of code might take a dependency on the property names, and translating them would break that dependency. If we wanted the property names to *display* with translated column names, then we could utilize a custom view to do that.

Take a look at the following listing, where we've added a data section to contain our default strings.

Listing 21.2 Adding a data section to Global.psm1

```
$msgTable = Data {                                          Data
    # culture="en-US"                              ❶        section
    ConvertFrom-StringData @'
        attempting = Attempting
        connectionTo = Connection to
        failed = failed
        succeeded = succeeded
        starting = Starting Get-OSInfo
        ending = Ending Get-OSInfo
'@
}

function Get-OSInfo {
    [CmdletBinding()]
    param(
        [Parameter(Mandatory=$True,ValueFromPipeline=$True)]
        [string[]]$computerName
    )
```

```
    BEGIN {
        Write-Verbose $msgTable.starting                    ◁──┐  Using a
    }                                                          ② string
    PROCESS {
        ForEach ($computer in $computername) {
            try {
                $connected = $True
                Write-Verbose "$($msgTable.attempting) $computer"
                $os = Get-WmiObject -ComputerName $computer `
                                    -class Win32_OperatingSystem `
                                    -EA Stop
            } catch {
                $connected = $false
                Write-Verbose "$($msgTable.connectionTo) $computer
➥$($msgTable.failed)"
            }
            if ($connected) {
                Write-Verbose "$($msgTable.connectionTo) to $computer
➥$($msgTable.succeeded)"
                $cs = Get-WmiObject -ComputerName $computer `
                                    -class Win32_ComputerSystem
                $props = @{ComputerName=$computer;
                           OSVersion=$os.version;
                           Manufacturer=$cs.manufacturer;
                           Model=$cs.model}
                $obj = New-Object -TypeName PSObject -Property $props
                Write-Output $obj
            }
        }
    }
    END {
        Write-Verbose $msgTable.ending
    }
}
                                                         ❸  Export-
Export-ModuleMember -function "Get-OSInfo"           ◁──┘  ModuleMember
```

We've added a data section at ❶. This utilizes the ConvertFrom-StringData cmdlet
to convert a here-string into a hashtable. The result is a $msgTable object, with prop-
erties named connectionTo, starting, ending, and so on. The properties will contain
the English-language values shown in the script. We can then use those properties
at ❷, whenever we want to display the associated text. Because this is a script module,
it would ordinarily make the $msgTable variable accessible to the global shell, once
the module is imported. We don't want that; we'd rather $msgTable remain internal
use only within this module. So we also added an Export-ModuleMember call at ❸. By
exporting our Get-OSInfo function, everything else, that is, everything we don't
explicitly export, remains private to the module and accessible only to other things
within the script file.

We're going to test this by removing the module, reimporting it, and then running
it. We'll make sure to use the –Verbose switch so that we can test our localized output.
Here's what it should look like:

```
PS C:\> remove-module global
PS C:\> import-module global
PS C:\> Get-OSInfo -computerName localhost

Manufacturer       OSVersion        ComputerName      Model
------------       ---------        ------------      -----
VMware, Inc.       6.1.7601         localhost         VMware Virtua...

PS C:\> Get-OSInfo -computerName localhost -verbose
VERBOSE: Starting Get-OSInfo
VERBOSE: Attempting localhost
VERBOSE: Connection to to localhost succeeded

Manufacturer       OSVersion        ComputerName      Model
------------       ---------        ------------      -----
VMware, Inc.       6.1.7601         localhost         VMware Virtua...
VERBOSE: Ending Get-OSInfo
```

As you can see, our changes seem to be successful. Our verbose output is displaying with the correct English-language strings. Now we can move on to the next step: creating translated versions of those strings.

21.3 *Storing translated strings*

We need to set up some new text files and a directory structure to store the translated strings. Each text file will contain a copy of our data section. We'll start by creating the following new directories and files:

- \Documents\WindowsPowerShell\Modules\Tools\de-DE\Tools.psd1
- \Documents\WindowsPowerShell\Modules\Tools\es\Tools.psd1

This creates two localized languages, German and Spanish. The *es* and *de-DE*, as well as the *en-US* used in our data section, are language codes defined by Microsoft. You have to use the correct codes, so be sure to consult the list at http://msdn.microsoft.com/en-us/library/ms533052(v=vs.85).aspx.

With the files created, we're going to copy our `ConvertFrom-StringData` command from the original script and into the two new .psd1 files. We'll then translate the strings. The next two listings show our final result. As we said earlier, we're just using Google Translate here; we're sure the results will be amusing to anyone who knows what these actually mean!

Listing 21.3   de-DE version of Global.psd1

```
ConvertFrom-StringData @'
    attempting = Versuch
    connectionTo = Der anschluss an
    failed = gescheitert
    succeeded = gelungen
    starting = Ab Get-OSInfo
    ending = Ende Get-OSInfo
'@
```

Listing 21.4   es version of Global.psd1

```
ConvertFrom-StringData @'
    attempting = Intentar
    connectionTo = Conexion a
    failed = fracasado
    succeeded = exito
    starting = A partir Get-OSInfo
    ending = Final Get-OSInfo
'@
```

NOTE   The way in which you type the here-strings is specific. The closing `'@` can't be indented; it must be typed in the first two characters of a line, all by itself. Read `about_here_strings` in PowerShell for more information on these.

We're not quite ready to retest our script; we need to modify it to load the translated data. That's done with the `Import-LocalizedData` cmdlet, and one of the two built-in variables we mentioned earlier will play a role. The cmdlet automatically uses `$PSUICulture`'s contents to figure out which .psd1 file to import. That means this can be tricky to test on a single-language Windows installation! We used our international MVP contacts, who own localized versions of Windows, to help us test this. The following listing shows the changes to Global.psm1 that we've made.

Listing 21.5   Modifying Global.psm1 to import the current language

```
$msgTable = Data {
    # culture="en-US"
    ConvertFrom-StringData @'
        attempting = Attempting
        connectionTo = Connection to
        failed = failed
        succeeded = succeeded
        starting = Starting Get-OSInfo
        ending = Ending Get-OSInfo
'@
}
Import-LocalizedData -BindingVariable $msgTable                    ❶ Importing the
                                                                    current language
function Get-OSInfo {
    [CmdletBinding()]
    param(
        [Parameter(Mandatory=$True,ValueFromPipeline=$True)]
        [string[]]$computerName
    )
    BEGIN {
        Write-Verbose $msgTable.starting
    }
    PROCESS {
        ForEach ($computer in $computername) {
            try {
                $connected = $True
```

```
                        Write-Verbose "$($msgTable.attempting) $computer"
                        $os = Get-WmiObject -ComputerName $computer `
                                            -class Win32_OperatingSystem `
                                            -EA Stop
                    } catch {
                        $connected = $false
                        Write-Verbose "$($msgTable.connectionTo) $computer
        $($msgTable.failed)"
                    }
                    if ($connected) {
                        Write-Verbose "$($msgTable.connectionTo) to $computer
        $($msgTable.succeeded)"
                        $cs = Get-WmiObject -ComputerName $computer `
                                            -class Win32_ComputerSystem
                        $props = @{ComputerName=$computer;
                                   OSVersion=$os.version;
                                   Manufacturer=$cs.manufacturer;
                                   Model=$cs.model}
                        $obj = New-Object -TypeName PSObject -Property $props
                        Write-Output $obj
                    }
                }
            }
        }
        END {
            Write-Verbose $msgTable.ending
        }
    }

Export-ModuleMember -function "Get-OSInfo"
```

You can see where we added the `Import-LocalizedData` command at ❶. Because this isn't contained in a function, it's executed when our module is loaded. The neat thing about this command is that it automatically reads $PSUICulture, which we mentioned, and looks for the .psd1 file in the appropriate subfolder. If it doesn't find the right file, then it doesn't do anything. That leaves $msgTable populated with our original English-language strings, making those our defaults.

A bit more about data sections

The data section in our script has a strict syntax. In general, it can contain only supported cmdlets like `ConvertFrom-StringData`. It can also support PowerShell operators (except `-match`), so that you can do some logical decision making using the `If...ElseIf...Else` construct; no other scripting language constructs are permitted. You can access the `$PSCulture`, `$PSUICulture`, `$True`, `$False`, and `$Null` built-in variables but no others. You can add comments, too. There's a bit more to them, but that's the general overview of what's allowed. You're not meant to put much code in there; data sections are intended to separate string data from your code, not to contain a bunch *more code.*

21.4   *Do you need to globalize?*

We don't see a lot of cases where administrators need to write localized scripts, but we can certainly imagine them. Larger, international organizations might well want to make the effort to localize scripts, especially when the output will be shown to end users rather than other administrators. PowerShell's built-in support for handling multi-language scripts is fairly straightforward to use, and as you've seen here, it's not even difficult to convert a single-language script to this multi-language format.

21.5   *Lab*

As we mentioned in this chapter, we don't see a lot of instances where administrators need to use globalization. For that reason, we're not giving you a lab for this chapter. But we do encourage you to follow along with the example in this chapter, so that you know how globalization works in the event you ever have a use for it.

Crossing the line: utilizing the .NET Framework

Until now, we've focused on keeping you entirely within PowerShell. Everything we've shown you to this point has utilized native PowerShell commands, techniques, and capabilities. The sole exception was our brief dip into databases, which required us to utilize the underlying .NET Framework. In that case, we still tried to hide the Framework a bit by providing you with PowerShell-style functions to use for database access. We've taken this approach because we truly believe that PowerShell is at its easiest and most consistent when you use it in the way we've been doing.

In this chapter, we're going to cross the line and use the Framework more directly. This isn't an approach that we advocate when you can accomplish your task using native PowerShell capabilities, but we recognize that sometimes you can't rely solely on what's built into, and for, PowerShell. There's a price to pay for using the Framework, though: We're exiting the somewhat tidy world of PowerShell. There will be no built-in help, and the online documentation we'll rely on is written for professional programmers, not administrators or scripters. Our PowerShell scripts will necessarily start to look more like C# applications, and we'll have to rely more on programming techniques than on command-line approaches.

22.1 .NET classes and instances

The .NET Framework is organized into a massive set of classes. A *class* is basically a hunk of code that handles some specific set of related tasks. For example, the Framework includes a class named System.Math, which provides capabilities for performing arithmetic calculations. Most Framework classes have a multipart name

217

like that, indicating that the Math class is part of the System namespace. For the most part, a *namespace* is an organizational element, much like a filesystem directory.

You get an instance when you load a class into memory, often giving it parameters to tie it to a specific element or behavior. For example, when you run this

```
$var = 'Hello!'
```

you create a new instance of System.String and store it in the variable $var. This instance of System.String is unique and stands independently of any other instances you may have created.

Classes define a number of properties, methods, and events for themselves, which are collectively referred to as its *members*. You've already worked extensively with properties and methods in PowerShell, because the objects generated by most PowerShell commands are just instances of some Framework class. For example, Get-Process produces instances of the System.Diagnostics.Process class, and those instances have all of the properties and methods that you're accustomed to working with.

22.2 *Static methods of a class*

Many classes—System.Math being one example—have static methods. A static method is one that's accessible as part of the class itself, without actually creating an instance of the class. Static methods often perform generic tasks that can be completed entirely by the arguments passed to the method. For example, the Abs() method of the Math class returns the absolute value of a given number:

```
PS C:\> [System.Math]::Abs(-5)
5
```

That also shows the syntax for accessing a static method: Include the complete class name in square brackets. Follow the closing bracket with two colons, and then specify the method name. Methods are always followed by parentheses, which contain a comma-separated list of the method's arguments. There should be no spaces anywhere in this syntax; everything must run together as we've shown.

Usually, you can shorten the class name:

```
PS C:\> [math]::abs(-5)
5
```

This is typically permitted when you're working with a class that has a unique, unambiguous name, meaning the Framework can figure out what you're asking for without wondering, "Do you mean System.Math or SomethingElse.Math?"

The Framework is enormous and isn't all physically loaded into PowerShell by default. On disk, the Framework's code is divided among a variety of *assemblies*, which are typically DLL files. We've found that most of the classes under the top-level System namespace are available by default, but for other namespaces you may need to explicitly load the necessary assembly in order to begin using the classes. For example, the Microsoft.VisualBasic.VBMath class isn't loaded by default, as you can see from the error message when we try to use its Rnd() method:

```
PS C:\> [microsoft.visualbasic.vbmath]::rnd()
Unable to find type [microsoft.visualbasic.vbmath]: make sure that the
assembly containing this type is loaded.
At line:1 char:1
+ [microsoft.visualbasic.vbmath]::rnd()
+ ~~~~~~~~~~~~~~~~~~~~~~~~~~~~~~~~~~~~~~~
    + CategoryInfo          : InvalidOperation: (microsoft.visualbasic.vb
  math:TypeName) [], RuntimeException
    + FullyQualifiedErrorId : TypeNotFound
```

In these cases, you can manually load the necessary assembly:

```
PS C:\> [system.reflection.assembly]::loadwithpartialname('Microsoft.Visual
Basic') | Out-Null
```

Here, we've piped the output to `Out-Null` to suppress that output. We usually do that when loading assemblies in a script, so that the output of `LoadWithPartialName()` doesn't mess up our script's intended output.

We should note that using `LoadWithPartialName()` is easy but is considered a poor practice. The .NET Framework documentation lists the method as *deprecated*, meaning it may be removed from future versions of the Framework. There's a great blog post by one of PowerShell's developers, Lee Holmes, that explains the details and offers alternatives (and a helper script) at http://www.leeholmes.com/blog/2006/01/17/how-do-i-easily-load-assemblies-when-loadwithpartialname-has-been-deprecated/. We admit that we continue to use `LoadWithPartialName()` because it's so much simpler and because we're willing to do any necessary debugging on the rare occasions when it doesn't work the way we need it to.

22.3 *Instantiating a class*

PowerShell's `New-Object` cmdlet creates a new instance of a class. It does this by calling a class's constructor, which may require you to supply one or more arguments in order to create the instance. For example, the only constructor for the `System.IO.DriveInfo` class requires you to provide a drive name:

```
PS C:\> $drive = New-Object -TypeName System.IO.DriveInfo -Argument 'C:'
```

When multiple arguments are required, provide them to the `-ArgumentList` parameter as a comma-separated list. Some classes have multiple constructors; `New-Object` will choose the correct one based upon the arguments you provide. For example, the `System.String` class offers a variety of constructors. Here are a few:

- `String(Char)`
- `String(Char[])`
- `String(Char, Int32)`
- `String(Char[], Int32, Int32)`

Each of these constructs a new `System.String` based on slightly different input. The last one, for example, accepts an array of characters and then constructs a string starting at the designated character and including the specified number of characters.

This can get pretty complex, but the point is that the *type of data* you provide in your arguments and the *order* in which you list those arguments must line up to one of the provided constructors. You couldn't construct a new System.String using an argument list like 1,2,3 because none of the class's constructors are expecting three integers in a row.

22.4   *Using Reflection*

PowerShell's super-handy Get-Member cmdlet utilizes a .NET Framework feature called *Reflection*. In essence, Reflection lets you see an object's members—its properties, methods, and events—simply by looking at it. Any .NET Framework instance can be piped to Get-Member, and the cmdlet will show you what you're dealing with. This applies only to instances, not to static classes; running [System.Math] | Get-Member won't produce useful output.

For example, we'll create an instance of the System.IO.DriveInfo class, pointing it to our C: drive, and then ask Get-Member to show us the instance's members:

```
PS C:\> $drive = New-Object -TypeName System.IO.DriveInfo -ArgumentList 'C:'
PS C:\> $drive | Get-Member


    TypeName: System.IO.DriveInfo

Name               MemberType Definition
----               ---------- ----------
Equals             Method     bool Equals(System.Object obj)
GetHashCode        Method     int GetHashCode()
GetObjectData      Method     System.Void GetObjectData(System.Runtime....
GetType            Method     type GetType()
ToString           Method     string ToString()
AvailableFreeSpace Property   long AvailableFreeSpace {get;}
DriveFormat        Property   string DriveFormat {get;}
DriveType          Property   System.IO.DriveType DriveType {get;}
IsReady            Property   bool IsReady {get;}
Name               Property   string Name {get;}
RootDirectory      Property   System.IO.DirectoryInfo RootDirectory {get;}
TotalFreeSpace     Property   long TotalFreeSpace {get;}
TotalSize          Property   long TotalSize {get;}
VolumeLabel        Property   string VolumeLabel {get;set;}
```

This same information is available on the class's documentation page at http://msdn.microsoft.com/en-us/library/system.io.driveinfo, but being able to access it from within the shell is convenient.

22.5   *Finding class documentation*

Google, Bing, or some other search engine is your best bet for finding .NET Framework documentation. You can also start at http://msdn.microsoft.com/en-us/library/gg145045, which is the top-level page (at the time of this writing) for the entire Framework's documentation library.

Figure 22.1 shows a portion of one class's documentation page. As you can see, the top of the page lists the class name (Math, part of the System namespace), and we've

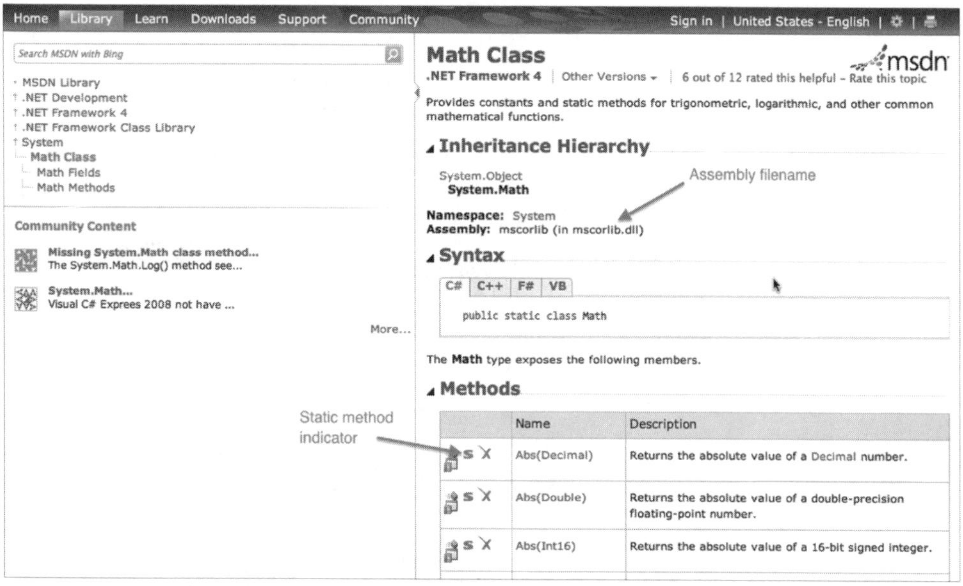

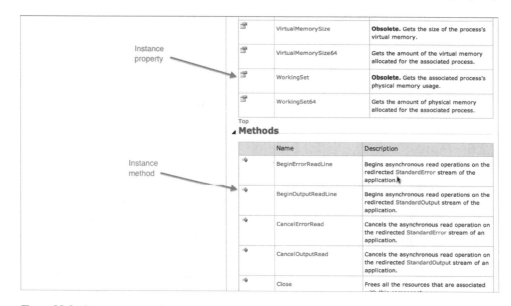

Figure 22.1   Finding a class's assembly name and its static methods

highlighted a static member of the class. The big *S* icon next to the method name tells us that this is a static method; we could click the method name to learn more about how to use it.

In figure 22.2, we've switched to the `System.Diagnostics` namespace and the `Process` class contained therein. We've highlighted both an instance property

Figure 22.2   Instance properties and methods

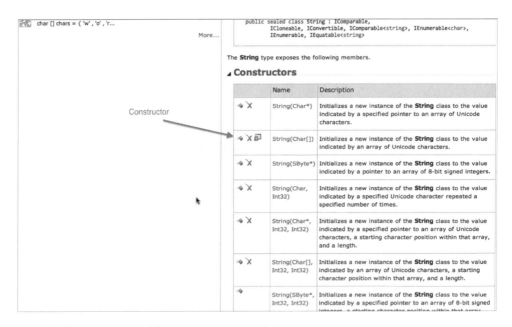

Figure 22.3   Constructors of the `System.String` class

(`WorkingSet`) and an instance method (`BeginOutputReadLine()`). Remember that both of these are accessible only from an active instance of the class, rather than as static members.

Finally, in figure 22.3 we're showing the `System.String` class and highlighting some of its constructors. These constructors provide various ways of creating a new instance of the class.

If the documentation looks a little programmer-ish, well, it's supposed to. Remember, we've left the comfortable confines of PowerShell and ventured into the programmers' world. We're using their stuff, so we have to read their docs.

Note that there are more than a few versions of the .NET Framework out there; PowerShell v3 uses Framework v4, so you'll often want to look specifically at documentation for version 4.

22.6   *PowerShell vs. Visual Studio*

The more extensively you use the .NET Framework, the less efficient PowerShell becomes at helping you do so. That's because PowerShell wasn't designed as a .NET development environment; Microsoft offers Visual Studio for that. If you find that you need to borrow a bit of the Framework in a PowerShell script, you're probably fine; if you're looking at a PowerShell script that's grown to hundreds of lines and consists mainly of Framework stuff, you'd probably have an easier time switching to Visual Studio and embracing C# or another .NET language (like Visual Basic). We've seen administrators crank out hundreds of lines of what is essentially simplified C# code (PowerShell's syntax is, after all, based in part on C# syntax), offering the excuse, "I don't have time to learn C#." The time savings Visual Studio could have offered them would have more than made up for the learning curve. Visual Studio offers a development environment, tools, debugging experience, and so on that are specifically designed for working with .NET.

This is something we want you to keep in mind. If working with .NET in PowerShell seems a bit tricky sometimes, it's because PowerShell wasn't ever designed to make that a super-smooth experience. The ability to access the Framework from PowerShell is something you should think of as bonus functionality, not PowerShell's primary mission.

22.7 *Lab*

The .NET Framework contains a class named `Dns`, which lives within the `System.Net` namespace. Read its documentation at http://msdn.microsoft.com/en-us/library/system.net.dns. Pay special attention to the static `GetHostEntry()` method. Use this method to return the IP address of www.MoreLunches.com.

Part 4

Creating tools for
delegated administration

In this last part of the book, we're going to look at toolmaking from one of its most common use cases: delegated administration. We're going to show you how to build tools that are intended for less-technical or less-privileged users. Whether you're deploying a GUI-based tool to end users or setting up delegated administration for your organization's help desk, these techniques are ones you'll use again and again.

These techniques get more complex than what we've covered up to this point, and they draw on a wide range of technologies that are technically outside of PowerShell itself. We're going to stick with our mission of not trying to be comprehensive but rather of focusing on the basics and helping you understand them thoroughly. These chapters will leave plenty of room for further independent exploration, but we'll make sure you know enough to be effective at that.

Creating a GUI tool, part 1: the GUI

In this chapter and the two after it, we're going to show you how to use PowerShell to build a graphical user interface (GUI) application, suitable for distribution to end users. Note that there's no way to compile this into an executable that doesn't need PowerShell in order to run, but we'll be able to make this look a lot like a real Windows application.

Before writing this chapter, we thought long and hard about what directions to take, because when it comes to building a GUI we have several. We decided to use Windows Forms (WinForms), one of two .NET Framework GUI systems. We also decided, for the most part, to rely on a commercial tool named PowerShell Studio (http://primaltools.com) to build this GUI application. We won't belabor the reasons behind those decisions here; we'd rather get on with the task at hand. But you should understand our reasoning and your other options, so we've written a brief appendix to this book, which you'll find online at http://www.manning.com/LearnPowerShellToolmakinginaMonthofLunches. There we explain the different choices we were faced with and why we went the way we did. We realize that there's a financial investment with PowerShell Studio, but we assume most of our readers are IT professionals working in a corporate environment, where presumably there's a budget for tools to do your job.

23.1   *Introduction to WinForms*

WinForms is the older of Microsoft's two GUI systems in the .NET Framework. It was joined in .NET v3.5 by Windows Presentation Foundation (WPF), which is an independent system. WPF doesn't replace WinForms, but it does offer somewhat more modern capabilities. We find WinForms to be simpler to work with, so that's what we decided to use.

WinForms applications are based on the idea of a *form*, or window. Each window in your application—a dialog box, an output screen, or whatever—is a form. Each item on a form is referred to as a *control*, and they might include things like buttons, labels, text boxes, radio buttons, check boxes, and all of the other familiar Windows GUI elements.

Each form and control has a variety of *properties* that control their appearance and in some regards their behavior. Controls are just a kind of object, much like the objects produced by PowerShell commands. Like objects, they have properties. They also have *events*, which represent things that can happen to the control. For example, clicking a button *fires* a specific event for that control. We can attach PowerShell commands as *event handlers*, and WinForms will execute those commands in response to the event. That's how we'll make our form interactive.

Forms and controls are created by *instantiating* an instance of their respective class. Once you have an instance of a control, you can set its properties and attach event handlers. Controls are given *names*, which enable you to refer to them more easily. In PowerShell, we'll store the controls in a variable, so that referring to them is easier yet. The controls on a form include properties that tell WinForms where to position the control on the form. By manipulating those properties, you can create the exact layout that you need.

We should point out that we're not going to try to make you a WinForms expert in this series of three chapters—we'd need an entire book for that. Our goal is to introduce you to the technology and its techniques through a simple example, as a way of getting you started. From there, you can continue to learn and explore on your own. We suggest Microsoft's own MSDN Library as a great reference to WinForms; visit http://msdn.microsoft.com/en-us/library/cc656767 for the WinForms Portal.

23.2   *Using a GUI to create the GUI*

It's entirely possible to create a GUI using nothing more than PowerShell's native ISE editor, but it's a huge pain in the neck. We're going to show you how to do that anyway, but we're going to start with a tool that takes most of the pain out of the process. That tool, PowerShell Studio, is a commercial tool, meaning you have to pay for it. It does have a free 45-day trial, so we're hoping that'll be sufficient to get you through this book. Its maker, SAPIEN Technologies, also offers a free community edition of the tool's predecessor, PrimalForms. That version is a bit less functional, but if you're only worried about creating simple scripts that utilize a single form (window), then it'll probably do a great job for you. In this series of chapters, we'll be relying on Power-Shell Studio 2012; if you're using a different version, then expect your screen shots to be at least somewhat different.

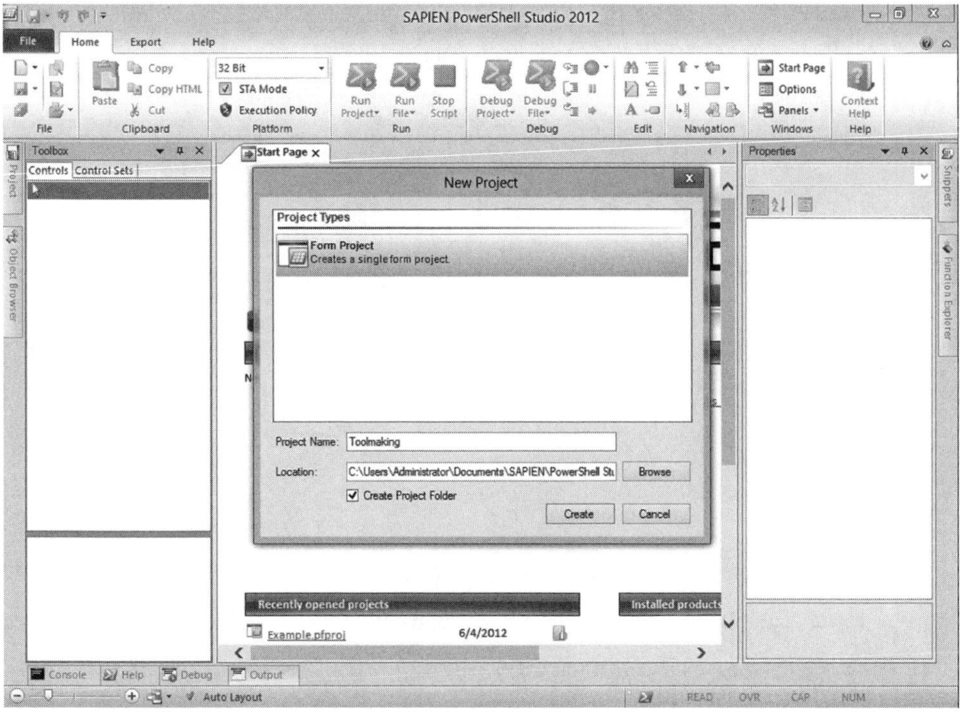

Figure 23.1   Starting a new forms project in PowerShell Studio

As shown in figure 23.1, we'll start by creating a new forms project. This gives us a basic, blank form to start with.

TRY IT NOW   We strongly encourage you to follow along with this step-by-step demonstration. Doing so will give you a better feel for the toolset and help get you working on your own projects a lot more quickly.

We'll then customize the form a bit. We won't bother resizing it right now—we'll wait until we get some controls in place to do that—but we will configure some of its other appearances and behaviors. Using the Properties list on the right-hand side of the application, we'll set the following:

- `FormBorderStyle` to `FixedDialog`—This makes a non-resizable form, although we'll still be able to adjust the size we want while we're designing it.
- `MinimizeBox` and `MaximizeBox` to `False`—These remove the window title bar's minimize and maximize buttons but leave the close button.
- `StartPosition` to `CenterScreen`—This controls where the form appears when it first opens.
- `Text` to "Toolmaking Demo"—This customizes the text in the window title bar.

TIP   It's often easier if you change the Property list to list properties alphabetically, by clicking the A-Z button just above the list.

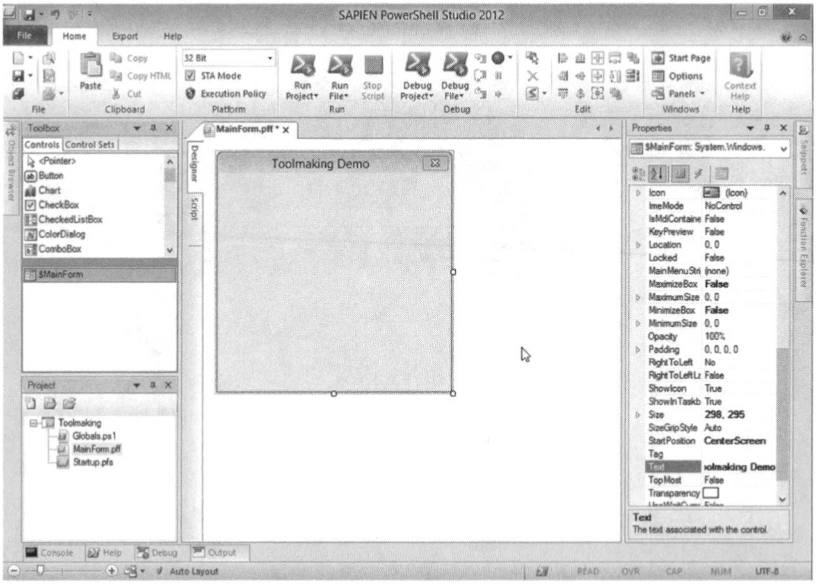

Figure 23.2   Our WinForms project so far, with the form appearance customized

Figure 23.2 shows the form so far.

Now we'll add some controls, as shown in figure 23.3. We've added two Labels, a TextBox, a ComboBox, and a Button. These were dragged out of the Toolbox, which is on the left-hand side of the application's window.

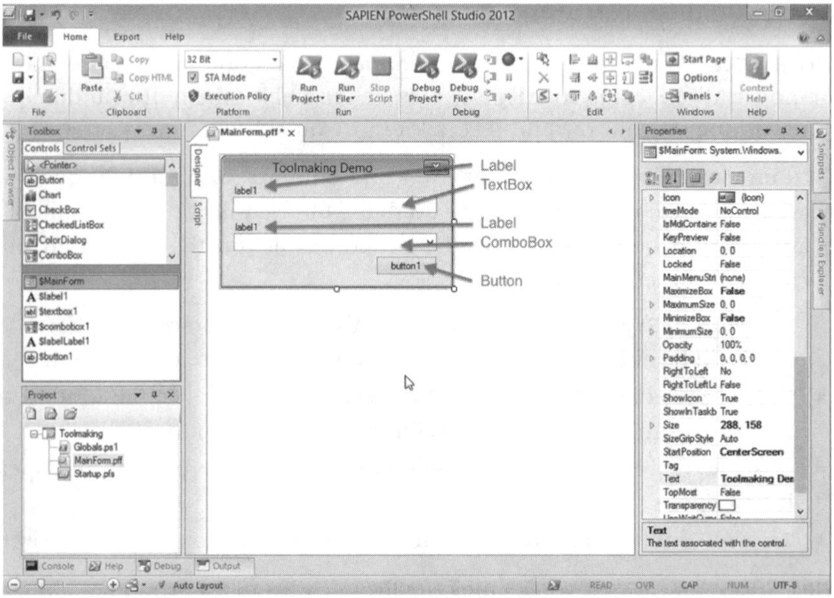

Figure 23.3   Laying out the controls on the form

Now we need to adjust the properties of these controls.

- First `Label`:
  - Set Text to "Enter computer name:"
- `TextBox`:
  - Set Name to "ComputerName"
- Second `Label`:
  - Set Text to "Select Event Log:"
  - Set Visible to False
- `ComboBox`:
  - Set Name to "EventLogName"
  - Set DropDownStyle to "DropDownList"
  - Set Visible to False
- `Button`:
  - Set Name to "OKButton"
  - Set Text to "OK"

Figure 23.4 shows the revised form layout.

That's basically all we need to do! We'll make sure to save the project at this point, so that we don't lose anything if something goes wrong, but the overall form design is done. Note that we did need to think about what this would do, and we haven't shared that design process with you because we're focusing now on the mechanics of getting this done.

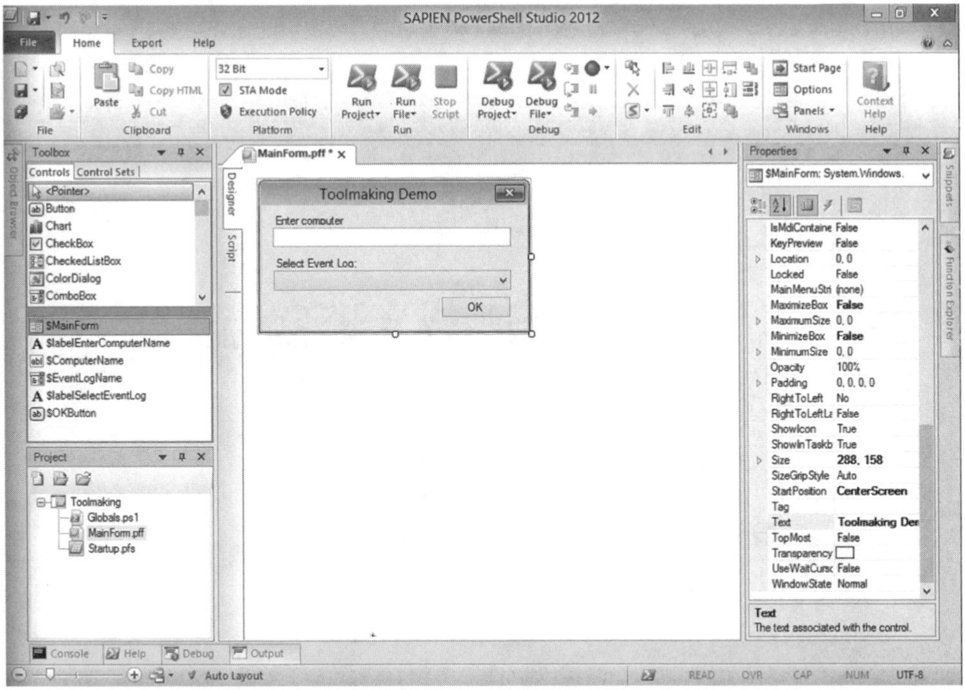

Figure 23.4 Finalizing the form design

23.3   *Manually coding the GUI*

The neat thing about PowerShell Studio is that it can create the PowerShell script needed to implement the GUI we've designed. We used its Export to Clipboard File option to create the script shown in figure 23.5.

This script is massive: almost 230 lines are required just to create the simple GUI that we designed. We're not going to list the entire thing here, but we do want to call your attention to a few snippets. First is the section that loads the .NET Framework pieces required to create the GUI:

```
[void] [reflection.assembly] ::Load("System, Version=2.0.0.0,
  Culture=neutral, PublicKeyToken=b77a5c561934e089")
[void] [reflection.assembly] ::Load("System.Windows.Forms, Version=2.0.0.0,
  Culture=neutral, PublicKeyToken=b77a5c561934e089")
[void] [reflection.assembly] ::Load("System.Drawing, Version=2.0.0.0,
  Culture=neutral, PublicKeyToken=b03f5f7f11d50a3a")
[void] [reflection.assembly] ::Load("mscorlib, Version=2.0.0.0,
  Culture=neutral, PublicKeyToken=b77a5c561934e089")
[void] [reflection.assembly] ::Load("System.Data, Version=2.0.0.0,
  Culture=neutral, PublicKeyToken=b77a5c561934e089")
[void] [reflection.assembly] ::Load("System.Xml, Version=2.0.0.0,
  Culture=neutral, PublicKeyToken=b77a5c561934e089")
[void] [reflection.assembly] ::Load("System.DirectoryServices,
  Version=2.0.0.0, Culture=neutral, PublicKeyToken=b03f5f7f11d50a3a")
```

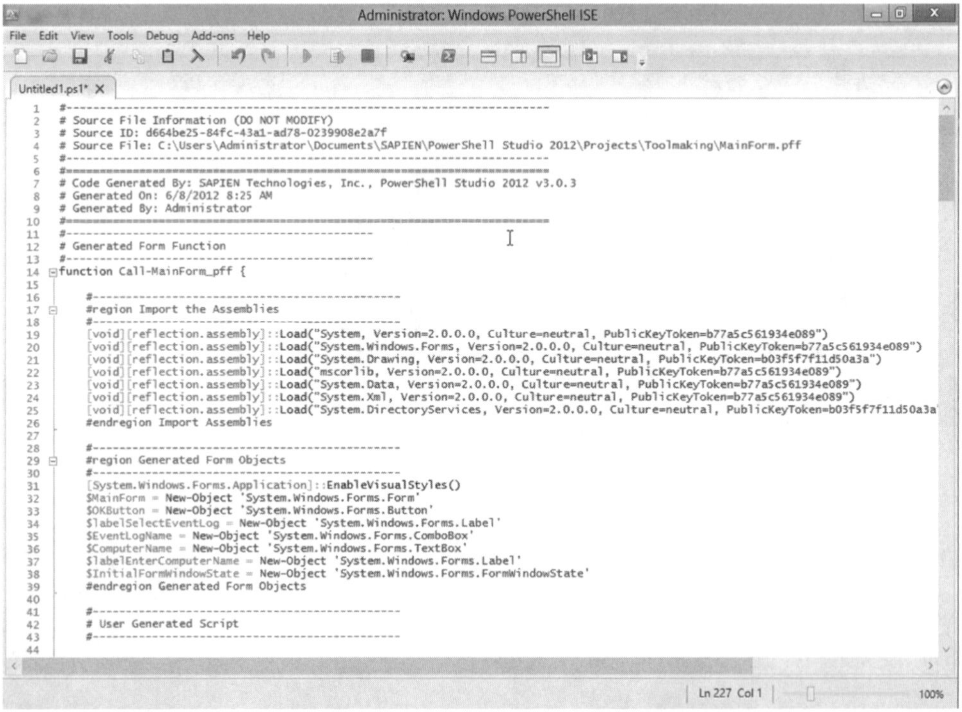

Figure 23.5   Here's how the GUI gets created in code, rather than in a GUI designer tool.

Next is the code to create the various GUI elements we designed. Notice that the variable names reflect the Name property that we assigned in PowerShell Studio. Our button, for example, is represented by $OKButton and our text box by $ComputerName. The elements for which we didn't assign a specific name have been given generic names, such as $LabelSelectEventLog.

```
[System.Windows.Forms.Application]::EnableVisualStyles()
$MainForm = New-Object 'System.Windows.Forms.Form'
$OKButton = New-Object 'System.Windows.Forms.Button'
$labelSelectEventLog = New-Object 'System.Windows.Forms.Label'
$EventLogName = New-Object 'System.Windows.Forms.ComboBox'
$ComputerName = New-Object 'System.Windows.Forms.TextBox'
$labelEnterComputerName = New-Object 'System.Windows.Forms.Label'
$InitialFormWindowState = New-Object
  'System.Windows.Forms.FormWindowState'
```

Finally, there are several sections that assign our initial property values. Here, for example, are the properties for the main form and for our button:

```
#
# MainForm
#
$MainForm.Controls.Add($OKButton)
$MainForm.Controls.Add($labelSelectEventLog)
$MainForm.Controls.Add($EventLogName)
$MainForm.Controls.Add($ComputerName)
$MainForm.Controls.Add($labelEnterComputerName)
$MainForm.ClientSize = '282, 129'
$MainForm.FormBorderStyle = 'FixedDialog'
$MainForm.MaximizeBox = $False
$MainForm.MinimizeBox = $False
$MainForm.Name = "MainForm"
$MainForm.StartPosition = 'CenterScreen'
$MainForm.Text = "Toolmaking Demo"
$MainForm.add_Load($OnLoadFormEvent)
#
# OKButton
#
$OKButton.Location = '190, 94'
$OKButton.Name = "OKButton"
$OKButton.Size = '75, 23'
$OKButton.TabIndex = 4
$OKButton.Text = "OK"
$OKButton.UseVisualStyleBackColor = $True
```

That's exactly what hand-coding this GUI would look like. As you can see, it's pretty extensive. There's also a lot of trial and error involved, especially around the controls' Location and Size properties. To be blunt, we've done this hand-coded stuff before, and we'll never do it again. The price for PowerShell Studio is more than fair considering how much time we've wasted trying to hand-code these little things in the past.

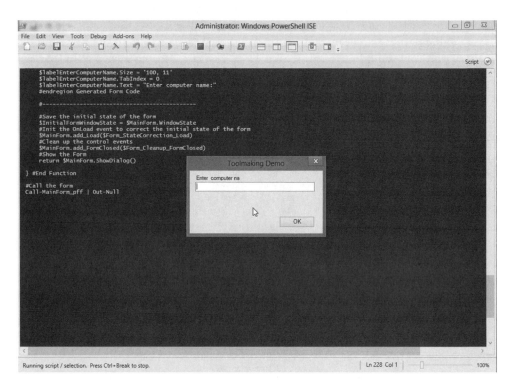

Figure 23.6   Running the GUI-based script for the first time

23.4   *Showing the GUI*

Showing the GUI is a simple matter of running the script. We can do this right within PowerShell Studio, by clicking Run Project on the Home tab of its ribbon. Or, because we've already exported the script to the clipboard and pasted it into the PowerShell ISE, we could run it there. When we do so, we get the display shown in figure 23.6.

Everything isn't perfect. As you can see, our Enter Computer Name: label is cut off a bit. That was visible in PowerShell Studio earlier, and we declined to fix it then. We can go ahead and do that now, while making any other visual tweaks that are needed. Our Select Event Log label, for example, was a bit short, so the bottom of the *g* was getting cut off. That's also easy to fix, by adjusting the label back in PowerShell Studio. After making all of our visual tweaks, we're finished with the form and ready to move on to the code.

TRY IT NOW   We're going to continue building on this GUI example in the next two chapters, so we encourage you to make sure you're following along.

23.5   *Lab*

In this lab you're going to start a project that you'll work with over the next few chapters, so you'll want to make sure you have a working solution before moving on. Developing a graphical PowerShell script is always easier if you have a working command-line script. We've already done that part for you in the following listing.

Listing 23.1   Command-line PowerShell script

```
Function Get-ServiceData {
[cmdletbinding()]
Param(
[parameter(Position=0,Mandatory=$True,HelpMessage="Enter a computername")]
[ValidateNotNullorEmpty()]
[string]$Computername,
[Parameter(Position=1)]
[ValidateSet("Running","Stopped","All","%")]
[string]$Filter="All"
)

Try {
    Write-Verbose "Getting $filter services from $computername"
    if ($Filter -eq "All") {
        $filter='%'
        Write-Verbose "Using WMI filter: state Like '$Filter'"
    }
    $services=Get-WmiObject -Class Win32_Service -ComputerName $Computername
    -filter "State Like '$Filter'"
    #write selected results to the pipeline
    $services | Select Name,Displayname,State,StartMode,StartName
}
Catch {
    Write-Warning "Failed to get services from $Computername.
    $_.Exception.Message"
}

} #end function
```

You can either retype or download the script from MoreLunches.com.

The function takes a computer name as a parameter and gets services via WMI based on user-supplied filter criteria. The function writes a subset of data to the pipeline. From the command line it might be used like this:

```
Get-servicedata $env:computername -filter running | Out-GridView
```

Your task in this lab is to create the graphical form using PowerShell Studio. You should end up with something like the form shown in figure 23.7.

Make the Running radio button checked by default. You'll find it easier later if you put the radio buttons in a GroupBox control, plus it looks cooler. The script you're creating doesn't have to do anything for this lab except display this form.

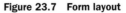

Figure 23.7   Form layout

Creating a GUI tool, part 2: the code

In the previous chapter, we created the graphical user interface for our PowerShell script; in this chapter, we'll start adding the code needed to make that GUI functional. We'll continue working in PowerShell Studio. But everything we're doing will be much more code intensive, meaning you could choose to use the tool just to create the GUI, copy and paste the GUI-creation code into the PowerShell ISE, and then work in the ISE from there.

24.1 *Addressing GUI objects*

When we had PowerShell Studio create the script that implements the GUI, it assigned our GUI controls to variables. Those variables were named based on what we assigned to the Name property of our controls, so our Computername text box is in the $ComputerName variable. For controls we didn't name explicitly, the tool made up a name—often based on the controls' Text property, such as $LabelEnterComputerName. We always make a point to explicitly name any control we plan to work with or have users interact with, so that we can have a concise and sensible variable name.

We'll use those variables to address and access the GUI controls, or objects. When followed by a period, they'll let us access properties, such as $ComputerName.Text, which provides access to whatever was typed in the text box.

24.2 *Example: text boxes*

The text box is a good example. We don't need to worry when the user is doing something with it; we'll just let them type whatever they want. When they're finished, they'll click the OK button, and we'll read the contents of the text box—that is, whatever they typed—by using $ComputerName.Text.

There might be times when you do care about user interaction with a text box; you might, for example, want to be able to take some action as a user is typing. You can definitely do that; just double-click the text box in PowerShell Studio, and you'll open an empty event handler for the text box's Change event, which fires every time the contents of the text box change. Be careful with that, because if from within that event handler you change the contents of the text box, you'll trigger another Change event, which can result in an infinite loop.

> **TIP** If you want a computer name text box to default to the local computer, in the script panel find the form Load function and add a line of code to update the Text value of your control like this:

```
$formMenu_Load={
    #TODO: Initialize Form Controls here
    $Computername.text=$env:computername

}
```

We suggest using the environmental variable instead of localhost because some commands won't recognize localhost as a computer name.

24.3 *Example: button clicks*

The OK button is a bit different. We *do* care about user interactions with that control. We're going to have it do double duty, meaning we'll have users click it once to populate and display our drop-down list box and again to query a list of event log entries.

In PowerShell Studio, we'll double-click the button to create and open an event handler for the button's Click event. This takes us into a code, or script, view, where we can enter the commands we want to run when the button is clicked. For now, we'll put in a few pieces of code, as shown in figure 24.1. But we'll be populating most of this code in the next section when we deal with our list box.

Our code so far looks like this:

```
$OKButton_Click={
    if ($EventLogName.Visible) {
        # retrieve event log
    } else {
        # populate event log list
        $logs = Get-EventLog -ComputerName $ComputerName.Text `
                             -List
    }
}
```

What we're doing is checking the state of our $EventLogName drop-down list box, specifically, the state of its Visible property. If the drop-down list isn't visible (which it isn't to start with, because we set that property to False when we designed the GUI in the previous chapter), then we'll populate the drop-down list with event log names.

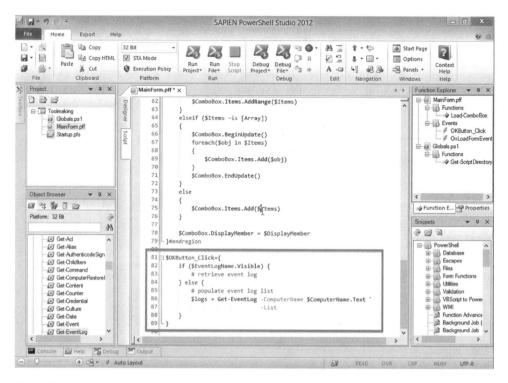

Figure 24.1   Populating the button's `Click` event handler

We'll eventually add code to make the list visible. If the list is visible when OK is clicked, then we'll retrieve the selected event log.

Clicks aren't the only type of event a button can fire. Most controls trigger dozens of events—everything from the mouse moving over the control to various control-specific events like clicks or changes. The point is that you only attach event handlers to the events you care about—those events that you want to have some prepro-grammed response for. In PowerShell Studio, you can right-click any control in the design view, select Add Event, and get a complete list of available events. The MSDN Library (we provided a link in the previous chapter to that) documents what events each control offers and what each event is for.

24.4   *Example: list boxes*

This is the tricky part of our script. Fortunately, PowerShell Studio gives us a helper function that makes it easier to populate our drop-down list. To use that, we'll need to retrieve a list of event log names as plain strings, which we'll store in the variable $logs:

```
$logs = Get-EventLog -ComputerName $ComputerName.Text `
                     -List |
        Select-Object -ExpandProperty Log
```

Note that the -ExpandProperty parameter of Select-Object is crucial here. Normally, Get-EventLog returns a collection of objects, and the event log name is in the Log property of those objects. We need to extract that information so that it's a plain String, because plain Strings are what we need to put into the drop-down list box.

We then call the Load-ComboBox helper function. Again, that's inserted by Power-Shell Studio whenever we include a ComboBox control in our project; this isn't a native PowerShell command. Here's how we'll use that helper function and how we'll make the drop-down list and its label visible afterward:

```
Load-ComboBox -ComboBox $EventLogName `
              -Items $logs
$EventLogName.Visible = $true
$labelSelectEventLog.Visible = $true
```

What if we weren't using PowerShell Studio and didn't have that Load-ComboBox helper function? Populating the list box still isn't that difficult. Again assuming that the list of log names is in the variable $logs, exactly as just shown, we'd do this to populate the list box:

```
Foreach ($log in $logs) {
    $EventLogName.Items.Add($log)
}
```

The key is to try to add only plain Strings to the drop-down list; you can't add any other kind of complex object. If you're working with complex objects, such as the original list of event logs returned by Get-EventLog, you'll have to first extract the desired property contents, which we did using Select-Object –ExpandProperty.

Once the list is populated and visible, the user will be able to select a log and click OK again. We don't want them clicking OK unless a log has been selected from the list; the way to check for that is to look at the drop-down list's SelectedIndex property. It'll be -1 if no item is selected. So we'll build a quick check for that:

```
if ($EventLogName.SelectedIndex -gt -1) {

}
```

That way, if OK is clicked with no item selected, nothing will happen. From there, we need to have the script query the selected log:

```
if ($EventLogName.SelectedIndex -gt -1) {
    $entries = Get-EventLog -ComputerName $ComputerName.Text `
                            -LogName $EventLogName.SelectedItem
}
```

We've used the drop-down list's SelectedItem property to access the text of the currently selected list item. Because we know that's a valid log name (we got if from Get-EventLog, remember), it should work fine. Note that the validity concern is why we changed this from a normal ComboBox to a DropDownList when we designed the GUI. A ComboBox would allow the user to select an item from the list or enter a value of their own. We didn't want that; we wanted to limit their choices to those log names returned by Get-EventLog.

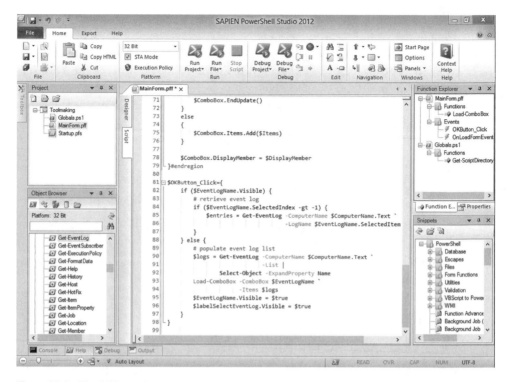

Figure 24.2   The OK button's `Click` event handler

As you can see, we're combining familiar PowerShell commands with the properties of our GUI controls. It takes a bit of getting used to, but with a bit of practice you'll get there.

At this point, we've saved the requested event log entries into the variable $entries, and we're ready to do something with that information. Figure 24.2 shows our OK button's Click event handler so far.

TRY IT NOW   Make sure you're following along. In the next chapter, we'll continue to build on this, so we don't want to lose you!

Here's the complete code (we've truncated it a little):

```
$OKButton_Click={
    if ($EventLogName.Visible) {
        # retrieve event log
        if ($EventLogName.SelectedIndex -gt -1) {
            $entries = Get-EventLog -Computer $ComputerName.Text `
                                    -Log $EventLogName.SelectedItem
        }
    } else {
        # populate event log list
        $logs = Get-EventLog -ComputerName $ComputerName.Text `
                        -List |
```

```
                    Select-Object -ExpandProperty Log
            Load-ComboBox -ComboBox $EventLogName `
                          -Items $logs
            $EventLogName.Visible = $true
            $labelSelectEventLog.Visible = $true
        }
    }
```

NOTE If you're using PowerShell Studio, make sure you download the sample code for this book from http://MoreLunches.com. We've included the complete PowerShell Studio project file for the completed project, so you can pop it open and run it for yourself.

24.5 Example: radio buttons

The example we've been working with doesn't need them, but we want to make sure you see a few more controls in action that you're likely to use. First are radio buttons. A radio button is a set of mutually exclusive choices. By that we mean that only one radio button can be checked at a time. The control has a Checked property that you can test or set. The value is either $True or $False. Here's a sample form in figure 24.3.

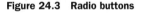

Figure 24.3 Radio buttons

We recommend setting a default radio button for your form. To use, test each radio button to see if it is checked. Here's a code sample that goes behind this form:

```
$buttonOK_Click={
    #TODO: Place custom script here
    if ($radiobuttonServices.Checked) {
        $Title="Services for $($computername.Text)"
        Get-Service -ComputerName $Computername.Text | Out-GridView -Title
➥ $Title
    }
    elseif ($radiobuttonProcesses.Checked) {
        $Title="Processes for $($computername.Text)"
        Get-Process -ComputerName $Computername.Text | Out-GridView -Title
➥ $Title
    }
    elseif ($radiobuttonDiskSpace.Checked) {
        $Title="DiskSpace for $($computername.Text)"
        Get-WMIObject -Class Win32_LogicalDisk -Filter "DriveType=3" -
    ComputerName $Computername.Text |
        Select DeviceID,Size,Freespace,Volume Out-GridView -Title $Title
    }
    else {
        #this should never happen
        Write-Warning "Failed to determine what radio button is checked"
    }

}
```

Remember we said that you can have only one radio button checked at a time? That's per form or grouping. If you have a set of radio buttons, you can add a `GroupBox` control and drop your radio buttons into it. Within the grouping you can only have one radio button checked. Figure 24.4 demonstrates what this might look like.

You still need to test the `Checked` property of each radio button control.

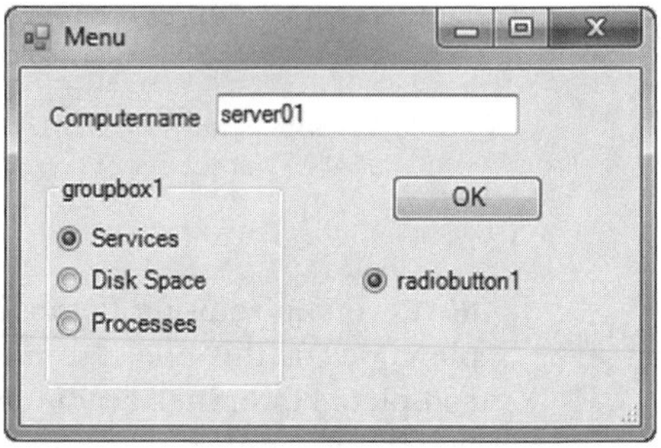

Figure 24.4   **Grouped radio buttons**

24.6   *Example: check boxes*

Another similar control is the check box. Whereas radio buttons are mutually exclusive, you can have as many boxes checked as you'd like. These too have a `Checked` property that you can set and test. Figure 24.5 illustrates what a check box form might look like.

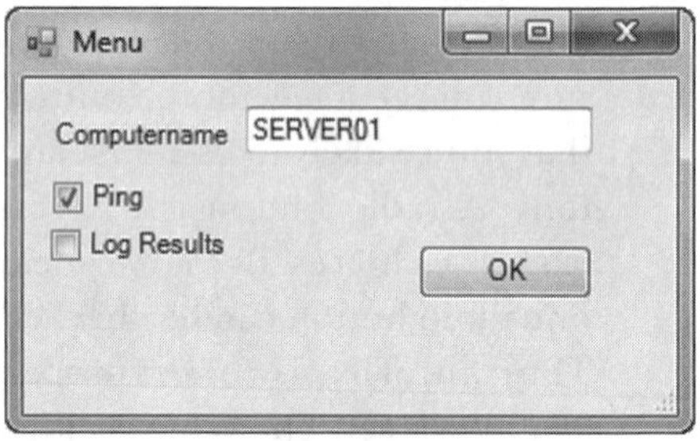

As with radio buttons, you can test the `Checked` property and respond accordingly.

Figure 24.5   **Check boxes**

```
$buttonOK_Click={
    #TODO: Place custom script here
    if ($checkboxPing.Checked) {
      if (Test-Connection -ComputerName $Computername.Text -Quiet) {
          $pinged=$true
        }
      else {
          Write-Warning "Failed to ping $($computername.text)"
          $pinged=$False
      }
    }
    else {
        #don't test ping, assume we can.
        $pinged=$True
    }

    If ($pinged) {
    $data=Get-WmiObject -Class Win32_ComputerSystem -ComputerName
     $Computername.Text
    }
    if ($checkboxLogResults.Checked) {
        $export=Join-Path -Path "$env:userprofile\documents" -ChildPath
➥  "$($Computername.Text)-CS.xml"
        $data | Export-Clixml -Path $export
        Get-Item $export | out-gridview
```

```
    }
    else {
        $data | out-gridview
    }
}
```

For complex forms, you can also drop check boxes into GroupBox controls.

> **NOTE** PowerShell Studio obviously offers more controls than we can cover here. You can right-click a control and get help on it. The Help menu also has a link to a number of samples, so you can see many of these controls in action.

24.7 Lab

In this lab you're going to continue where you left off in chapter 23. If you didn't finish, please do so first or download the sample solution from MoreLunches.com. Now you need to wire up your form and put some actions behind the controls.

First, set the Computername text box so that it defaults to the actual local computer name. Don't use localhost.

> **TIP** Look for the form's Load event function.

Then, connect the OK button so that it runs the Get-ServiceData function from the lab in chapter 23 and pipes the results to the pipeline. You can modify the function if you want. Use the form controls to pass parameters to the function.

> **TIP** You can avoid errors if you set the default behavior to search for running services.

You can test your form by sending output to Out-String and then Write-Host. For example, in your form you could end up with a line like this:

```
<code to get data> | Out-String | Write-Host
```

In the next chapter you'll learn better ways to handle form output.

Creating a GUI tool, part 3: the output

In the previous two chapters, we showed you how to create a GUI and add functionality to it. In this chapter, we'll take that functionality and use it to create some output for the application's user. We'll focus on two techniques: the easy, built-in way of generically displaying output and the harder, more customized way of building your own output form.

25.1 Using Out-GridView

We'll start by using the `Out-GridView` cmdlet, which will be available on any computer that has the PowerShell ISE installed. We'll make one minor change to our application's OK button handler; the complete handler is listed here:

```
$OKButton_Click={
    if ($EventLogName.Visible) {
        # retrieve event log
        if ($EventLogName.SelectedIndex -gt -1) {
            $entries = Get-EventLog -Computer $ComputerName.Text `
                                    -Log $EventLogName.SelectedItem
            $entries | Out-GridView
        }
    } else {
        # populate event log list
        $logs = Get-EventLog -ComputerName $ComputerName.Text `
                        -List |
                Select-Object -ExpandProperty Log
        Load-ComboBox -ComboBox $EventLogName `
                        -Items $logs
        $EventLogName.Visible = $true
        $labelSelectEventLog.Visible = $true
    }
}
```

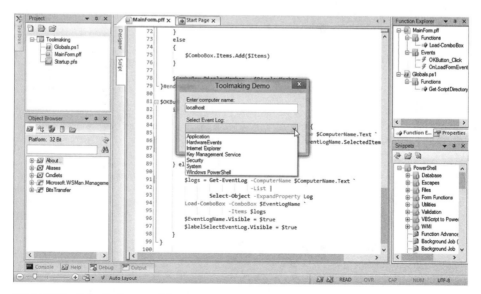

Figure 25.1 Running our script displays the first form.

We've piped $entries to Out-GridView. We could have piped the output of Get-EventLog directly to Out-GridView, but having the log entries in the $entries variable will make it easier for us to demonstrate the next output technique. Now we'll run our script for the first time, by clicking Run Project inside PowerShell Studio. Figure 25.1 shows the first form that appears.

We'll enter "localhost" and click OK. As shown in figure 25.2, we're then given a drop-down list of all available application logs from that computer. We'll select Application, and click OK a second time.

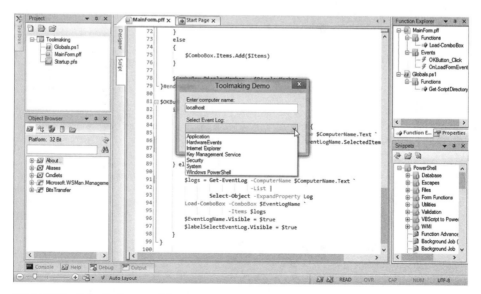

Figure 25.2 Selecting an event log

Finally, figure 25.3 shows what Out-GridView does: It displays our output in a sortable, filterable, interactive grid. We think this is a great way to display even complex output to end users, because it lets them continue to work with the data and requires zero effort on our part!

Now for some troubleshooting notes:

- PowerShell Studio can run scripts in one of two modes on a 64-bit system: 32-bit and 64-bit. On our 64-bit Windows 8 computer, we needed to run the script in 64-bit mode in order for Out-GridView to work. You can choose this mode using a drop-down list in the Home tab of PowerShell Studio.

- The Get-EventLog cmdlet requires the Remote Registry Service on remote computers (even if you're connecting to localhost), which was disabled on our Windows 8 computer. We had to enable and start the service in order for the cmdlet to work. When we didn't, we got an error when trying to populate the drop-down list.

- If User Account Control (UAC) is on, you may need to run your scripts in Elevated mode. That's also chosen from the drop-down list on PowerShell Studio's Home tab.

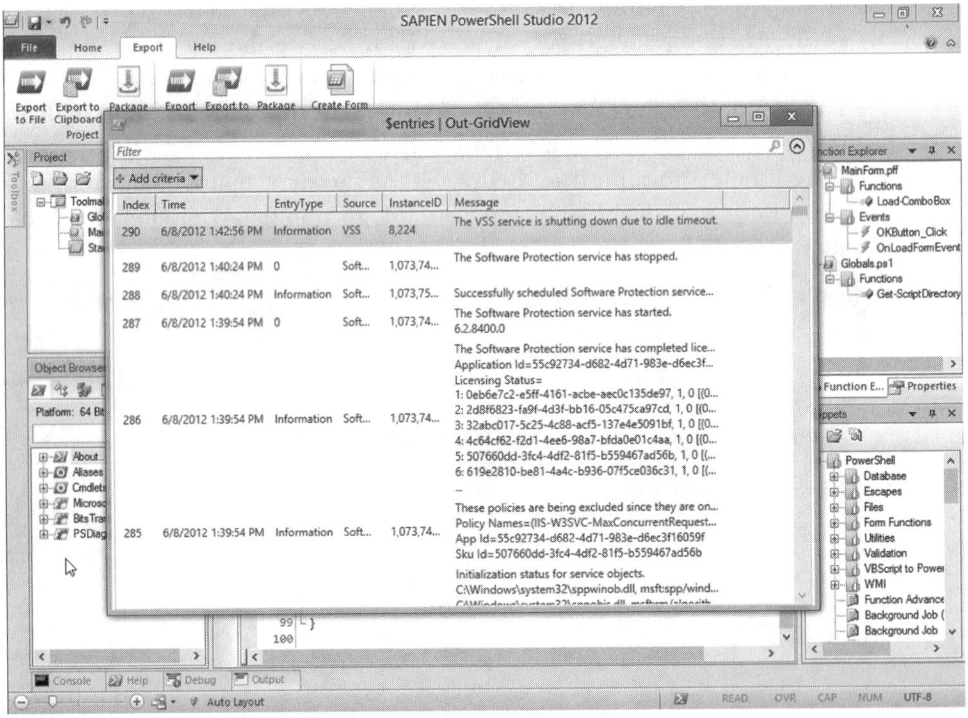

Figure 25.3   The results, shown in Out-GridView

25.2 Creating a form for output

If you choose not to use Out-GridView, or if it isn't suitable for your needs, then you'll need to "roll your own" output form. To continue our example, we're going to comment out the Out-GridView command in our OK button's event handler:

```
$OKButton_Click={
    if ($EventLogName.Visible) {
        # retrieve event log
        if ($EventLogName.SelectedIndex -gt -1) {
            $entries = Get-EventLog -Computer $ComputerName.Text `
                                    -Log $EventLogName.SelectedItem
            # $entries | Out-GridView
        }
    } else {
        # populate event log list
        $logs = Get-EventLog -ComputerName $ComputerName.Text `
                            -List |
                Select-Object -ExpandProperty Log
        Load-ComboBox -ComboBox $EventLogName `
                     -Items $logs
        $EventLogName.Visible = $true
        $labelSelectEventLog.Visible = $true
    }
}
```

That way, we can take an entirely new approach. We're going to construct a second form inside our PowerShell Studio project. This form will also be a fixed dialog box, and it'll just display the computer name and the number of event log entries that were found in the specified log. In figure 25.4, you'll see that we used the File tab to open the New menu, selecting New Form.

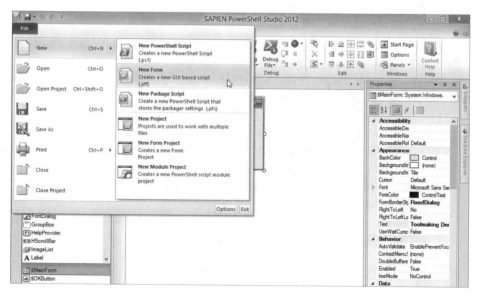

Figure 25.4   Creating a new form for our project

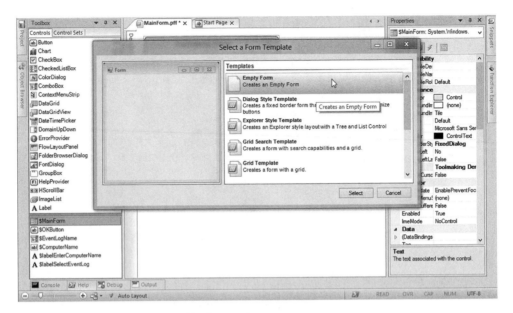

Figure 25.5   Selecting the template for the new form

Figure 25.5 shows that PowerShell Studio offers a number of ready-made form templates. We'll start with a blank one.

We'll set the following properties for the form:

- Name: Results
- ControlBox: False
- FormBorderStyle: FixedDialog
- Text: Results

Next, we'll add three labels and a button to the form, which is shown in figure 25.6. You'll notice that we changed the TextAlign property of all three labels to MiddleCenter. We also named them (from top to bottom) ComputerNameLabel, LogNameLabel, EventCountLabel. We named the button OKButton2, and set its Text property to OK. We saved everything to be safe.

It's important to remember that each form in our project gets bundled into its own standalone function, and these functions are bundled together into the final script. Because each function has its own scope, no one form can "see" anything from inside the other forms. That can make it a bit tricky to move data from one form to another, but that's what we'll show you how to do next.

First, we need to add our new Results form to our Toolmaking project. Because we created the new form from the File tab, it was created as a standalone file. So now, in the application's Project Explorer (on the left), we'll right-click our Toolmaking project and select Add Existing File, as shown in figure 25.7.

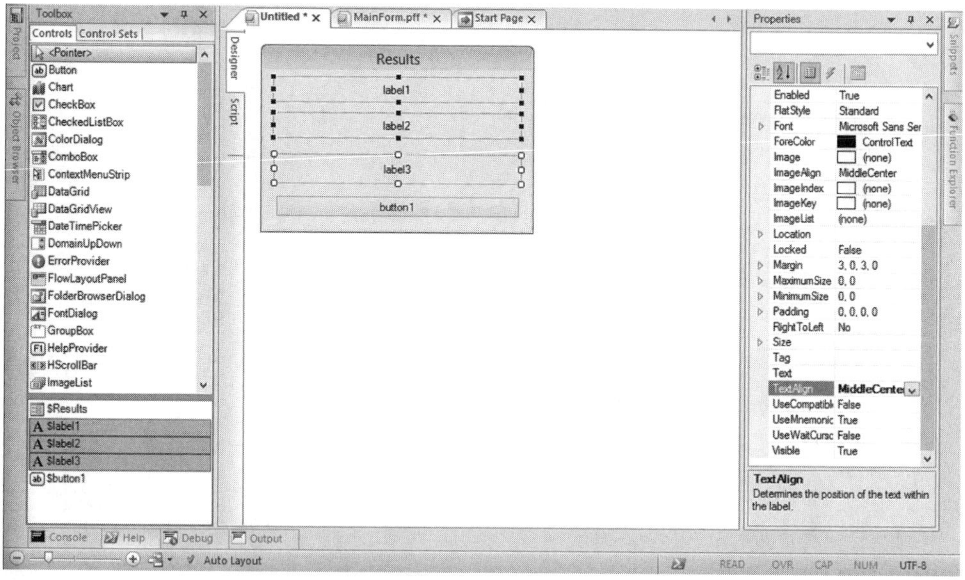

Figure 25.6 Adding controls to the form

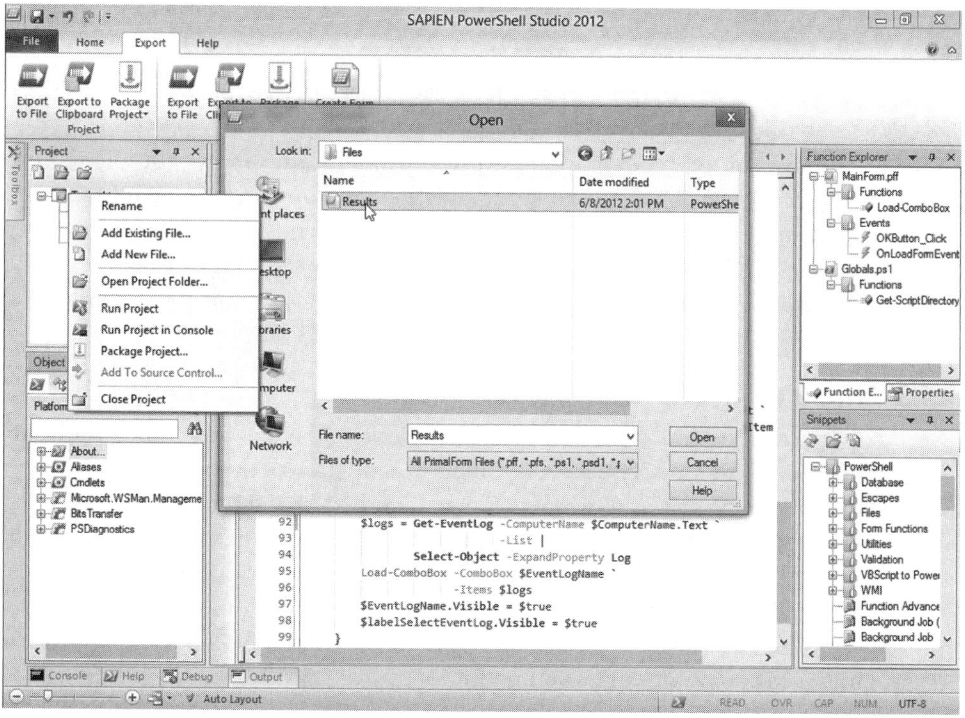

Figure 25.7 Adding the Results form file to our Toolmaking project

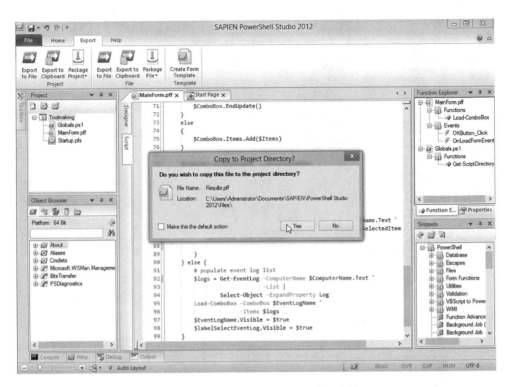

Figure 25.8   Copying the Results form file to the Toolmaking project folder

As shown in figure 25.8, we'll also select the option to have the file copied into the project's folder. That way, all of the files are contained in a single folder, which is more convenient. Now, we certainly could have created the form right within the project to begin with, by right-clicking the Toolmaking project folder inside PowerShell Studio and selecting Add New File from there. But the way we did it is a common approach, and we wanted to make sure you know how to deal with it.

25.3   *Populating and showing the output*

Our script, should we export the entire project to a .PS1 script file, would now consist of three functions. The Main() function is what gets the script up and running and displays the initial form window. That's handled by the Call-MainForm_pff function. A second function, Call-Results_pff, now implements the new Results form. Because all three of these functions live within the script, they can "see" each other, although they can't see *inside* each other. Our Results form and all of its controls don't even exist until Call-Results_pff is called, so that'll be the first thing we have to do in our main OK button event handler:

```
$OKButton_Click={
    if ($EventLogName.Visible) {
        # retrieve event log
        if ($EventLogName.SelectedIndex -gt -1) {
```

```
                $entries = Get-EventLog -Computer $ComputerName.Text `
                                     -Log $EventLogName.SelectedItem
              #$entries | Out-GridView
              Call-Results_pff
          }
      } else {
          # populate event log list
          $logs = Get-EventLog -ComputerName $ComputerName.Text `
                            -List |
                  Select-Object -ExpandProperty Log
          Load-ComboBox -ComboBox $EventLogName `
                        -Items $logs
          $EventLogName.Visible = $true
          $labelSelectEventLog.Visible = $true
      }
  }
```

Doing that instantly shows the form as well, which doesn't look so good right now because we haven't populated it. The trick will be to somehow pass our information into the new function, so that the Results form can "see" the information we want it to use. There are a lot of ways in which we could do that, but we're going to do it by opening the Globals.ps1 file that PowerShell Studio automatically created in our project. At the top, we'll declare a new variable named `$global_events` and set it to be an empty array. Figure 25.9 shows this addition.

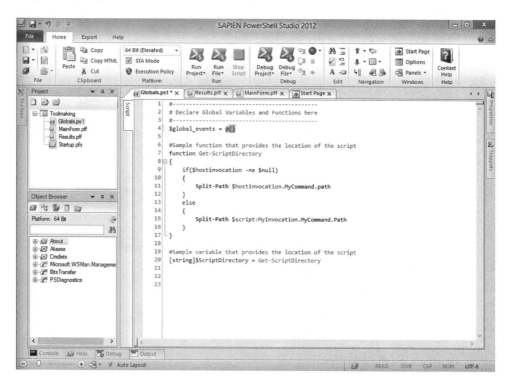

Figure 25.9 Adding the `$global_events` variable to Globals.ps1 in our project

Figure 25.10   Putting the event log results into the new global variable

Back in our OK button event handler, we'll now put the results of Get-EventLog into $global_events instead of $entries. Figure 25.10 shows this modification.

Because $global_events is global, it'll be visible to our Results form, too. There's already an event handler in the Results form's script that will run when the form is loaded. Figure 25.11 shows what we've added to it.

Figure 25.11   Populating the Results form's Load event handler

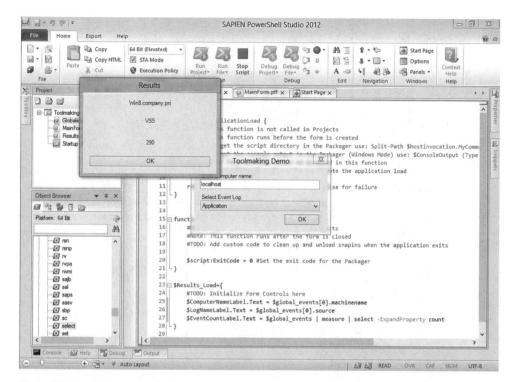

Figure 25.12   A quick test run of the new script

We'll run this quickly to see what it's looking like, and figure 25.12 shows the results.

Because we haven't yet added code to our OK button on the Results form, we have to use the red Stop Script button in PowerShell Studio to close the script. Right now, we have another problem, too. We were able to pull the computer name from the event log entries, but the entries themselves don't contain any record of what log they're from. We populated the second label with the Source property of an event, but that didn't turn out to be the log name. Here's what we'll need to do to finish this project:

- Create a new variable, $global_logname, in Globals.ps1.
- In the OK event handler in the main form, set $global_logname equal to $EventLogName.SelectedItem prior to running Call-Results_pff.
- In the Results form's Load event handler, use $global_logname to set $LogNameLabel.Text.
- Add a Click event handler for the Results form's OK button, and add $Results.Close() to it.

TIP   To see all of these changes, download this book's sample scripts from MoreLunches.com. We've provided the original PowerShell Studio files for this project as well as the complete chapter 25 script, which you can run as is from PowerShell or the PowerShell ISE. If you open that script in the ISE, you can also see the exact code we added to finish this project.

In-form options

If you don't want to create additional forms, there are several controls you can use within the form itself to display your results. You can use a `Label` control for a simple one-line result. Just set the `Text` property.

```
$labelDeviceID.Text=$data.deviceID
$labelFreespace.Text=$data.FreeGB
$labelSize.Text=$data.SizeGB
$labelVolume.Text=$data.Volumename
```

You could use a `RichTextBox` control. This control has some interesting visual properties you can experiment with. If you use this control, set the font to a fixed-width font like Consolas, especially if you want to display PowerShell output. Both of these controls expect strings, so you might need to reformat any PowerShell output by piping it to `Out-String`.

```
#clear any existing text box values
$RichTextBoxResults.Clear()
$data=<my command>
$RichTextBoxResults.Text=$data | Out-String
```

The last option, although the most complicated of the bunch, is a `DataGridView` control. This is like what you get when you pipe results to `Out-Gridview`, except the table is in your form. You put data in the control via its `DataSource` property, which is an array of binding values. Fortunately, PowerShell Studio has a helper function called `Load-DataGridView` that makes it easier to populate it. Here's a code snippet of what that might look like:

```
#clear the grid
    $datagridview1.ClearSelection()
    #get data
    $data=Get-WmiObject Win32_LogicalDisk -Filter "drivetype=3"
        -ComputerName $Computername.Text |
    Select "DeviceID",@{Name="SizeGB";Expression={"{0:N2}" -f ($_.Size/
        1GB)}},
    @{Name="FreeGB";Expression={"{0:N2}" -f ($_.Freespace/
        1GB)}},"VolumeName"
    #add the data to the control
    Load-DataGridView -DataGridView $datagridview1 -Item $data
```

You'll find demo PowerShell Studio project files for these controls on MoreLunches.com.

25.4   Lab

We'll keep things pretty simple for this lab. Using the PowerShell Studio lab project from chapter 24, add a `RichTextBox` control to display the results. Here are some things to remember:

- Configure the control to use a fixed-width font like Consolas or Courier New.
- The `Text` property must be a string, so explicitly format data as strings by using `Out-String`.

- Use the control's `Clear()` method to reset it or clear out any existing results.
- If you need to move things around on your form, that's okay.

You can download a sample solution at MoreLunches.com.

Creating proxy functions

A proxy function acts as a wrapper around an existing function, cmdlet, or other command. In its simplest form, a proxy function passes all parameter input through to the wrapped command. Proxy functions are commonly used to add parameters, remove parameters, or otherwise expand or restrict the underlying command, becoming a useful tool for delegated administration. For example, you might provide users with a proxy function that removes a command parameter that you don't want the user to have access to. When loaded, a proxy function somewhat hides the real, wrapped command. Combined with techniques like constrained remoting endpoints (which we cover in the next chapter), proxy functions can completely hide the wrapped command, becoming the only means by which a user can accomplish a given task.

26.1 What are proxy functions?

A proxy function, which some folks call a wrapper function, is designed to sit on top of an existing command. For example, if you create a proxy function named ConvertTo-HTML, it will hide the real ConvertTo-HTML cmdlet. Whatever parameters you provide as part of the proxy function will become the only ones available to users, enabling you to take away functionality, add functionality, and so forth.

Proxy functions can also be used to create entirely new commands that, under the hood, leverage the functionality of an existing command. For example, we'll show you how to create an Export-HTML command that internally utilizes ConvertTo-HTML and Out-File, while still leaving both of those native cmdlets independently accessible.

26.2 *Creating the proxy function template*

The first step in creating a proxy function is to create the template. PowerShell does this for you, so it's a pretty easy step. The result is a function that looks and works exactly like the original one—essentially a copy of it. You'll use this template as a starting point for renaming the function, adding parameters, or removing parameters.

We're going to start with the ConvertTo-HTML cmdlet. Our goal is to create a proxy function named Export-HTML, which adds a -FilePath parameter so that the converted HTML can be written directly to a file. We're also going to remove the entire parameter set that includes the -Fragment parameter, because it doesn't make sense (for our use case, at least) to write an HTML fragment to a file. Because we're not naming our function ConvertTo-HTML, the original cmdlet will remain accessible.

We'll start by running these two commands:

```
PS C:\> $metadata = New-Object System.Management.Automation.CommandMetaData
 (Get-Command ConvertTo-HTML)
PS C:\> [System.Management.Automation.ProxyCommand]::Create($metadata) | Ou
t-File NewScript.ps1
```

> **TRY IT NOW** We strongly encourage you to follow along with our commands and script edits. The script produced by PowerShell doesn't fit neatly within the pages of this book, but we'll limit the number of changes we make to that formatting to try to keep our script as consistent as possible to what you'll see if you do this on your own.

This results in a file, NewScript.ps1, which is shown in the following listing. You'll notice that this is just a script, not an actual function.

Listing 26.1 NewScript.ps1

```
[CmdletBinding(DefaultParameterSetName='Page', HelpUri='http://
    go.microsoft.com/fwlink/?LinkID=113290', RemotingCapability='None')]
param(
    [Parameter(ValueFromPipeline=$true)]
    [psobject]
    ${InputObject},

    [Parameter(Position=0)]
    [System.Object[]]
    ${Property},

    [Parameter(ParameterSetName='Page', Position=3)]
    [string[]]
    ${Body},

    [Parameter(ParameterSetName='Page', Position=1)]
    [string[]]
    ${Head},

    [Parameter(ParameterSetName='Page', Position=2)]
    [ValidateNotNullOrEmpty()]
    [string]
    ${Title},
```

```
        [ValidateNotNullOrEmpty()]
        [ValidateSet('Table','List')]
        [string]
        ${As},

        [Parameter(ParameterSetName='Page')]
        [Alias('cu','uri')]
        [ValidateNotNullOrEmpty()]
        [System.Uri]
        ${CssUri},

        [Parameter(ParameterSetName='Fragment')]
        [ValidateNotNullOrEmpty()]
        [switch]
        ${Fragment},

        [ValidateNotNullOrEmpty()]
        [string[]]
        ${PostContent},

        [ValidateNotNullOrEmpty()]
        [string[]]
        ${PreContent})
begin
{
    try {
        $outBuffer = $null
        if ($PSBoundParameters.TryGetValue('OutBuffer', [ref]$outBuffer))
        {
            $PSBoundParameters['OutBuffer'] = 1
        }
        $wrappedCmd = $ExecutionContext.InvokeCommand.GetCommand('ConvertTo-
    Html', [System.Management.Automation.CommandTypes]::Cmdlet)
        $scriptCmd = {& $wrappedCmd @PSBoundParameters }
        $steppablePipeline =
    $scriptCmd.GetSteppablePipeline($myInvocation.CommandOrigin)
        $steppablePipeline.Begin($PSCmdlet)
    } catch {
        throw
    }
}

process
{
    try {
        $steppablePipeline.Process($_)
    } catch {
        throw
    }
}

end
{
    try {
        $steppablePipeline.End()
    } catch {
        throw
```

```
        }
}
<#

.ForwardHelpTargetName ConvertTo-Html
.ForwardHelpCategory Cmdlet

#>
```

We're going to wrap this in a function named `Export-HTML`. Also, to make this a bit easier to load and use, we'll immediately resave the file as a script module. We'll save the file as ..\Documents\WindowsPowerShell\Modules\Proxies\Proxies.psm1.

We're also going to go ahead and rename the proxy function, as shown in listing 26.2, because this proxy no longer uses the same syntax as the original command. While we're at it, we'll also remove the link to Microsoft's online command documentation. Changes in the following listing are shown in boldface.

Listing 26.2   Renaming the proxy function to `Export-HTML`

```
function Export-HTML {
    [CmdletBinding(DefaultParameterSetName='Page',
                   RemotingCapability='None')]
    param(
        [Parameter(ValueFromPipeline=$true)]
        [psobject]
        ${InputObject},

        [Parameter(Position=0)]
        [System.Object[]]
        ${Property},

        [Parameter(ParameterSetName='Page', Position=3)]
        [string[]]
        ${Body},

        [Parameter(ParameterSetName='Page', Position=1)]
        [string[]]
        ${Head},

        [Parameter(ParameterSetName='Page', Position=2)]
        [ValidateNotNullOrEmpty()]
        [string]
        ${Title},

        [ValidateNotNullOrEmpty()]
        [ValidateSet('Table','List')]
        [string]
        ${As},

        [Parameter(ParameterSetName='Page')]
        [Alias('cu','uri')]
        [ValidateNotNullOrEmpty()]
        [System.Uri]
        ${CssUri},

        [Parameter(ParameterSetName='Fragment')]
        [ValidateNotNullOrEmpty()]
```

```
        [switch]
        ${Fragment},

        [ValidateNotNullOrEmpty()]
        [string[]]
        ${PostContent},

        [ValidateNotNullOrEmpty()]
        [string[]]
        ${PreContent})
begin
{
    try {
        $outBuffer = $null
        if ($PSBoundParameters.TryGetValue('OutBuffer', [ref]$outBuffer))
        {
            $PSBoundParameters['OutBuffer'] = 1
        }
        $wrappedCmd =
$ExecutionContext.InvokeCommand.GetCommand('ConvertTo-Html',
[System.Management.Automation.CommandTypes]::Cmdlet)
        $scriptCmd = {& $wrappedCmd @PSBoundParameters }
        $steppablePipeline =
$scriptCmd.GetSteppablePipeline($myInvocation.CommandOrigin)
        $steppablePipeline.Begin($PSCmdlet)
    } catch {
        throw
    }
}

process
{
    try {
        $steppablePipeline.Process($_)
    } catch {
        throw
    }
}

end
{
    try {
        $steppablePipeline.End()
    } catch {
        throw
    }
}
<#

.ForwardHelpTargetName ConvertTo-Html
.ForwardHelpCategory Cmdlet

#>
}
```

26.3 Removing a parameter

We'll start by removing the -Fragment parameter, which is the only parameter in the Fragment parameter set. It's the third-to-last parameter defined in the script right now, after $CssUri and before $PostContent. The next listing shows the modified Proxies.psm1 file, which now lacks a -Fragment parameter.

Listing 26.3 Removing the -Fragment parameter

```
function Export-HTML {
    [CmdletBinding(DefaultParameterSetName='Page',
                  RemotingCapability='None')]
    param(
        [Parameter(ValueFromPipeline=$true)]
        [psobject]
        ${InputObject},

        [Parameter(Position=0)]
        [System.Object[]]
        ${Property},

        [Parameter(ParameterSetName='Page', Position=3)]
        [string[]]
        ${Body},

        [Parameter(ParameterSetName='Page', Position=1)]
        [string[]]
        ${Head},

        [Parameter(ParameterSetName='Page', Position=2)]
        [ValidateNotNullOrEmpty()]
        [string]
        ${Title},

        [ValidateNotNullOrEmpty()]
        [ValidateSet('Table','List')]
        [string]
        ${As},

        [Parameter(ParameterSetName='Page')]
        [Alias('cu','uri')]
        [ValidateNotNullOrEmpty()]
        [System.Uri]
        ${CssUri},

        [ValidateNotNullOrEmpty()]
        [string[]]
        ${PostContent},

        [ValidateNotNullOrEmpty()]
        [string[]]
        ${PreContent})

    begin
    {
        try {
            $outBuffer = $null
            if ($PSBoundParameters.TryGetValue('OutBuffer', [ref]$outBuffer))
```

```
        {
            $PSBoundParameters['OutBuffer'] = 1
        }
        $wrappedCmd =
$ExecutionContext.InvokeCommand.GetCommand('ConvertTo-Html',
[System.Management.Automation.CommandTypes]::Cmdlet)
        $scriptCmd = {& $wrappedCmd @PSBoundParameters }
        $steppablePipeline =
$scriptCmd.GetSteppablePipeline($myInvocation.CommandOrigin)
        $steppablePipeline.Begin($PSCmdlet)
    } catch {
        throw
    }
}

process
{
    try {
        $steppablePipeline.Process($_)
    } catch {
        throw
    }
}

end
{
    try {
        $steppablePipeline.End()
    } catch {
        throw
    }
}
<#

.ForwardHelpTargetName ConvertTo-Html
.ForwardHelpCategory Cmdlet

#>
}
```

At this point, we can hop into the shell and try this out:

```
PS C:\> import-module proxies
PS C:\> help export-html

NAME
    ConvertTo-Html

SYNTAX
    ConvertTo-Html [[-Property] <Object[]>] [[-Head] <string[]>]
    [[-Title] <string>] [[-Body] <string[]>] [-InputObject <psobject>]
    [-As <string> {Table | List}] [-CssUri <Uri>] [-PostContent
    <string[]>] [-PreContent <string[]>]  [<CommonParameters>]

    ConvertTo-Html [[-Property] <Object[]>] [-InputObject <psobject>]
    [-As <string> {Table | List}] [-Fragment] [-PostContent <string[]>]
    [-PreContent <string[]>]  [<CommonParameters>]
```

You can see that the help content is still showing ConvertTo-HTML, and the -Fragment parameter is still showing up. That's okay; what's important is that the shell recognized our Export-HTML command. The help file confusion is coming from these two lines at the end of the function:

```
<#

.ForwardHelpTargetName ConvertTo-Html
.ForwardHelpCategory Cmdlet

#>
```

We'll remove those two lines now, resave the script, and try it again:

```
PS C:\> remove-module proxies; import-module proxies
PS C:\> help export-html

NAME
    Export-HTML

SYNTAX
    Export-HTML [[-Property] <Object[]>] [[-Head] <string[]>] [[-Title]
    <string>] [[-Body] <string[]>] [-InputObject <psobject>] [-As
    <string> {Table | List}] [-CssUri <Uri>] [-PostContent <string[]>]
    [-PreContent <string[]>]  [<CommonParameters>]
```

Ah, that's much better. The Fragment parameter set is gone, and the help correctly shows our function's name.

26.4 Adding a parameter

We'll start by declaring a -FilePath parameter. We'll do this at the end of the existing parameter list, so we'll show you the last original parameter by way of reference. Note that we needed to add a comma after the last original parameter, so that the parameter list would continue to include our new one. We also needed to move the closing) from the Param block:

```
[ValidateNotNullOrEmpty()]        Original -PreContent
[string[]]                        parameter
${PreContent},

[Parameter(Mandatory=$True)]
[ValidateNotNullOrEmpty()]        New -FilePath
[string]                          parameter
$FilePath)
```

We used $FilePath rather than ${FilePath}; both have the same effect. The template produced by PowerShell uses only the curly brackets as a kind of better-safe-than-sorry precaution; we know that $FilePath is a legal variable name, so we don't need the curly brackets.

Now we need to make our new parameter work. To do that, locate this section of the template:

```
begin
{
    try {
        $outBuffer = $null
        if ($PSBoundParameters.TryGetValue('OutBuffer', [ref]$outBuffer))
        {
            $PSBoundParameters['OutBuffer'] = 1
        }
        $wrappedCmd =
$ExecutionContext.InvokeCommand.GetCommand('ConvertTo-Html',
[System.Management.Automation.CommandTypes]::Cmdlet)
        $scriptCmd = {& $wrappedCmd @PSBoundParameters }
        $steppablePipeline =
$scriptCmd.GetSteppablePipeline($myInvocation.CommandOrigin)
        $steppablePipeline.Begin($PSCmdlet)
    } catch {
        throw
    }
}
```

We only need to modify around this one line:

```
$scriptCmd = {& $wrappedCmd @PSBoundParameters }
```

The new code will look like this:

```
$PSBoundParameters.Remove('FilePath') | Out-Null
$scriptCmd = {& $wrappedCmd @PSBoundParameters | Out-File $filePath }
```

This removes our –FilePath parameter from the parameter collection, because the underlying ConvertTo-HTML won't know what to do with it. We then allow the original ConvertTo-HTML to run but pipe its output to Out-File and provide Out-File with our $filePath parameter's value. Whatever other parameters were specified to our function will all be in $PSBoundParameters, and because they're all valid with ConvertTo-HTML, we're just passing them along by "splatting" them as @PSBoundParameters. The following listing shows the revised Proxies.psm1.

Listing 26.4   The final Proxies.psm1

```
function Export-HTML {
    [CmdletBinding(DefaultParameterSetName='Page',
                  RemotingCapability='None')]
    param(
        [Parameter(ValueFromPipeline=$true)]
        [psobject]
        ${InputObject},

        [Parameter(Position=0)]
        [System.Object[]]
        ${Property},

        [Parameter(ParameterSetName='Page', Position=3)]
        [string[]]
        ${Body},
```

```
        [Parameter(ParameterSetName='Page', Position=1)]
        [string[]]
        ${Head},

        [Parameter(ParameterSetName='Page', Position=2)]
        [ValidateNotNullOrEmpty()]
        [string]
        ${Title},

        [ValidateNotNullOrEmpty()]
        [ValidateSet('Table','List')]
        [string]
        ${As},

        [Parameter(ParameterSetName='Page')]
        [Alias('cu','uri')]
        [ValidateNotNullOrEmpty()]
        [System.Uri]
        ${CssUri},

        [ValidateNotNullOrEmpty()]
        [string[]]
        ${PostContent},

        [ValidateNotNullOrEmpty()]
        [string[]]
        ${PreContent},

        [Parameter(Mandatory=$True)]
        [ValidateNotNullOrEmpty()]
        [string]
        $FilePath)
begin
{
    try {
        $outBuffer = $null
        if ($PSBoundParameters.TryGetValue('OutBuffer', [ref]$outBuffer))
        {
            $PSBoundParameters['OutBuffer'] = 1
        }
        $wrappedCmd =
$ExecutionContext.InvokeCommand.GetCommand('ConvertTo-Html',
[System.Management.Automation.CommandTypes]::Cmdlet)
        $PSBoundParameters.Remove('FilePath') | Out-Null
        $scriptCmd = {& $wrappedCmd @PSBoundParameters | Out-File
$filePath }
        $steppablePipeline =
$scriptCmd.GetSteppablePipeline($myInvocation.CommandOrigin)
        $steppablePipeline.Begin($PSCmdlet)
    } catch {
        throw
    }
}

process
{
```

```
        try {
            $steppablePipeline.Process($_)
        } catch {
            throw
        }
    }

    end
    {
        try {
            $steppablePipeline.End()
        } catch {
            throw
        }
    }
}
```

As a quick test, we reimported our module and tried to export a list of running processes to HTML. Figure 26.1 shows the results. At the bottom of the screen you can see the commands we ran, and Internet Explorer shows the resulting file.

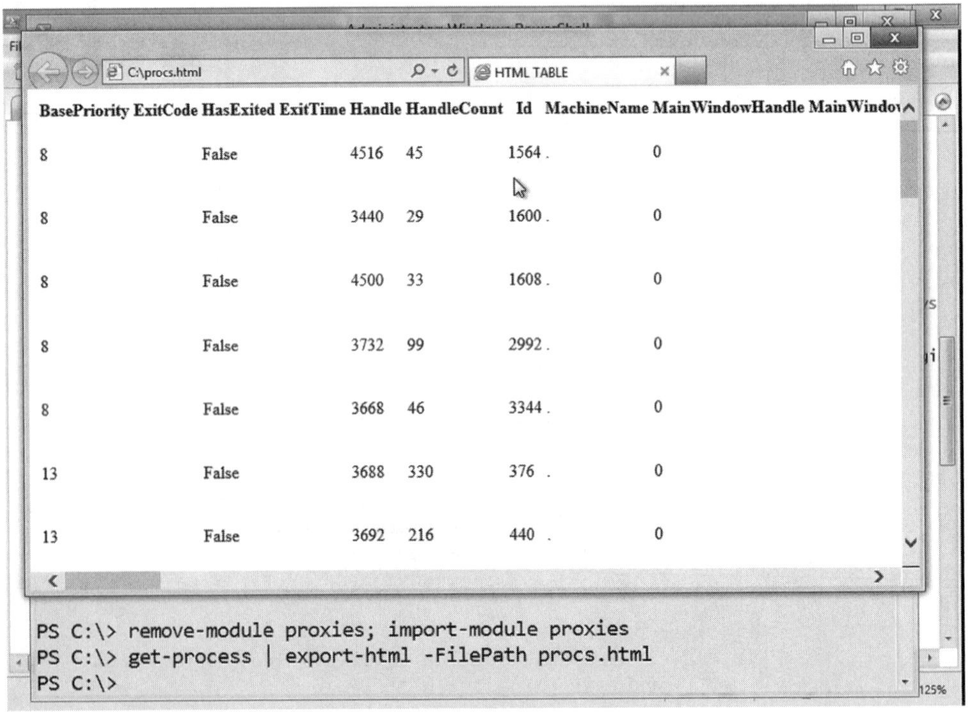

Figure 26.1   Testing the `Export-HTML` command

26.5   *Loading the proxy function*

There are a few rules regarding proxy functions when it comes time to load them. Because our example used a new command name, `Export-HTML`, it's able to coexist with the original wrapped command, `ConvertTo-HTML`.

But if we'd named our function `ConvertTo-HTML`, then we'd have effectively removed easy access to the original `ConvertTo-HTML`. When two loaded commands have the same name, PowerShell runs the last one loaded by default. To run the original, we'd have had to run something like this:

```
PS C:\> Get-Process | Microsoft.PowerShell.Utility\ConvertTo-HTML
```

By specifying the name of the module that the original command lives in, we can access it and bypass a proxy function that uses the same name. Of course, this ability to bypass the proxy function might not be something you want to allow. In that case, you'd need to only provide access to your proxy function via Remoting. By creating a constrained Remoting endpoint (that's the topic of the next chapter), you can allow only your proxy function to be visible to users, denying them access to the original command while still enabling the proxy function to utilize the original command's functionality.

26.6   *Lab*

Create a proxy function for the `Export-CSV` cmdlet. Name the proxy function `Export-TDF`. Remove the `-Delimiter` parameter, and instead hardcode it to always use `-Delimiter "`t"` (that's a backtick, followed by the letter *t*, in double quotation marks).

Work with the proxy function in a script file. At the bottom of the file, after the closing } of the function, put the following to test the function:

```
Get-Service | Export-TDF c:\services.tdf
```

Run the script to test the function, and verify that it creates a tab-delimited file named c:\services.tdf.

Setting up constrained
remoting endpoints

The ability to create constrained endpoints has existed since PowerShell v2, but PowerShell v3 makes them easier to create and makes them an effective way to set up delegated administration capabilities within your environment. We'll walk you through the complete process of creating and configuring these and give you some ideas for how you might utilize them in your own organization.

27.1 Refresher: Remoting architecture

Figure 27.1 provides a quick overview of PowerShell's Remoting architecture. You use the Web Services for Management (WS-MAN) protocol to communicate between computers (or even between two services on the same computer). WS-MAN utilizes either HTTP or HTTPS, with HTTP being the default. On the remote computer, a Windows Remote Management (WinRM) service receives the incoming WS-MAN traffic and routes that traffic to one or more *endpoints*. When those endpoints connect to PowerShell, a *session configuration* determines the capabilities of that particular connection. The default session configurations created when you enable Remoting (by running `Enable-PSRemoting`) are basically unrestricted and may only be utilized by Administrators.

> **NOTE** For a more in-depth look at how Remoting works, we recommend *Learn Windows PowerShell 3 in a Month of Lunches*. You can also refer to Don's free *Secrets of PowerShell Remoting* guide, which is available at http://PowerShellBooks.com.

For this chapter, we'll assume that the computer you're working on already has Remoting enabled (run `Enable-PSRemoting` as an Administrator accepting all defaults, and ensure that the command completes without error).

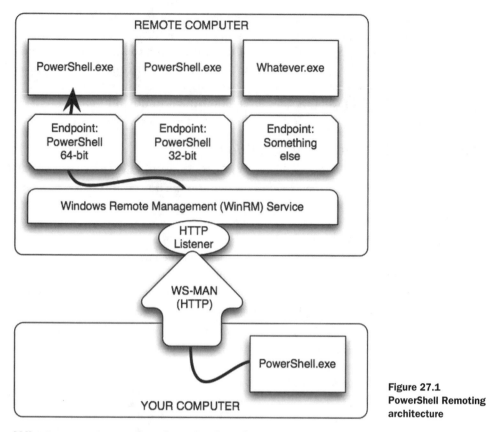

**Figure 27.1
PowerShell Remoting
architecture**

27.2 *What are constrained endpoints?*

A constrained endpoint, or constrained session configuration, is an endpoint that has limited capabilities. You can also create endpoints that run all commands under a specified user credential, rather than running commands under the credential of the connected user (which is the default behavior).

Limitations can include preloading specified PowerShell modules or scripts, restricting the commands visible to the connected user, limiting or eliminating PowerShell's scripting language (which enables the endpoint only to run commands), and so on.

Why might you do any of these things? Delegated administration is perhaps the perfect example. Suppose that we've created a user group named NetTechs and populated it with users who we want to be able to perform specific network-related tasks on a computer. We don't, however, want to give those users permission to perform those tasks. We could set up a constrained endpoint that includes only the commands we want them to run and configure the endpoint to run all commands under an alternate credential—one that *does* have permissions to run those commands. We'd further restrict the endpoint to accept only connections from that NetTechs group. Members of that group would be able to connect and run the supplied commands but not do anything else—a perfect example of delegated administration. By not giving them direct permission to run those commands, we'd ensure that they could run them *only* through the endpoint we provide them. That would allow us to severely restrict their capabilities to a closely defined set of tasks. We could, for example, load the endpoint with proxy functions, forcing our NetTechs users to perform their tasks through whatever limited interface we provide. That would help ensure they didn't stray outside the boundaries of what we wanted to allow them to do and help prevent them from causing collateral damage on the computers they were working with.

27.3 *Creating the endpoint definition*

There are two steps to creating the endpoint, and the first is to create its definition, which PowerShell calls a session configuration. The result of this is a configuration file, which contains information on the endpoint's capabilities. The fact that this is created in a file is a crucial advantage in automation endpoint creation: You can create a single-session configuration file and then copy it to multiple computers or even store it in a shared folder on the network. Multiple computers can then register a new endpoint using that configuration file, helping to make each of them consistent.

The file is created by running New-PSSessionConfigurationFile; we'll leave it to you to read the command's help to explore its full set of capabilities. For now, here's the command we'll run:

```
New-PSSessionConfigurationFile -Path C:\NetTechEndpoint.pssc `
                               -Description 'For NetTech use' `
                               -ExecutionPolicy Restricted `
                               -ModulesToImport NetAdapter,NetSecurity `
                               -PowerShellVersion 3.0 `
                               -VisibleFunctions 'Get-NetAdapter',
                                                 'Set-NetAdapter',
                                                 'Show-NetFirewallRule' `
                               -VisibleProviders FileSystem `
                               -SessionType RestrictedRemoteServer
```

> **TRY IT NOW** If you're using a Windows 8 or Windows Server 2012 computer, you should be able to run this command exactly as is. We recommend that you do so, so that you can follow along with this chapter's overall example.

Briefly, our new endpoint will include only two modules, NetAdapter and NetSecurity. Further, it will expose only three commands from those modules. It will not permit script execution. It will only run PowerShell v3 and will only permit PSDrives to be mapped to regular filesystem drives, meaning the registry, WS-MAN configuration, and other drives won't be available within the endpoint. The –SessionType parameter is especially important: Rather than choosing Default, which loads most PowerShell cmdlets, or Empty, which loads none, we've selected RestrictedRemoteServer. That adds a set of about eight core cmdlets, including ones that let a connected user disconnect from the session and close it.

You must be very careful when deciding what commands to make visible. The New-PSSessionConfigurationFile cmdlet will let you limit cmdlets (-VisibleCmdlets) or functions (-VisibleFunctions). You have to know the command type. Don't assume that everything in a module is a cmdlet. In the previous example, the `Get-NetAdapter` command is a function, which you can verify with `Get-Command`. If we'd used `-VisibleCmdlets`, it would have had no effect and nothing would have been restricted.

The other potential gotcha is that sometimes you can still end up with unexpected visible commands. When you do, as in the NetTechs example, if you run `Get-Command` you'll still see some cmdlets. That's because the `NetSecurity` module contains both functions and cmdlets. Even though we're limiting functions from the module, all the cmdlets are still visible. We haven't found any way using `New-PSSessionConfigurationFile` to set `-VisibleCmdlets` to nothing. The best workaround we can offer is to manually edit the .pscc file, remove the comment character in front of `VisibleCmdlets`, and set it equal to `''`. Next we'll cover connecting to the endpoint.

27.4 Registering the endpoint

This is the second step in creating a custom endpoint, and it reads in the session configuration file that we just created. It then registers that configuration with the WinRM service, officially putting the endpoint into action. We'll run this command:

```
Register-PSSessionConfiguration -Path C:\NetTechEndpoint.pssc `
                                -Name NetTechs `
                                -ShowSecurityDescriptorUI `
                                -AccessMode Remote `
                                -RunAsCredential Administrator
```

A few things happen when we run this. First, as shown in figure 27.2, we're prompted for the password of the Run As credential that we specified. This password will be

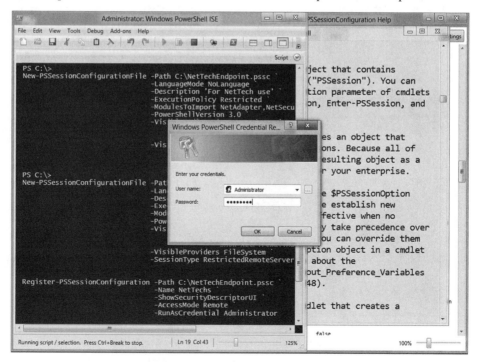

Figure 27.2 Providing the Run As account password

securely embedded within the endpoint's configuration, and that account will be used to execute all commands within the endpoint. Note that the command will ultimately fail, and the endpoint won't be registered, if you don't provide the correct password.

As shown in figure 27.3, we're also prompted to register the endpoint and then again to restart the WinRM service. This is necessary in order to make the new endpoint active. An additional parameter of `Register-PSSessionConfiguration` will suppress this prompt and not restart the service, but the new endpoint won't be active until either the service or the entire computer is restarted.

Finally, as shown in figure 27.4, we're prompted to set the security of the endpoint. We'll add the NetTechs user group and give them Read and Execute permissions. This dialog was displayed because we specified `-ShowSecurityDescriptorUI`. Had we not done so, we'd have needed to provide the endpoint's permissions using the Security Descriptor Definition Language (SDDL), which we can never make heads or tails of. Using the UI is a lot easier for us and helps us get the exact permissions we want on the endpoint.

TRY IT NOW If you're following along, then you'll need to make sure you provide the correct password for your computer's Administrator account. If you want to skip adding the specific permissions for a local NetTechs group, then just accept the defaults on the permissions dialog. That user group doesn't exist by default, but you can certainly create it on your computer and add a user account to it if you'd like to test it.

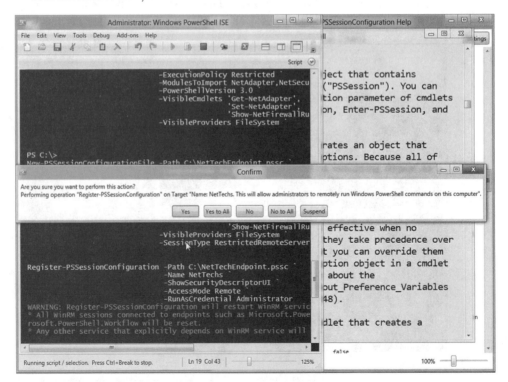

Figure 27.3   The "Are you sure?" prompt to register the endpoint

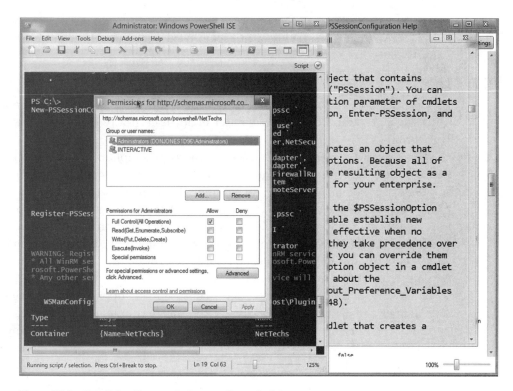

Figure 27.4 Specifying the permissions on the endpoint

If all goes well, you should be able to retrieve the endpoint once it's created:

```
PS C:\> Get-PSSessionConfiguration -Name Net*

Name          : NetTechs
PSVersion     : 3.0
StartupScript :
RunAsUser     : Administrator
Permission    :
```

27.5   *Connecting to the endpoint*

To connect to a custom endpoint, use `Invoke-Command` or `Enter-PSSession`, providing the `–ConfigurationName` parameter to specify the configuration name. Without that parameter, you'll connect to the computer's default PowerShell endpoint, which is fully functional and (by default) restricted to Administrator use.

```
PS C:\> Enter-PSSession -ComputerName localhost -ConfigurationName nettechs
```

You need to run this command in a session that's running under credentials for a user who belongs to the NetTechs group or use the `–Credential` parameter to specify the credentials. Once connected, you can run `Get-Command` to verify that only your desired commands are visible within the endpoint. If you try to run an unapproved command like `Get-Service`, you'll get an error, which is exactly what we wanted.

TIP   Normally in a remote session, you can use Exit to leave the session. But in a constrained session this is an unapproved command. Instead, use the Exit-PSSession cmdlet.

27.6   *Lab*

Create a new, local user named TestMan on your computer. Be sure to assign a password to the account. Don't place the user in any user groups other than the default Users group.

Then, create a constrained endpoint on your computer. Name the endpoint ConstrainTest. Design it to include only the SmbShare module and to make only the Get-SmbShare command visible (in addition to a small core set of cmdlets like Exit-PSSession, Select-Object, and so forth). After creating the session configuration, register the endpoint. Configure the endpoint to permit only TestMan to connect (with Read and Execute permissions), and configure it to run all commands as your local Administrator account. Be sure to provide the correct password for Administrator when you're prompted.

Use Enter-PSSession to connect to the constrained endpoint. When doing so, use the -Credential parameter to specify the TestMan account, and provide the proper password when prompted. Ensure that you can run Get-SmbShare but not any other command (such as Get-SmbShareAccess).

Never the end

28

Welcome to the end! Well, the end of the book—this is just the beginning of your career as a PowerShell toolmaker!

28.1 Welcome to toolmaking

At the outset of this book, we defined *toolmaking* as a second kind of PowerShell audience. You're now a part of that audience; you're no longer constrained to using the tools and commands provided to you by others but can instead combine those to make your own task-specific tools. Whether those are tools you'll use on your own or ones you'll delegate to other less-technical or less-privileged users, you're now in a position to harness the shell to automate tasks within your environment.

What's next? The third PowerShell audience—after tool *users* and tool *makers*—is *developers*. Those are the folks who use Visual Studio to develop applications that host PowerShell and harness its powers or who make more complex tools by programming in C#, Visual Basic, or another .NET Framework language. Frankly, we find that we can usually get just about anything we need done using the techniques we've presented in this book.

We want to reiterate one thing from this book's introduction: Our goal wasn't to provide a comprehensive reference to you. Instead, we wanted to provide a tutorial of the core toolmaking techniques, and that's what we've done. Almost everything we've shown you can be expanded, tweaked, and extended to do more and to meet specific scenarios. For example, there are lots of other things you can do with advanced function parameters, more you can do with custom views, a ton more you can do with workflow, and so on. We'll leave it up to you to research those additional capabilities; now that you have the basics under your belt, adopting additional techniques should come pretty easily.

28.2   *Cool ideas for tools*

You probably already have existing PowerShell or VBScript scripts that might benefit from a makeover into a reusable tool. Or if you are looking for some suggestions, see if you can develop a PowerShell tool for the following tasks:

- Get the password age of the local Administrator account from a remote computer.
- Create a drive report tool that shows you drive utilization on a server's drives.
- Create a tool to back up and clear event logs on remote computers.
- Create a tool to display file usage by owner for a given folder on a given computer.
- Create a tool to display uptime and last boot time for a group of mission-critical servers.
- Try your hand at developing a PowerShell workflow that configures several services, creates a folder structure, copies some files, and creates a new local Administrator account.
- Create a tool to query a computer for services running under a local or domain account.
- Create a tool to query a computer for all expired certificates.

Note that some of these might even benefit from a GUI treatment.

28.3   *What's your next step?*

Our best advice is to *dig in*. Come up with an idea for a tool that you can use in your own environment, and start writing it. You'll likely get stuck at some point, and you're welcome to hop on http://bit.ly/AskDon to post a question to us (both of us answer questions there). We'll do our best to help. You'll find other topical expertise at http://powershell.com/cs/forums/default.aspx?GroupID=24, so you'll be able to get help for domain-specific topics like IIS, SQL Server, SharePoint, Windows, Exchange, and more.

Above all, *don't delay.* You should still have a lot of fresh material in your mind from this book, and the time to put it to use is *now.* Of course, you can always flip back through the pages of this book to refresh your memory. We'll caution you a bit about doing so: Keep in mind that, in many chapters, we provided scripts that actually had errors, so that we could run across those and fix them. Make sure you're not referring to an erroneous script! We'll also give you a biased recommendation: Get a copy of *PowerShell In Depth: An Administrator's Guide,* which we co-authored with fellow MVP Richard Siddaway. It's intended more as a long-term reference than this book (which is meant as a tutorial), and it covers just about everything you might need to do in PowerShell.

Good luck!

appendix
GUI technologies
and PowerShell

In chapters 23–25, we showed you how to build a graphical user interface (GUI) as part of a PowerShell script. We chose to use the WinForms technologies, and we made heavy use of a tool called PowerShell Studio (formerly PrimalForms), sold by SAPIEN Technologies (http://sapien.com). In this appendix, we want to briefly explain some of those decisions in more detail. Frankly, there's very little technology associated with those decisions—they're more practical and political—which is why we've pulled this discussion into an appendix, so that we didn't have to interrupt the main narrative of the book.

A.1   *WinForms vs. WPF*

We had to choose between two distinct ways of building the GUI: Windows Forms, which folks refer to as WinForms, or Windows Presentation Foundation, which is usually called WPF.

WinForms is the older technology, dating back to the first version of the .NET Framework. It utilizes GUI components that are, for the most part, native to Windows itself; the .NET Framework is merely a way of accessing them. We find Win-Forms to be fairly straightforward to work with and more than sufficient for building the more straightforward tools that administrators usually want to create.

WPF is a newer technology, having been introduced in .NET Framework v3.5. It's capable of creating much more complex and richer GUIs and has a number of unique capabilities, like the ability to quickly change a GUI's overall appearance (but not layout) by "skinning" the UI elements. Some developers refer to these capabilities as eye candy, although WPF is a bit deeper than that.

In WPF, the GUI is defined in an XML file using a format called XAML. That means the definition of the GUI—what elements are located where—is separate from the code that makes the GUI work. Developers tend to like that separation, because it enables a lot of different workflows, such as having a designer create the GUI and letting a developer focus on bringing the GUI to life.

WPF provides more and better capabilities for working with media, documents, 3D content, and more. You can get additional information on the major differences at http://joshsmithonwpf.wordpress.com/2007/09/05/wpf-vs-windows-forms/. It's an older article, and WPF has certainly come a long way since then, but it's still a good, concise summation of some key differences.

Given that we wanted to focus on pretty simple GUIs, WinForms was more than sufficient, which is a big part of why we chose it. But that wasn't the only reason.

A.2   *PrimalForms / PowerShell Studio*

We tell you, it killed us to have to write a book around a commercial, third-party tool. Not that PowerShell Studio isn't worth your consideration—we think it's great. We just hate that you bought this book to learn to do something, and now we're telling you to shell out another few hundred bucks for this tool. Why are we doing that?

As far as we've been able to discover, PowerShell Studio is the only tool of its kind in the world. It provides a GUI-based experience for designing your GUI, which we feel is absolutely essential. Hand-coding the elements in a GUI gets complicated if you have anything more than a text box and a button; we wouldn't have even put chapters 23–25 in the book if we'd been forced to hand-code everything we did. Bottom line: We wouldn't touch PowerShell-based GUI development without a tool like PowerShell Studio, and it's the only one there is.

We've assuaged our guilt on this score by noting that SAPIEN continues to provide a free Community Edition of the older PrimalForms product (you have to log in to their website in order to access their Downloads section, and that's where you'll find the free tools).

Our decision to use WinForms was driven in part by the fact that PowerShell Studio outputs WinForms-based code. We feel that (a) you need a tool to do the GUI design, (b) the only tool out there uses WinForms, and so (c) we tend to stick with WinForms.

Some of PowerShell Studio's other features seal the deal for us in terms of using the tool, like its ability to bundle your script into an encrypted executable that can run under alternate credentials. Because that particular feature is exactly what we, as administrators, want to do with our scripts, it pretty much justifies the tool's purchase price. Don't forget: You can download the software and try it out for yourself during a trial period.

A.3   *Other options*

Our decision to use PowerShell Studio doesn't necessarily need to be your decision. We do recognize that it's a pricey tool, although we do enough work with it that, for us, it's well worth the price given how much time it saves us.

You could elect to use WinForms and hand code everything. You could also get a free Visual Studio Express edition from Microsoft, use its graphical GUI builder, and translate the resulting C# or Visual Basic code into PowerShell. Microsoft may not always offer a free version of Visual Studio that does WinForms development, though, so that—as well as the time it takes to translate the C# or Visual Basic code to Power-Shell—is something to keep in mind.

You could also elect to use WPF. Again, you could use Visual Studio to graphically develop your UI and just take the resulting XAML and somehow use it in a PowerShell script. There's an open source effort called Show-UI that's built around the idea of using WPF from within PowerShell; http://show-ui.com provides a basic starting point and download link, and searching for "Show-UI" in your favorite Internet search engine will turn up tutorials and walkthroughs. Your resulting script will have a dependency on the Show-UI module, which means you'll have to find a way to distribute that along with your scripts in order for them to work.

Whatever you decide is fine with us. Most of the concepts we've shown you in this book carry over no matter what you decide to do.

index

WF (Workflow Foundation) 183
-WhatIf parameter 163
$WhatIfPreference variable 166
While constructs. *See* Do...While constructs
–wildcard option 22
Win32_ComputerSystem class 65
Win32_OperatingSystem class 32, 55, 64–65, 164, 174
Win32Shutdown method 174
Windows Management Instrumentation. *See* WMI
Windows Presentation Foundation. *See* WPF
Windows Remote Management. *See* WinRM
Windows Workflow Foundation 183
Windows, English version of 86
WindowsPowerShell folder 85
WinForms 228

WinRM (Windows Remote Management) 268
WMI (Windows Management Instrumentation) 7, 54, 163
WMI command 163, 168
WMI queries 73, 98, 100
WMI Win32_Volume class 51
$workflow:myvar 191
Workflow Foundation. *See* WF
workflow keyword 183–184
$workflow scope identifier 191
workflows 183–191
    activities concept in 185–186
    designing 188
    example of 189–190
    overview 183–184
    parallelism of 187–188
    parameters for 184
    persisting state 186
    remoting with 186–187
    resuming 186
    suspending 186
    vs. functions 190–191

WPF (Windows Presentation Foundation) 228
Write-Debug command 109
Write-Debug statements 114
Write-Host command 72
Write-Output command 56, 58–63
Write-Verbose command 68–69
Write-Warning $_.Exception.Message 97
WS-MAN (Web Services for Management) protocol 164, 268

X

$x variable 39
XML editor 8
XML file 85–86, 121, 123, 128–129, 179, 191
XML formats 85
XML tags 120
XML-based help 84–86

MORE TITLES FROM MANNING

PowerShell in Depth
An administrator's guide
by Don Jones, Richard Siddaway,
  and Jeffery Hicks

ISBN: 978-1-617290-55-8
525 pages
$49.99
December 2012

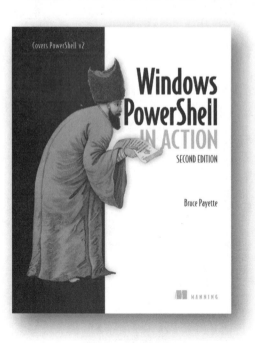

Windows PowerShell in Action
Second Edition
by Bruce Payette

ISBN: 978-1-935182-13-9
1016 pages
$59.99
May 2011

For ordering information go to www.manning.com

MORE TITLES FROM MANNING

PowerShell in Practice

by Richard Siddaway

ISBN: 978-1-935182-00-9
584 pages
$49.99
June 2010

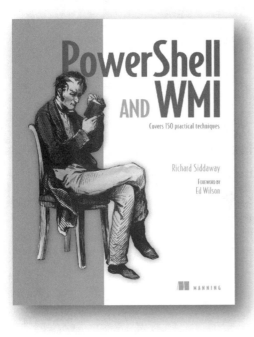

PowerShell and WMI

by Richard Siddaway

ISBN: 978-1-617290-11-4
552 pages
$59.99
April 2012

For ordering information go to www.manning.com

MORE TITLES FROM MANNING

Learn Windows PowerShell 3
in a Month of Lunches,
Second Edition

by Don Jones and Jeffery D. Hicks

ISBN: 978-1-617291-08-1
368 pages
$44.99
November 2012

Learn SQL Server 2012
in a Month of Lunches

by Grant B. Fritchey

ISBN: 978-1-617290-63-3
325 pages
$44.99
July 2013

For ordering information go to www.manning.com